MW00390053

This is for anyone who's ever been the underdog.

If you're the kind of person who excels when someone says "you can't do that"... and if striving to be the best, especially against all odds, is important to you... then you will *love* this book.

Because in the end, being successful is about living life on *your* terms and nothing more.

After all, isn't that why you went into business for yourself, in the first place?

Read This

This is the third printing of this book.

The response to it has been so warm and welcoming, and the changes it's encouraged people to make and the corresponding results they've seen... has far surpassed what I ever imagined.

If I've learned one thing about business, and about life, in general... it's this: usually, the things that have the biggest impact on you, were often unexpected.

It is my sincere hope, you look back one day and think about this book, as one of those things that had an unexpected "big impact" on your business... and hopefully on your life, as well.

Thanks for your support, and thank you for your business.

See you inside.

Craig Garber

How To Make Maximum Money With Minimum Customers
21 Proven Direct-Marketing Strategies Anyone Can Use!

All Rights Reserved. No part of this product may be reproduced, transmitted in any form or by any means -- whether physical or electronic -- or stored in any kind of information storage or retrieval system, or photocopied or recorded using any other means, without express written permission from the publisher.

The individual purchaser is the sole authorized user of the information in this publication. If you reproduce or transmit this product using *any* format or *any* kind of medium, or if you sell it, you are in violation of copyright laws and **WILL** be prosecuted to the fullest extent of the laws of the United States of America.

This means you can NOT sell this on eBay when you're done with it!

Legal Notices and Limit Of Liability: While all attempts have been made to provide effective and verifiable information in this product, the author and publisher assume NO responsibility for any errors, inaccuracies, or omissions, nor is any liability assumed for ANY damages resulting from the use of the information contained inside, or the ideas implied or derived from this information.

This product is ultimately designed for educational purposes only. It is sold with this understanding, and the understanding that the author and publisher are not engaged in rendering any kind of legal, accounting, regulatory, compliance or other professional services. If legal advice or other expert assistance is required, you must seek out the services of competent professionals in this area.

Due to the nature of direct response marketing and the wide variety of rules and regulations related to business activities in different industries and in different locales, some of the advice or ideas suggested in this product may be deemed unlawful in certain circumstances and/or locations. Also, since federal and local laws differ widely, as do codes of conduct for members of various professional organizations and agencies, you as the reader, accept **FULL** responsibility for determining the legality, appropriateness, and/or ethical propriety of any and all business transactions or practices used in your particular business and geographic location, whether or not these transactions and/or practices are suggested or implied, either directly or indirectly in this product. As with any business advice, you are also strongly encouraged to seek professional counsel before you start taking ANY action. Also, **NO guarantees of income or profits are intended by this information** -- there are simply too many variables going on that will, or may affect each individual's results, and your results may vary greatly from any examples given or illustrated. Neither Craig Garber nor kingofcopy.com® can promise or even imply your personal success, especially since they have no control over your decisions or actions, or your circumstances, or the marketplace and the economy, and therefore they can not accept any responsibility for your results. YOU are the only one who can take the action you need to get the results you want!

© kingofcopy.com® 2009

THIRD PRINTING, MARCH 2011

Published by:
kingofcopy.com®
3959 Van Dyke Road #253
Lutz, Florida 33558

ISBN 978-0-9841255-1-7

Contents

Foreword

My name is Christian Godefroy and I have been involved in the fascinating world of direct-response marketing for over 37 years. During this time, I have been an entrepreneur using direct marketing and a student of it, as well. But of course, the most successful entrepreneurs are always life-long students, aren't they?

I have also, during this time, sold in excess of $300 Million dollars worth of goods and services around the world, primarily in Europe where I've spent most of my life. I am not telling you this to brag, simply to let you know what I am about to say isn't based on theory or education. It is based on practical wisdom gained from spending 37 years out there in the trenches, every day.

I had the good fortune of meeting Craig Garber a little over three years ago. I ordered one of his courses and Craig recognized my name and contacted me. Unbeknownst to me at that time, Craig was a student of my material, the same way I was a student of his.

During these last three years, I have come to know Craig professionally *and* personally -- and my life is definitely better because of this. After reading this manual, you will *also* know Craig personally and professionally, and I promise, *your* business life, and *your* personal life, will be equally enriched.

Reading this manual will be like studying Craig under a magnifying glass, spying on him every day, stealing his best ideas and taking microfilms of his best sales copy.

Even better, you will be reading his mind to understand how you can achieve such outstanding results with a small online list of less than 5,000 names -- which is simply unheard of.

Let me tell you, it takes courage and dedication to read 357 pages, even when it is so well written. But your courage and dedication will pay off, many times over.

First of all, this book is FILLED with diamonds. In fact, it is a veritable diamond mine, with nuggets liberally scattered all over. And you will easily be able to bend down and scoop these diamonds up into your hands, page after page after page. I urge you to write them down and apply them, immediately.

Second, Craig is one of the brightest guys I have ever met in my life. Although he reveals a lot about himself, he never brags about himself or about his intelligence -- even though he easily could. I love brilliant guys, because they always have new ways of seeing things, clever shortcuts to use, and breakthrough systems that are easily applied. And, they are very practical in their vision.

You will find Craig is exactly like that.

Third, I don't need to tell you there are people you meet who drain your energy, even when they are writing. Craig, on the other hand, is like a powerful dynamo. He leaves you filled with MORE energy than you started with before your interaction with him. In fact, the more you read him, the more energy you have and the more motivation grows inside of you. The clearer you think, the smarter you will act, and the more money you will make.

In fact, last year, using just two of Craig's Strategies in this manual (Strategy # 4 and Strategy # 6), I pulled in $304,044.82 in 7 days alone. At 90% profit, I am forever grateful to him for sharing these Strategies, which are now yours for the taking.

Fourth, Craig is the most generous guest - or host - you could have. When I met Craig here in Europe, his arms were filled with gifts for my kids, my wife and myself. And these gifts were so carefully selected we were full of joy and gratitude. We still are.

And this is how you will feel after reading this manual. You will have the "sense" Craig has just given you some of the most valuable gifts and treasures you may ever stumble across.

The bonus section by itself is worth several times the price you paid for the entire manual. Many concepts and strategies are so deep and so well explained, you'll have sudden insights that will bring you a rush of money from out of the blue, like in a casino when you hit the Jackpot or win the Grand Prize.

Fifth, Craig is ORIGINAL. He thinks like no one else thinks, and he will show you how to do the same. Why keep using old approaches when his new ones work 5 times better? And the nice thing is, Craig reveals everything about these secret strategies, holding nothing back.

I could go on like this for hours, because Craig's work is carefully crafted with the same precision Stradivarius uses to craft a custom violin. There are *very* few men like him on earth.

He always finds a way of surprising me with the deepness of how he thinks about life, about business, and about money. And you too, will be moved in this same way.

Craig is the Leonardo da Vinci of direct marketing: creative, easy to understand, a beautiful soul, and successful in all aspects of his life.

Follow him!

Christian H. Godefroy - Chesieres, Switzerland
Copywriter and Infopreneur
www.positive-club.com

About This Book

If you love marketing, selling, and making money, or if marketing intimidates you right now, but you'd *desperately* love to consistently be making *gobs* of money in your business using effective marketing, then this is the most **exciting** and **important** manual you will ever read!

Here's the thing, though. In a sense, this book is a classic "con," and here's why: It sucks you in with the promise of making money, but... what you're ultimately going to find is that a little ways into the whole deal... the bait's been switched on you!

See, what starts out as a money-making proposition, rapidly turns into much more than that. It turns into a way of living and a way of running your business and your life, that takes you on the most exciting journey you could ever imagine!

This journey ultimately lets you do things your way, and live a happier and more fulfilling life as a result. Which is exactly what happens when you build quality relationships with your customers using the strategies inside this manual. They become more like extended family members you get to drop in on every once in a while, only without all the dysfunctional behavior.

The truth is, you're about to discover some of the most powerful selling secrets in existence! Many of them have been used throughout the ages to create and build treasure troves of cash. And almost all of them are based on pushing your prospects emotional buy-buttons, which ultimately, is the cornerstone concept to your success in selling and marketing, regardless of what business you're in.

This book gives you all the insight you need, all delivered in plain and simple English, so you can easily apply these strategies to *any* business. And I do mean ANY business.

If I were you, I'd make sure you have three things with you at all times when you're reading this book. One, a highlighter to outline the most critical information you're going to want to use right away. And two and three, a pen or pencil and a yellow pad to take down all the ideas that are going to come to you as you go through this information.

See, the most common feedback I hear from consulting clients and from the members of my various coaching groups, is... "After speaking with you, I couldn't sleep. I was up all night -- my head was *spinning* with ideas!"

So be forewarned, and heat up your coffee pot right now, because you will *most definitely* wind up experiencing the very same thing as you go through this book.

I have tried to present these ideas in order from the more simplistic to the more advanced, but since I have no idea where you personally are at in your business or in your marketing knowledge, your mileage may vary on this.

In any event, batten down the hatches and buckle your seatbelts, because if you're the kind of person who likes to shoot for the moon every once in a while, then you just may be in for... the most *thrilling* ride... of your life!

Now just trust me to do my thing, and you'll remember and benefit from the experience you're about to have, for as long as you live. And you and I will probably have a *very* long and *very* meaningful relationship.

And now... let's get on with the show.

Introduction

I am Mr. Nobody, from nowhere, and here's my story. It can very well be your story, too, if you'd like.

My name is Craig Garber. I'm a publisher and a direct-marketing consultant, and many people say I'm one of the best copywriters in America.

I'm also one of the most unusual people you will ever meet. On the surface, I'm as much of a hardass as anyone you'll ever find in business. However, get to know me and you're more likely to see me cuddling my little daughter in my arms, than getting all hot and bothered over a deal I'm involved with.

But hold on a moment, I'm getting ahead of myself here.

There are two defining moments in business for me, you should probably know about.

The first came when I was 14 years old, during the early part of the summer of 1977.

That year, Led Zeppelin played their last concert, in Oakland... Talking Heads released their first album... and the Porsche 928 made its debut, as well.

In general, 1977 was a hectic year for America, and an uncommonly scary year for my hometown of New York City, in particular.

We had a 25 hour blackout in New York City, where people went completely wild, looting stores and robbing anything in sight that wasn't nailed to the ground.

I remember watching people literally smashing the storefront windows of Crazy Eddie on Fordham Road, and then walking down the street lugging their new television sets under their arms, with a sense of entitlement about it. Society's rules of conventional social behavior were stripped away during this blackout. It was, thankfully, a rare glimpse of human nature at its worst.

That summer, David Berkowitz, also known as the "Son Of Sam" was busy killing women and couples, one by one, in the outer boroughs of the Bronx and Brooklyn. During this time, all the kids in my neighborhood ended our nights early, rather than risk becoming another victim of this nut, who was eventually caught on August 10th, tracked down by a conscientious officer following up on an unlikely parking ticket.

In October, my beloved Yankees won the World Series (you can't grow up in The Bronx and not be a Yankee fan), and Reggie Jackson validated his "Mr. October" title, one more time.

That summer, I also got my first job. Somehow, my father's uncle, who owned an advertising agency in Manhattan, got me a job as a foot messenger working somewhere around midtown. If my memory serves me correctly, it was near 46th Street and 5th Avenue, just around the corner from Rockefeller Center.

Making minimum wage, which I believe was $2.90 an hour back then, I'd take parcels from one office to another, or from one office back to the dispatcher, who would then call forth another foot messenger to take this package somewhere else.

Most of these packages were blueprints or documents, and of course, this was long before fax machines and e-mail. And Federal Express, although available, was far too expensive for most businesses to use regularly, back then.

Working at this job, smack dab in the middle of Manhattan was a hell of an experience for me -- a real eye-opener. For starters, I expected to see tons of young kids working there, just like me. But lo and behold, most of the full-timers who worked there were grown men. There were only a few summer workers like myself.

And let me tell you, these full-time guys were as strange as can be.

This was a job several steps south of any other job you can get. You pick up a package "here"... and you bring it "there." If dogs or homing pigeons were bigger, they'd have revolutionized the industry.

Having said that, everyone there was very nice and no one ever bothered you as long as you stayed busy, which meant, "stayed out of the office."

I thought the name of the game was to pound out as many deliveries as possible, but I learned very quickly, that I was dead wrong.

I remember it was my second day of work, and I called up my father from a pay phone. I think I was somewhere down in the West Village or perhaps even in SOHO

(Before it was SOHO as you know it today. Back then it was nothing but abandoned lofts and shooting galleries.) I was crying into the phone telling him I couldn't walk any more.

And I meant what I was telling him. See, I'd delivered so many packages in these first two days, the rubber soles of my Pro-Keds sneakers had literally worn bare, and I had absolutely enormous throbbing blisters all over the soles of my feet.

My dad, not one for compassion, yelled at me and told me I'd better stick it out, or else. Smart enough to know he was not the sharpest guy around, but not brave enough to challenge him (yet), I gathered myself and somehow got through the rest of the week.

I remember asking one of the full-timers what to do about this situation. "Butch," a sinewy black man in his late 30's, very kind and soft-spoken, and who had an air of respect about him when he bopped up and down the street, had some solid advice for me, for sure.

Butch told me I had this job all wrong. That the name of the game wasn't to deliver as many packages as possible, but to take your time delivering only those you could comfortably handle. After all, they're only paying you minimum wage, right?

Butch said I needed to "relax... and chill..."

According to Butch, after you get your package, you're just supposed to sit and chill for a while. Smoke a cigarette (I didn't smoke.), go chat up some ladies (I was 14.)... stop into a bar and have a drink (I was 14.)... go and grab yourself a meal (I was making minimum wage and brought my lunch to work every day in a brown bag.).

Sensing Butch was on to something, and yet, wanting to take his suggestions and sort of incorporate them with my own work ethic, I came up with the following. I'd definitely start walking much slower -- not as slow as any of the full-time guys, but significantly slower than the rest of New York. And if I was hungry or thirsty, or even if I just wanted a break, from now on I'd sit down for a few minutes and have a soda or something, and enjoy one of the biggest benefits of growing up in New York City: people-watching.

I also discovered one of the most fabulous pastimes and passions of my life -- browsing through the used record bins of the West Village retail music stores. Here, a world of music suddenly opened up to me that I never even knew existed, and from that time onward, I enthusiastically came home with three or four new LP records a week, on average.

In fact, back then, if you went hog wild and were prepared to spend maybe $20 or $30 dollars on records, and if you were a smart shopper, you could come back home with 12 to 15 good used records, and maybe even one or two new ones in the mix as well.

I wound up spending weekends downtown as well, showing all the neighborhood kids from the Bronx, all the really cool places to hang out in "the city." I saw the midnight Rocky Horror Show at the 8th Street Playhouse more times than I can count. And I copped loose joints and nickel bags from the dealers in Washington Square Park all night long. ("Yo, loose joints?") Back then, Washington Square Park had no curfew -- it was open all night long.

We smoked hash and drank those big one-gallon jugs of Ernest and Julio Gallo wine, before we went into see "Laser Rock" at the Hayden Planetarium. And we listened to the music of Pink Floyd, Led Zeppelin and The Doors all night long.

I came of age that summer, and to this day, there's a place in my heart for the West Village and Manhattan, that's even hard for me to explain.

In the wintertime, I'd eat steaming hot salted pretzels from the street vendors, for only a quarter, and wash it down with a cup of hot cocoa with marshmallows in it for another quarter. If I was there early in the day, I'd go into one of the many Greek diners that used to populate Manhattan, and order a toasted corn muffin and a cup of coffee. That was back before all the Koreans moved in and opened their salad bars and breakfast nooks which now dot Manhattan like sand on your beach towel.

And if I had "big money on me," maybe I could afford to buy a bag of chestnuts from one of the hot dog vendors along 5th Avenue.

During the summer, it was slices from Pizza Box on Bleecker Street (which is still there today), Cannoli's from Rocco's Pastry further west on Bleecker, and a cup of cherry shaved ice from the Dominican guys back home in the Bronx.

But I digress. Let's get back to my first defining moment in business...

A few weeks into the summer, once I'd gotten the work routine down and was finally enjoying my life, my father happened to look at one of my paychecks, and he saw it was signed by a man named "Norman Lederman."

My dad tells me he went to school with a kid called Norman Lederman, and so the following week I go to work and ask the dispatcher if I can somehow meet this Norman Lederman fellow, to ask him if he knows my dad.

The dispatcher, who for some reason likes me -- probably because even with my "new" work ethic I was still 100% more productive than anyone else -- says no problem and then calls the big boss on the phone, to confer with him.

I'm immediately whisked away to some mysterious back-room elevator, which very slowly ascends a few floors to Norman Lederman's lair.

I don't remember what his office looked like, but I do remember I was scared shitless standing there talking to him. He was my first boss after all -- in fact, not just my boss, but my bosses boss! He was a giant of a man with an acne'd face, and a Fastaffian look about him I still remember vividly.

He tells me he does know my father, and that he'd like to take my dad and I out to lunch the following week.

So where's the defining moment?

It happened at lunch. My dad, who was an arrogant, ignorant blue-collar worker his whole life, and who poo-poohed the rich and anyone even remotely successful, whenever he could... predictably sat down with that same smug arrogance during the meal.

I was astounded, even at this young age, how my father couldn't possibly be curious about this man's success. Instead, he sat there with an air of entitlement that said, "This guy's lucky I agreed to go to lunch with him." My father, the toll collector...

But my dad's another story for another day.

All I wanted to know, as we were sitting there at that table eating lunch, was "How do you get to own a business?" I would have LOVED to find out how this guy was making so much money he was able to employ over a dozen people full-time, here in midtown Manhattan.

This was a real person -- someone I actually now knew -- who really owned his own business. Wow!

How'd he manage to do this? How'd he get from high school in the Bronx to here? What was the secret formula? How can someone else do it? Do you need permission? Is there a class? Tell me, tell me, tell me!

How can I do it?

This was my first sense of understanding that the world was bigger (and probably a lot better) than what my old man had been telling me for as long as I could remember. That something was wrong back home in Wonderland. That there was more to life than my apartment housing project in the Bronx, and the cast of characters who lived there. That living in the hood or having an apartment in midtown wasn't preordained. That destiny really was in your own hands, and that you could change your financial situation.

That who you were yesterday, really has nothing to do with who you are today.

Why was Butch working for Mr. Lederman and not the other way around? I *had* to find the answers to these questions, but I knew I'd never find them sitting around my house waiting for the answers. It was from this point on, I knew my road to salvation was not in the Bronx, but "somewhere else" outside my apartment in the projects.

I didn't know where to go, what to do, or how to get there, but God help me, I knew I'd find the answers to these questions, somehow.

Defining moment number two, occurred in 2000. I was knee-deep into my beginning experiences with emotional direct-response marketing, and I had no clue that the future would hold money and riches far beyond what I'd ever experienced before, or what I truly even believed was possible.

I was a struggling financial planner running my own business, and a member of a monthly telephone coaching program about marketing. To a great extent, the coaching program really was just an opportunity for various guests to get on the call, educate you for 45 minutes, and then try and sell you their product.

Which isn't necessarily a bad thing, it's just not what a $397 monthly coaching program should be. (Which is probably why I've never EVER pitched or done anything but deliver content in any of my coaching programs.) Nevertheless, every month, on every call, I listened as intensely a safe-cracker trying to hear the ticks of the tumblers, sucking every single ounce of information out of each call.

On one call, the proctor said something that really pissed me off. He said something like, "Most people set up their personal lives and plan their free time, based on what their business leaves them with. Why do you do this? Why don't you plan out what kind of a lifestyle you want to have, and then design your business around that particular lifestyle?"

Well, I have to tell you, I was livid when I heard this. I thought to myself, "Sure, I want to go fishing, smoke cigars, and read books all day long, in between making love to my wife. And then I can schedule in an hour or so of work here and there, and life will be great."

The speaker came off a little arrogant and presumptuous, and he could have communicated the same message with a little more empathy and guidance. But... I felt so challenged and had such a strong sense of righteous indignation over this, I vowed to myself, I was going to figure out how to make this statement, my reality.

Come hell or high water, I *was* going to figure this one out.

Like many things I've done, someone telling me I couldn't do something, or someone challenging me, or making me feel "less than" because I wasn't in control over my situation at that particular point in time, motivated me to ultimately succeed.

Who knows, you may be no different when it comes to being challenged. After all, the most successful people usually love a good challenge, right?

I wrote my first sales letter right around the same time I took on this challenge. Three years later, I closed my financial planning business and took on another challenge -- to grow a direct response marketing and consulting practice, and become one of the world's best copywriters.

Now I'm not going to sit here and tell you that I finally got it "all figured out." Because I don't think you've ever got it all figured out. The more knowledge and wisdom I seem to accumulate, the more I realize how little I know and how much more there is out there for me to learn.

But I do live life more on my own terms nowadays, and although I work a lot of hours, I only work with those people I want to work with, and I only work on those activities I want to work on. And this is true regardless of whether they're my own projects or projects with clients.

And I do all this working out of my home overlooking my lake, so I really can't complain.

This book contains the lion's share of the most effective strategies I've profited from, during this 9-½ year journey.

Now don't get me wrong. There are a lot of people who make a lot more money than I do. But these strategies allowed me to make almost $600,000 with a small list of less than 5,000 names in a non-niched marketplace. And I don't know *anyone* who's done anything even *remotely* close to that, so you probably want to pay very close attention from here on in.

I've used these techniques to make myself and my clients a small fortune, and if you use even *some* of them, your bottom line has nowhere to go, but up, up, up! In fact, if you use even *half*, or *one-quarter* of the information inside this book, you're in for a real treat! You'll see the impact of these strategies on your business, and on your life, *very* rapidly.

I'd like to tell you this has been an easy journey, but if I told you that, I'd be lying. I've worked my ass off, and frankly, few people are willing to work as hard and as consistently as I do.

But as far as I can tell, life's not easy for anyone. So if you're going to have challenges to face anyway, then you might as well be facing them with a fistful of dollars in your pocket, and a vault full of cash in your bank account, right?

The truth is, life's **much** easier when you have money. The only people who say this isn't true -- the ones who say "Money can't buy you happiness" -- are always broke.

Money does buy you happiness because it buys you choices. And choices, in most cases, buy you freedom.

I wish you nothing but good luck and good fortune on your journey.

Now, let's go sell something.

Craig Garber

Craig Garber
July 25, 2009

Dedication

In spite of my perceived callous exterior and my biting sense of humor, there are a few things in life I hold precious and above all others. Number one is my family.

I can honestly say I wouldn't have the drive or the motivation to do what I do, and to perform at the consistent level of intensity I do it at, if it weren't for my wife and three kids. They are always on my mind, and have supported and encouraged me, through good times and bad. And believe me when I tell you, we've had some very bad times, for sure.

I want to thank my loving wife Anne for everything. Anne, you have encouraged and supported me, pushing me to places far beyond what I ever could have expected or done on my own, and you never gave up on me, even when I was ready to give up on myself. You put up with me even when I am an asshole. You are my true soul mate, and you are a wonderful mom.

You are a very brave woman and I respect you and love you for that. Don't ever question yourself, you have more smarts than anyone I know! Always go with your gut, babe. I will always love you and take care of you, and look after you forever. Oh, and I know I tell you this all the time, but you are also one smokin' hot blonde.

You've dealt with my completely screwed up ex-wife, my nutty dogs, my boundless and crazy energy, and my driven and unrelenting work ethic, better than anyone else can.

Either you are crazy or I am one hell of a catch.

Don't answer that one.

And to my children. Thanks for putting up with me even though I overreact some times, even though I yell too much (I am getting better, right?) and for loving me through thick and thin. You will *never* know how much it meant to me when we were dead-broke and I told you guys, and all you said was "So what. We know you'll make something happen."

Nick, I will always remember when you came with me to Costco for the business expo and nobody showed up. You were so enthusiastic and optimistic the entire day, you'd have thought we were fighting off the crowds swarming around us, even though we didn't get one prospect all day. Even when those old ladies kept coming over and taking the free pens and Hershey's Kisses, you acted like we just hit a homerun to win the World Series in the bottom of the 9th inning. You and I have been in the foxhole together on more than one occasion, and ultimately we've always managed to climb out winners, even though sometimes it looked pretty bleak.

I know you are having a tough time right now. But I hope you somehow manage to find the strength to believe in yourself as much as you believed in me that day at Costco. And, as much as we all believe in you.

Life isn't easy Nick. But for you life isn't just difficult, sometimes it's overwhelming. That's O.K. though. Sometimes it's overwhelming for me, too. But be strong and fight. I will *always* be here for you when you need me, through thick and thin. But you have to be here for yourself, first. I know you can do it, Nicholas. Daylight's coming soon, and I love you very much and I know you can do anything.

Casey, you are an inspiration to me every single day you swim, run long distance, wrestle, and smile. Your optimism, persistence, and tolerance are incredible. You are truly "the man in the arena." Your commitment and dedication to what you do is motivation to all of us, and I sure wish I had your patience and your ability to forgive and forget, along with your tenacity. Whenever I picture you in my mind, it's always with a smile on your face. I am so very lucky you are my son.

I have missed precious time with you, thank you for the second chance. I promise you from the bottom of my heart, I won't blow it this time. I want you to know that whenever I am being pushed to my own limit, and I want to give up, I *always* picture you running around that track and getting ready to kick into your fourth and final big lap. I can never ever give up after thinking of this. You help me become even stronger.

You really have made me so incredibly proud, and I know this is just the beginning.

And Sam, you have the good and bad fortune to have the best and worst of your mother and I. You did hit the lottery though, because you got mom's looks! For me, there is no greater source of energy in this world than your own enthusiasm over life or over the things you learned in school that day... or simply when you say "Daddy."

I respect you so much for your decisiveness, your feistiness, and your drive. Keep marching to the beat of your own drum -- it's really the *only* beat that counts.

Now please stop fighting with your brothers.

I never had real parents to look up to, but **all of you** are my heroes.

I think of each one of you all day long.

Thanks, Love Dad

**This picture was taken in front of Lunch Counter Falls, the largest Class V rapids
on the Upper Snake River, just outside of Jackson, Wyoming.
Left to right, Nick, Anne, Samantha, Craig and Casey**

Who Is Craig Garber And Why Should You Care?

If you and I are going to develop any kind of a relationship, and if I'm going to have any kind of credibility with you, then you need to know who I am and why you should listen to anything I'm about to tell you, right?

O.K., so without going into my entire autobiography, I'll cover my professional and business career here. (You can find a lot more information about me personally on my website at kingofcopy.com, and in many of my daily missives.)

I graduated from the Bernard M. Baruch College (a division of City University of New York) in 1986, with a degree in Public Accounting, of all things. Back then, they affectionately used to call it UCLA, "University on the Corner of Lexington Avenue."

I actually graduated with honors from a well-known New York High School, The Bronx High School of Science. I did great on my SAT's and had good grades, but we were broke, so it was off to public school I went, when it came time to college. And at $23 bucks a credit, CUNY was the best deal going.

Before CUNY, I did a two-year stint at SUNY Binghamton (State University of New York), but after getting arrested by campus police for "allegedly" selling weed, I bailed. For a number of reasons, I was too immature to be away from home at the time, and I ran wild like an uncontrollable stallion.

The truth was, at 17, I already had too much emotional baggage. I'd suffered through years of physical abuse and emotional manipulation at the hands of my old man, and I wasn't socially equipped to go out into the world on my own at that time. Hanging around a bunch of spoiled affluent kids from Long Island wasn't something I was capable of handling. I was jealous and socially immature and completely unprepared to function on my own.

Today, after years of study and direct application, I can handle anything and anyone, and although I have a gruff exterior, I'm not confrontational at all. (Although if pushed...) But back then, I was *extremely* confrontational and angry. I had a chip on my shoulder the size of Montana, and anyone unfortunate enough to be around me at the wrong time, got the brunt end of it - usually for no reason and for no fault of their own.

In school upstate, kids would ask me questions like, "Do you have rats in your apartment?" "Were you in a gang?" "What's it like growing up in the projects?"

I just couldn't handle the ignorance, and I wasn't savvy enough to separate the kids who were condescending from the ones who were simply curious and unaware, which was probably most of them.

I was street smart, but not "money smart." I was in "limbo," as Al Lubrano says in his wonderful book *Limbo*, which every blue-collar kid who outgrows his neighborhood should read.

I was too smart to hang around the kids from my old neighborhood. They knew it, and weren't too keen on hanging out with the "college boy" anymore, either. But I also wasn't smart or wealthy enough to hang around with the kids from better neighborhoods, who grew up with better parents, and who knew what having a few dollars in their pockets felt like. And they weren't willing to accept me, either.

It's a middle ground you tend to live in for a while, until ultimately YOU make up your mind and decide who you want to be. The nice thing is, that choice is 100% yours.

I spent my first two post-college graduate years working as a CPA for Arthur Young, and then a third year with Ernst & Young after Ernst & Whinney merged with AY. I was very "technically competent" at my job in the audit department, but again... I had big problems fitting into the corporate culture.

Little social things tended to completely screw me up. While others sat down at the lunch or dinner table with their co-workers to enjoy a meal, things like which fork to use or where to put my water glass, were completely beyond me. And frankly, I didn't care about these things enough to learn them.

I wanted to fit in, but I wanted to fit in on my own terms. But that's simply not how the game is played in the beginning.

I never seemed to know what to talk about. Why were these people so consumed with business? What about the Yankees or how your family was doing?

A few people tried taking me under their wing, sensing I was a diamond in the rough, but I just wasn't ready for it.

Remember that chip on my shoulder?

Well, it held me back for a *l-o-n-g* time, until I was ready to deal with it, in my early 30's.

In 1989, after leaving the accounting firm, I got into sales. I'd moved to Florida at that time with my (now) ex-wife, and I was living in Plantation, which is a suburb of Ft. Lauderdale.

At the time, South Florida was the perfect place for me to live, actually, since it's absolutely the angriest place in America. The people in South Florida make New Yorkers look like big giant cuddly puffy clouds. When I left South Florida 16 years later in 2005, I promised myself I'd never return. Because my dad was such a hot-head, I'm like emotionally allergic to anger, and South Florida is just too angry and too toxic for me.

I didn't become successful at selling until 2000 when I got involved with emotional direct-response marketing, which means I had an 11-year gap where I was also flat-broke.

All the time.

Prior to this, for me, it seemed like in sales you're either making a killing, or living week to week and getting killed.

Oddly enough, it was my less than perfect childhood growing up in a housing project in the Bronx, with an abusive father at the helm, that ultimately allowed me to excel and made me such a "natural" at direct response marketing.

See, emotional direct response marketing is all about knowing what makes people tick and how to create certain reactions in your prospects. In this case, the reactions you want to create, are designed to either get someone to buy something, or... to get someone to "raise their hand" and let you know they're interested in hearing more about what you have to say.

In the first situation you're looking for buyers, and in the second, you're prospecting for qualified leads.

So you're either selling or generating leads, and in either case, you'd better be able to understand what causes people to do things, at an emotional level.

And here's where irony of my childhood comes in. Malcolm Gladwell explained it best in his best-selling book, *Blink*. Gladwell said, "People who have had highly abusive childhoods... have had to practice the difficult art of reading minds. In their case, the minds of violent parents."

And it's true. You see, I needed to know, within a split-second of the time I walked through the front door of my apartment, what was going to be coming at me, next.

Misjudging this, or saying the wrong thing, the wrong way, could mean the difference between peaceful co-existence with my father, and a weekend in Beirut.

See where I'm going with this? In my world, as a kid, you either got a pat on the back, or a smack across your face. There really wasn't any middle ground here.

I excelled at "knowing what makes people tick" when I was a kid, in order to survive... however I excel at this now, not to survive, but to prosper. Add to this the fact that I grew up in The Bronx, squandering tales of a misspent youth, and you've got a very unusual combination of street-smarts and intuition. And combining this with a 167 IQ, you simply cannot replicate this combination, any more than you can replicate Tiger Woods' golf swing.

The good news is, all of these things can be readily learned to the extent you need to learn them, by understanding a few simple principles of human behavior, and by putting the strategies inside this book to work for you.

You don't have to rewind your life and live with an abusive parent, to be good at emotional direct-response marketing or at Seductive Selling®. (Seductive Selling is my own, trademarked term for how I apply these strategies. It's also the name of the monthly offline newsletter I publish, and the name of my flagship marketing system that explains how to push your prospects emotional buy-buttons.)

However, because of my intuitive nature, once I stumbled across this kind of marketing, I realized I could parlay my understanding of human behavior into a small fortune, once I began applying all this knowledge to business.

Originally, I started in sales as a head-hunter, placing professional accountants, controllers and CFO's into various jobs in the corporate world. I enjoyed the selling process but that industry is rife with bad ethics, and the sales cycle for the higher-end jobs (the ones I always like working on, where you earn the most commission) is extremely long and very uncontrollable.

At that time, I was ill-equipped and had no clue how to get new business, or how to generate pre-qualified leads. Back then, to me, a referral meant the same thing it means to most people in sales. It meant "begging" for leads from "other professionals," or kissing some center of influence's ass for business.

And since neither of these things were very appealing to me, I never did any of them.

So... in spite of a great work ethic, I usually starved.

After that, I got involved with selling commercial liability insurance. The best thing that happened in this gig, and frankly, in my mind, the only reason why I was meant to have this job, was that I met my current wife there. She was one of my clients and Lord knows I give great client service.

One thing I just want to stop and make you aware of here, is that there will be things you do in life, and especially in business, that seem completely unproductive. Things you make no money at, and projects you work on that fail.

Don't worry about them. That's normal, it's just a part of life. In spite of what most gurus would have you believe, not everything works. In fact most things *don't* work the way you planned them. That's just the way it is.

Many of these experiences will just fall off your radar screen like yesterday's breakfast. But others will prove to be very important later on, so don't get down on yourself for things that failed or things that wasted your time. If you're awake and learning, nothing you do is ever wasted.

I hated my job selling insurance. I worked for some redneck former CPA who thought he was the cat's meow. The guy had the personality of a small soap dish, yet he seemed to think he was Moses coming down on high from the mountain with some secret tablets to offer his staff.

His idea of selling was to cold call as many people as possible and beg them for appointments.

So there I was, now 5 years into selling, close to 30 years old and still reduced to making cold calls.

So again... I usually starved.

But I got to my next destination from there, and for this, I'll always be grateful. Because ultimately, that led me to where I am now.

My point is that most things you do in life, usually do wind up making sense and having a purpose. The thing is, you don't always get to find out what that purpose is, until later. Remember, you can't connect the dots moving forward -- so sometimes it just takes a little while to figure out what was really going on.

Here's a little story that'll show you what I mean.

When I was a headhunter, there was an applicant I worked very closely with, trying to place him into a CFO slot. At the time he was a senior manager with Deloitte & Touche, and he wanted out.

Unfortunately for him, the deal we were working on didn't pan out, in spite of both of us working very hard to make it happen.

He did eventually land a job as a CFO, and I moved on to a new job selling commercial insurance. As luck would have it, a year or so later, his company was looking for a new insurance agent. We'd kept in touch on and off, so he called on me for help with his insurance program.

I set up an appointment to meet with the VP at his firm, who handled their insurance. I walk in to meet with the woman -- a very attractive blonde -- and we hit it off. Well, somebody up there must have been looking out for me, because here we are almost 17 years later and me and the attractive blonde will be celebrating our 15th wedding anniversary in a few months.

So don't worry about wasted effort. If you're smart, and if you're sincere and your intentions are pure, then your effort is never wasted. The results just don't always present themselves to you when you want them to.

O.K.?

Good, now let's get back to my spotty career. I'd just left my job as an insurance agent, and by this time, I'd come to the conclusion I wanted to sell some sort of financial services, since I understood money (CPA, passed the exam first time out.)... I could present complicated concepts in a very easy to understand way... and because I was interested in making bigger ticket commissions.

I also knew I only wanted to work with entrepreneurs, since I have no patience to wait around until someone else can "get back to you," because your contact isn't allowed to make decisions on their own.

I'm not very good dealing with committees, nor am I good at time-consuming meetings where nothing's really going on but a bunch of paper-shuffling and protocol following.

I enjoy dealing with decision-makers since I am a decision-maker. Not that I always make the right decisions, just that I'm not *afraid* to make decisions and take responsibility for them.

Plus I needed to be free. I'm about the last guy who's going to be able to sit in some sort of stupid rah-rah Monday morning meeting and sit their quietly obeying. I don't need to be kicked in the ass to get motivated.

I like doing things differently and I like being different, to the point where I am effectively, unemployable. I'm just fiercely independent.

I wasn't ready to work for myself, but I had to do something where I was as independent as a sales person could possibly be. So in 1994, right before Anne and I went off to Hawaii to get married, I took a job with a national financial planning firm that specialized in estate tax planning for high net worth individuals and business succession planning for entrepreneurs.

Par for the course with me, things started off on the wrong foot, immediately. The guy who hired me was someone who, for the first time in my life, I considered to be a mentor. A guy I could look up to, both career-wise, and a man who I respected as a person.

When I came back from my honeymoon, however, there had been some sort of a management shakeup, and this fellow was no longer running the local branch. He'd been demoted to being a regular producer just like me.

I was screwed right there and then.

Instead, they put some stereotypical young gung-ho corporate robot in there, who I got along with, about as easily as a school of divers gets along with a hungry shark. I wanted out of there and away from him as soon as possible.

Here's an example of the kind of relationship we had. At my first corporate Christmas party, he got really hammered and tried to hit on my wife. I can understand why he did it, he was in a miserable marriage and he was one of those guys who was perennially sexually frustrated. That was on a Thursday night.

On Friday morning I got up at the crack of dawn, put on my suit and tie, and was sitting down in his office waiting for him by 6:30 am. At about 7 o'clock, he comes strolling in, obviously surprised to see me there.

We greet each other cordially and he asks, "What's up?"

I close his door, sit down very calmly and slowly and look across his desk, directly into his eyes. I calmly and slowly say to him, "If you ever hit on my wife again, I will rip your head off. Do you understand me?" (He nods slowly and apologizes.)

"Are we clear on this?" ("Yes it will never happen again. I'm really sorry.")

I then get up and leave.

Needless to say, I never got employee of the month, but I really liked what I did and I wanted to learn as much as I could about the business. So I stuck around for about 4 ½ years and then on January 1st, 1999, I struck out on my own and started my own financial planning firm.

Although I had some good years, I was never extremely successful as a financial planner, again, because I had no marketing system. No predictable way of attracting pre-qualified clients who wanted to work with me.

And at the time, I was also knee-deep into a custody battle for my sons with my ex-wife, so needless to say I felt financial pressure every hour of every single day.

My decision to strike out on my own was based on the fact that I'd make more money simply because I no longer had to pay my office a percentage of the profits (which would more than double my commissions). And being very organized and detail-oriented, I'd have no problem taking care of all the regulatory and compliance issues, and all the required licensing and record-keeping, relevant to this business.

The problem was, the only business I ever really was able to pick up, was based on my tenacity to never stop following up with a lead, and not my ability to actually get leads. And because I sincerely cared about doing the right thing for my clients, once I did get in with a client, the payoff was usually large, but the problem was, they were few and far between.

I was, and I still am, someone who makes recommendations based on what's best for my customers and clients, and not what's best for me. If the two happen to intersect, that's great, and today my marketing is geared towards attracting those customers and clients where that's *most likely* to happen. After all, that's what good marketing should do. But no matter how broke I was, I've *never* placed my needs over a client's.

That's called "Making your problems someone else's problems," and that's just not how I roll. I'm into total self-responsibility. Chances are good, whatever's going on in your life, someone else didn't put you in that position, so it's not fair to expect or rely on someone else to get you out of it.

Now let me tell you, it's a blessing and a curse to be independent, and to be the kind of person who's always relied on your own wits to survive. The blessing obviously, is that you generally don't need anyone's help to move forward in life.

You're the guy people want to be in the foxhole with, because they know -- eventually -- they're getting out of there.

The curse is the same though. You think you don't need anyone's help, and you're reluctant to take it when it is offered. But the reality of life, and especially in business, is that there's **no way** you're going to make it on your own.

You need coaches, mentors, and a peer group to gather ideas from, bounce ideas off of, and to breathe creative "fresh air" into your mind. The ideal situation is having a mentor or two who can guide you through your trials and tribulations, or a partner who can short-cut your learning curve and spare you some losses.

Avoiding these kinds of relationships cost me a bundle and set my financial success back a number of years. Today, I no longer shy away from ideas, although I am quite selective about who I take them from.

After I set up my own firm, I (again, "accidentally") stumbled across a direct-marketing system that was supposed to help you get leads to sell life insurance. And as I began getting more involved with emotional direct-response marketing and writing sales copy, I "sensed" this was something I'd be good at. Again, because I understood what made people "tick," and this is the fundamental principle of direct-response marketing.

I never knew how to use this knowledge to make money. Before this, all I knew how to do was use it to survive on the streets and in my home growing up.

Well it turns out, the late Gary Halbert, one of the world's most well-known copywriters, and in my experience, one of the most brilliant marketing minds ever, lived about 25 minutes away from me. So, long story short, I contacted him and wound up working with him for 6 months.

After apprenticing with Gary Halbert, one night, after I wrote a long-form sales letter for him, he sends me this e-mail, which I've kept to this day:

"Craig, I think you have more natural talent for writing direct response copy than anyone else I've ever met. I've never said this to anyone else. You are GREAT and 100% ready. Actually, I think you might be better than me. You are a f*@%ing genius at this. Gary

We need to talk. Email me your number again and best time to call."

Gary then launched my career by promoting me at his seminars, and the rest, as they say... is history.

So now that you know where I came from, here are a few more things I've accomplished, that should make you want to soak up everything I'm about to tell you:

✓ I'll show you my income figures in just a minute, but appreciate that all my money is made with one full-time and one part-time employee. I have no office -- instead, I work out of my lake-front home overlooking my boat dock and my Jacuzzi. And I make all my money using the same exact strategies I reveal in detail, in this book, and each-and-every-month, inside my offline newsletter, also called Seductive Selling. I don't believe in keeping information like this hidden. Marketing, like good music, is all based on existing ideas, so if you don't learn them from me, you'll learn them from somebody else, so you might as well hear 'em from me, first.

Also, appreciate with the exception of a failed Google adwords campaign, I spent NO money on advertising at all. I'll get into this more a little later. All the leads I got basically came from organic search engine terms, posting articles online, and constantly updating my blog and my website with great information that people refer out.

✓ A while ago, I suggested to a private consulting client of mine, Brian Deacon, from Asheville, North Carolina that he "dump" his non-performing business, which was draining the life out of him, and instead get into one that would leverage his talents and relationships more effectively. To Brian's credit, he accepted my comments and did as I advised. **He also hired me to write his first mailer for this new business. Result: AN UNHEARD of 42.7% response on his FIRST mailing, and $152,751 in sales!** (And no, you are NOT misreading this.) Oh, and by-the-way, Brian (a former VP of Global Marketing at Microsoft, who worked side by side with Bill Gates) recently told me he expects this new business to bring him in over $3.5 Million dollars in revenue over the next 12 months. Not bad for a guy who at the time, was drowning in debt and just a few months away from having to abandon his dream of becoming a successful entrepreneur, is it?

✓ **A lead-generation piece I wrote for Chet Rowland, the owner of one of the largest independent pest -control companies here in West-Central Florida, produced a 7.5% lead-generation response, when mailed out to an ice-cold list in what was assumed to be "a completely unresponsive" marketplace!** In fact, we split-test no less than THREE different versions of letters I created, and all three of them came within a .7% response rate of each other!!

✓ Mike Miget, a residential mortgage broker in St. Louis, came to me because he needed help! His business is obviously *highly* competitive... he'd been studying direct-marketing for over 10 years and he'd also worked with a number of marketing "gurus" already, but yet, nothing would make his business budge. Using some sneaky (but 100% legal and ethical) techniques, **I developed a proprietary marketing system for Mike (which he has since trademarked), and the piece I wrote for him increased the number of leads he is now getting by *over* 50%. And since these new leads are also far better quality leads, his net profits are up well over 60%!** Mike's own loan officer coaching program went on to generate in excess of $1 Million dollars in net cash, using the strategies and marketing pieces I created, as the bedrock of his program..

✓ Another client of mine, Tom Foster from Phelps, New York -- has one of THE most boring and mundane businesses you could imagine, and he's actually located in the poorest county in New York State! Tom originally came to me, pretty much scared to death! In his mind, he'd already "surrendered" to his perceived destiny, which was to continue living week-to-week, barely paying the bills and just getting by. Today, however, Tom's no longer hopeless -- he's having the time of his life since **I "at least TRIPLED" his business**, according to Tom. Funny how even the most boring things in the world seem exciting when you've got serious and consistent cash-flow coming in, isn't it? (You can actually hear a recording of Tom at kingofcopy.com/ssnl - Warning: He does use some foul language on the call!)

✓ Before the real estate market went south, I created a Pre-foreclosure Lead Generation product (called the Pre-Foreclosure Success System), that has **no less than tripled the number of leads even the most successful Pre-foreclosure experts had been getting, using any other system or methods**. This was done prior to the current housing meltdown, when it was much harder for investors to find homes.

The best thing about this unconventional system, is that these leads call YOU, instead of you having to do the old dog-and-pony show, where you go out and start "convincing" sellers to do business with you. My system does ALL the convincing for you, and prospects are *thrilled* you're willing to work with them.

✓ This past year, I started a new niche business, consulting residential loan officers. **Before even lifting a finger to develop the marketing systems for our initial clients, I was able to collect $84,000 in fees, ahead of time!** (Oh, and by the way, this was the second time I did this. The first time, with the Pre-foreclosure Success System, I collected $45,000 in advance.) What made this particularly rewarding, was that 3 weeks prior to signing up, these participants (who paid me an average of $6,000 each), had never even so much as heard my name before!

This system has gone on to consistently generate a 2.5% lead generation response for those loan officers using it -- even in this horrible economy. That means for every 2,000 pieces of mail they send out, they are getting at least 50 fresh new *qualified* leads calling them. Before using this system, a 2,000 piece mailer might get them 10 leads, and *maybe* they were qualified leads... maybe they weren't.

✓ In the men's dating industry, **I sold $47,745 Dollars of low-priced information products in 3 weeks to a very small list (less than 1,000) online, with no pre-promotion or pre-sale warm-up, no teleseminar, and no teaser mailings!** Not a bad start for a new business that was just getting off the ground, now is it?

✓ I helped one of the members of my Mavericks Coaching group (Norm Blankenship from Meadow Vista, California) write a piece that pulled in a 17% response and a cool 80-to-1 return on his direct mail! **That means he made $80 from every dollar he spent on a mailing, and this was in a very difficult niche (small group insurance sales of a non-traditional product).**

✓ I wrote a yellow pages ad for a client up in a small town on the Washington state - Idaho border. The ad is currently pulling an insane **twelve-to-one** response -- during slow season, and in a low-margin business! He had two comments the third week after the ad broke: "My wife can't *believe* I'm bringing checks like this to the bank -- she almost doesn't think it's real." And, **"If I run the ad in the next county over, I am going to put my competition out of business!"** (Brad Bowman - Palouse-Empire, Washington)

After a very rough start in business, and an even rougher start in life, I'm living proof that your past has nothing to do with your future, unless you want it to. Like I said, who you were yesterday has nothing to do with who you are today, and certainly even far less to do with who you'll be tomorrow.

Today I am one of the most prolific and highest-paid freelance copywriters and direct-marketing consultants here in America. I see consulting clients only in my home office here in Tampa, at $7,500 a day, and I won't even think about sitting down and writing a marketing campaign for someone unless they're willing to pony up upwards of $60,000 plus ongoing royalties. I also run an active consulting practice working closely with entrepreneurs from all around the world, in a variety of coaching and Mastermind Groups.

What is far more important about me, than what I can tell you, is what others have to say, and if you want to see this, I'd again, encourage you to look through my website. Specifically, the following pages:

Seductive Selling Newsletter	kingofcopy.com/ssnl
Lead Generation Explosion	kingofcopy.com/leads
Seductive Selling System	kingofcopy.com/seductive
Success Stories	kingofcopy.com/testimonials.html
Telephone Consulting	kingofcopy.com/consulting
In-person Consulting	kingofcopy.com/consultingday
Mastermind Group	kingofcopy.com/mastermind
Mavericks Coaching Group	kingofcopy.com/mavericks
Success Stories	kingofcopy.com/testimonials.html

At this point, I hope I have your attention.

In the next Chapter, I'm going to show you one more thing about my business I think you'll find interesting, and then we're going to get down and do some work.

The Proof Is In The Pudding

Have you ever heard the expression, "The Proof Is In The Pudding?"

Well, interestingly enough, according to Ask Yahoo (on yahoo.com), here's the story behind this expression: Apparently, the phrase was originally "the proof of the pudding is in the eating." It dates back to at least 1615 when Miguel de Cervantes published *Don Quixote*.

And it means, the true value or quality of something can only be judged when it's put to use.

In other words, "results are what count."

So before we go anywhere, let me just show you my numbers from calendar year 2007, so you know what I'm about to tell you is factual and not some sort of exaggeration or overstatement I dreamt about, or created to make myself look like something more than I really am.

In 2007, I made $578,463.44 with a small online list of less than 5,000 names. On the next page, you'll see a snapshot of my shopping cart for that year. These numbers represent the bulk of my earnings online and do NOT include fees from consulting, copywriting, or royalties, which make up the remaining $116,427.68.

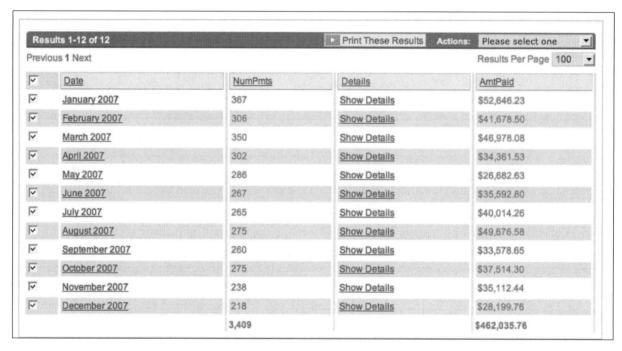

	Date	NumPmts	Details	AmtPaid
☑	January 2007	367	Show Details	$52,646.23
☑	February 2007	306	Show Details	$41,678.50
☑	March 2007	350	Show Details	$46,978.08
☑	April 2007	302	Show Details	$34,361.53
☑	May 2007	286	Show Details	$26,682.63
☑	June 2007	267	Show Details	$35,592.80
☑	July 2007	265	Show Details	$40,014.26
☑	August 2007	275	Show Details	$49,676.58
☑	September 2007	260	Show Details	$33,578.65
☑	October 2007	275	Show Details	$37,514.30
☑	November 2007	238	Show Details	$35,112.44
☑	December 2007	218	Show Details	$28,199.76
		3,409		$462,035.76

Again, total income grossed that year was $578,463.44.

Now don't get me wrong -- there are loads of people, especially online, who are making lots more money than I am. However, most of them were working with lists (meaning, the number of people they had to market to) *significantly* larger than mine or they are in unusually profitable "niche" markets.

And here's proof of the size of my list. This snapshot was taken on January 16th, 2008, and is actually the GROSS number of people on my list. Appreciate that this "gross" number includes 700-800 people who already had unsubscribed from my list at this point. Also, 816 of the people on this list had literally just been referred over to me by my friend Christian Godefroy after the first of the new year.

Autoresponder Name	Msgs in Series	Unique Clients
0-KingOfCopy.com Daily Tip	3	5675

So in reality, my list was much closer to 4,000 names than 5,000. Here, let's work the math:

Gross List	5,675 names
Unsubscribed list members	(700)
New names just received 2008	(816)

**Net number of names being
marketed to at the end of 2007**   **4,159**

Now let me share something else with you that's *very* instructive. It shows you how important it is to interact with, and constantly get feedback from mentors and other peers outside your own business, and outside of your own industry.

Originally, I had no particular idea what I accomplished was even of any significance. See, all I knew and thought about were all the other guys out there making more money than me, and how much further I had to go, and all the other plans I needed to put in place to get me there.

For instance, a very close friend of mine, Christian Godefroy, who I just mentioned a few minutes ago (he works primarily in the French marketplace, but you can find his English site at http://www.positive-club.com) earns well over a couple hundred thousand dollars every single month. But... he has 300,000 people on his list!

Christian's one of the few people I've looked up to as a mentor -- he's an absolutely brilliant marketer, in addition to being one of the classiest guys I know. He's one of the few people who when he speaks, I'm all ears.

I had the chance to spend some time with him at his beautiful oceanfront flat in Portugal, and the first day I got there, he sat me down and said to me, in his classy French accent, "Craig, please tell me. How did you make so much money with such a small list!?" He then said...

"This... is unheard of!"

And so that's when my appreciation of what I'd accomplished, started to kick in. **When a guy who's sold in excess of $300 Million dollars worth of goods and services, tells you he wants to learn something from you, you open your eyes. You don't need to be a brain surgeon to come to the conclusion that if a guy like this wants this information, then maybe you have something other people are going to want to know, as well.**

Now one thing I also must tell you is that I earned all this money *without* running any space advertising (display ads in newspapers or trade magazines)... and *without* using any direct mail other than to my existing customers (meaning, I didn't use direct mail to generate leads).

Today, I am doing each of these things currently, not only in my primary kingofcopy.com business, but in all my businesses.

And "Yes," this means this year and next year should be even more profitable as my list continues growing and as I get involved in more projects.

You should also know I RARELY ran any kinds of sales on my products, and I don't discount products or sell at unusually low prices. (We are currently in the process of testing lower-end product pricing specials at kingofcopy.com/special.) In fact, if you listen to an interview I did with Christian Godefroy himself (I'll give you the link to hear it, at the end of this Chapter.), you'll hear my pricing formula works like this:

For whatever product I'm selling, I look around the marketplace and see what else is out there from a competitive standpoint. Then, because I know my products and services are head-and-shoulders better than even my nearest "competitor" (I don't really believe in competition, I think if you're a good marketer, there's MORE than enough business for everyone.), I price my products significantly higher than their baseline.

I've been writing emotional direct-response copy since 2000, in sales since 1989, and working since I'm 14 (1977), and here's what I've consistently noticed: I always work harder and have more integrity about what I'm doing, than everyone else around me. Consistently delivering the best service, and doing what it takes to be the best, seems to be far more important to me, than to everyone else.

And based on my experience, people are more than willing to pay a premium for these traits. As a wise man once said, **"Price is only an issue in the absence of value."** And since my value is *always* greater than everyone else's, and more than what my buyers are expecting because of their previous experiences, charging and collecting premium prices for premium products and services, has never been a problem for me.

Also, I did a few joint ventures last year, but I didn't spend any money on advertising, with one exception. There was one time I tried Google Adwords. I got hooked up with a guy who promised he'd manage my account and get me *loads* of fresh, new pre-qualified leads. After paying him a hair over $3,000, and after him spending another $4,000 of my money on Google Adwords, I added a whopping 21 leads to my list over a three-month period.

Now I don't pretend to be a Google Adwords expert, and since then I've learned a hell of a lot about it. But I do know that spending $7 Grand for 21 leads in my business, is a crime.

So I terminated my relationship with this bozo rather quickly.

And just so you know I'm not any less immune to people trying to pull stuff on me than you are, when I told the guy I was pulling the plug on our relationship, he actually had the *balls* to engage me in the following conversation. What he said is in italics, *like this...* and my responses are in bold, **like this**:

"Look, I really could use your help writing copy for my clients. Why don't you keep me on as your Google Ad Words manager and you can write copy for my clients."

Are you kidding me?

Number one, what have you done for me that I'd even want to continue having a relationship with you? And number two, if you need my services, why don't you hire me, the same way I hired you?

"Well, there are some things I can do that will help you."

Isn't that what you were supposed to be doing with the $7 Grand I just dropped on you? How much money does someone have to spend with you before you actually do help them?

"Well, there's just things I can do."

How about this: Since I can't believe you actually have the balls to have this conversation with me, why don't we just agree this didn't work, and try and forget this whole thing ever took place, O.K.?

"Well... I'm kind of concerned about what kind of a reference you might give people about me."

That's the first intelligent thing you've said today. I gotta go.

Now first things first. Don't go calling my office up asking who this person is, and don't ask me who it is if you run into me, either. Just be careful who you're dealing with and abide by this adage and any losses you incur should be minimum: "Hire slow, and fire fast."

Second, the truth of the matter is, I should have seen this coming. The first thing this guy says to me after I hire him to work with me is, "So, how do you think we should market you using Google adwords."

29

And I don't know, maybe I'm stupid or something, but isn't that why I hired him? That's like your doctor asking you for some thoughts on how to reduce the bleeding in your stomach.

But I ignored this, and gave him way too much of a benefit of a doubt when I should have pulled the plug immediately.

I'm telling you all this because you need to know I'm not superhuman or anything like that. I make mistakes and I certainly don't always get it right. I'm *not* one of those people who has some sort of a magic touch, and Lord only knows everything I touch certainly does *not* turn to gold.

Yes, I have an unusual and special skill-set as a copywriter, and I do have an inherent understanding of what makes people tick, which I've applied to understanding how and why people buy. But even this talent was acquired from years of self-study and practice, NOT through formal education.

I don't belong to the internet marketing guru of the month club, and nobody with a big name has *ever* promoted me, online or offline, with the exception of Halbert, back in 2003.

In fact, I'm pretty stubborn when it comes down to it, and I've probably missed the opportunity to develop a lot of quality relationships simply because I like doing things "my way." And I'm not about to schmooze a bunch of people and tell them how wonderful they are, just so they invite me into their club.

Old habits die hard, I guess. But I've learned that if you just be yourself and be open to new ideas and new people... life has a way of sorting things out for you. You're going to have some hits and some misses along the way, but hang in there, and in the end, it'll all work out.

And now, without any further ado let's dig in!

Chapter References

- To listen to the 52-minute interview I did with Christian Godefroy, about my pricing models, go to http://www.kingofcopy.com/media/interviews/christian/index.html. There's no charge for this and you will get lots out of it.

Part One: What To Do

Strategy # 1

Why Hope Is NOT A Good Business Strategy (Don't wish for success, work for it.)

If you're looking for "easy," then this book *isn't* for you. Despite what you may read in sales letters and what fake gurus online might intimate or even come right out and say, making money *isn't* easy, not by a long-shot.

But that's life's filter for success. Those who are willing to work hard, get the money. Those who aren't, can piss and moan about *not* getting the money.

And despite all the horrible sales copy that says things like, "your computer will be spitting out money like an ATM"... and you'll be "sucking money out of your marketplace like a vacuum cleaner on steroids," making money takes serious planning and lots of thinking. And usually masterminding or at least bouncing your ideas off someone with experience, and then careful and meticulous execution of your plans.

"Easy" doesn't fit anywhere into this mix. Which is exactly why so few people have any kind of real money -- they're simply not willing to work hard for it.

I can tell you right now, out of all the money I made, very few of those dollars has come easy. I don't get much of the low-hanging fruit, and that's because most of it doesn't exist, especially in today's economy.

I had to constantly make new sales offers... position myself correctly... create new products and develop new ways of selling them... constantly make upsells, cross-sells, and bounce-back offers... do teleseminars, webinars, interviews and networking at events... survey and listen to my customers... deliver incredible content and top-quality products... continuously educate myself... and work an incredible amount of hours.

In fact, my work ethic is second to none, and this allows me to earn much more money than most people.

You see, sadly, most folks hear what they want to hear and they believe what they want to believe. They foolishly believe making money is "easy" because someone trying to sell them something, tells them it's easy.

What's easy is *thinking* about making money. What's easy is *thinking* you just need "one more thing" to grab the brass ring. One more skill-set, trick, strategy or tip, and *then* you'll "finally be ready" to go out and conquer the world.

This is complete nonsense. Don't get me wrong, I consistently invest thousands of dollars into my education, to make me smarter and to constantly nourish my mind with fresh creative ideas. **But the money is in the *execution*, not the *education*.**

I realize this may shake a few people up who are reading this, and that's why I put it first. If this is too much for you to handle -- if what you really want is another gateway telling you to buy more products and take more seminars -- that's fine, but it's not how I consistently make my small fortune, and it's not how anyone else I know makes theirs, either.

Of course, we all have fears and anxieties about taking on new ventures and even about making money. I'd be lying if I told you I didn't have some jitters before I mail a sales letter out, or before putting up a new web page.

But that's just like getting nervous before going out on stage, or having pre-game jitters before the finals. It's totally normal.

The only difference is, I know these jitters are normal and I also know whenever I get them, there's usually either a big breakthrough or lots of money waiting for me, around the corner. Or else I'm about to learn a valuable lesson about something that's going to make me a bushel of cash, soon.

So instead of freaking out, I embrace this anxiety and use it as energy to fuel my projects, instead of running from it.

But most people don't do that.

Reality is, for most people, "work" is a dirty four-letter word. However, if you aren't one of these people, then the journey ahead of you will be filled with excitement and prosperity. If you're afraid of working hard or you're just plain lazy, however, your journey will be filled with disappointment, constant complaining, and ultimately a lifetime of regrets over "what you could have done."

And I don't know about you, but for me, the one mistake I *never* want to make, is the mistake of *NOT* doing something that can potentially create emotional and financial satisfaction, personal growth and development, or validation of my effort, along with a sense of accomplishment.

If you feel the same way, then you and I are going to have a great relationship, and you're going to love the stories, strategies and tips inside this book.

I'll look forward to helping you on your journey -- let me know how it turns out.

Money-Making Action Steps Checklist

☐ **Be brutally honest and ask yourself whether or not your work ethic is as good as it could be.** You need to "get real" with yourself on this one. The answer may surprise you.

☐ **If your work ethic is truly solid, and you're still not where you want to be, then your problem or stumbling block is either a marketing weakness, or... it's a mindset issue, and we're going to cover both of these things inside this manual.**

☐ If you aren't working as hard as you can be - and I don't necessarily mean "long hours," although at some point in time, you're going to have to work long hours, at least for a little while -- **then why isn't your work ethic stronger?**

   ✓ **Perhaps you've never seen what it's like to work hard.** If so, find a role model and observe him or her, or interview them to find out what makes them tick. I think if you speak to, or read about successful people, you're going to find out they've all been through the ringer in one way or another. Ironically, while there are probably only 5 to 10 different things that drive all of us, yet there are thousands of excuses people make for not being successful.

   ✓ **Perhaps you simply need a defined goal.** Something like, "getting out of debt" isn't as powerful as "paying off your mortgage within the next three years." Remember, any time you set a deadline to do something, or anytime you start measuring whatever it is you're doing, your results will be incrementally improved.

   ✓ **Lastly, I'm not going to sit here and tell you to "visualize" your way to success.** Although this helps, and although you certainly can't be successful until you believe you deserve to be successful, at one point in time no one on earth was a better "visualizer" than me. And yet... I was dead broke. In fact, I was the wealthiest broke person in the world. I visualized myself being rich, but that's as close as the money ever came to me -- in my dreams.

In my case, it was a mindset issue -- I didn't feel "deserving" of success because of my background. But more on that later.

However, appreciate that if you're not working hard, then visualize this: **Where you are right now, is very likely to be where you're going to end up!** And until the pain of this reality is greater than the pain of finally getting your ass in gear and giving things your best effort, your situation will never change. And that's a fact.

✓ **Stop believing all those stupid sales letters you get in the mail or read online that say "it's easy."** That's just what everybody wants to hear. The truth though, is that hard work is necessary to accomplish anything in life that's worthwhile. Again, that's just life's filter for success in any field.

Chapter References

• If you want to hear all the sordid details about my own actual journey, including the good, the bad, and the ugly details of obstacles and trivia going on in my personal life, then check out "How To Make Your Dreams Come True" at kingofcopy.com/dreamscometrue. You'll get a good understanding of why it took so long for me to become successful, and hopefully you'll get to avoid some of the mistakes I made.

Strategy # 2

How To Make A HUGE Net Income
(Become a publisher and sell information.)

There is no other business I know of that delivers more money to your bottom line and into your pockets than the publishing business. Specifically, publishing niche information. And the nice thing is, you can even be in the information business as an adjunct to your regular business, if you know how to do it and if you're creative.

Here are some important insights on this topic from an article I published:

"The Most Profitable Product In The World You Can Ever Sell!"

Thank goodness, the most profitable product in the world you can ever sell also happens to be the easiest product to create.

Can you guess what I'm talking about?

Give up?

Well, that product is...

"Information!"

Let me give you some examples of what I mean: Most information is sold either through written words (books, e-books, special reports or full-blown systems, magazines and manuals), audios (CD's and MP3 downloads), videos (DVD's or online), or through computer programs (like software).

And can you guess how much it costs to burn a DVD? Or what it costs to make an audio CD?

The exciting truth is, in most situations it costs next to nothing. And if you're distributing your information online, even your distribution costs are close to zero, as well!

In fact, if you're selling information that can be downloaded online by your buyer, outside of a few pennies on the dollar for your merchant account and maybe $25 to $35 dollars a month to keep your website going, your overhead (outside of your marketing costs -- meaning, your cost to acquire your customers) are virtually "ZERO"!

That's why "information" is the most profitable product you can sell. And if your information offers good insight to your buyers, you're providing them with a great value and they're very likely to come back for more.

Plus, the amount of money you can make selling information isn't limited to your store hours, the number of hours you can physically work, or your inventory. You can create and publish something one time, and then you can sell it over and over again, forever.

Just look at Microsoft. Last year (these are older numbers, obviously) they did over $32 Million dollars in gross annual sales. Not a big deal, other companies are bigger. But there are few (if any) companies this size, that also have over $49 Million dollars of cash on-hand, and yet only a hair more than $1 Million dollars in long-term liabilities.

I don't know how familiar you are with asset-to-liability ratios (how much you own versus how much you owe), but theirs is astounding -- in fact, it's virtually unheard of.

And why are their numbers so strong?

Because of how much cash their products generate and how little it costs them to make it. Just think, it costs you $300 to buy the new Windows Operating System. How much do you think it cost Microsoft to burn a few CD's and toss in a manual or two?

Maybe $10 bucks?

Maybe?

And not to mention, in their case, many of these new customers are already existing customers simply upgrading their systems. So their customer acquisition costs are actually much lower than normal because of their high percentage of repeat buyers. (This is the main reason why all operating systems are continually upgraded, by the way.)

So how can YOU use this concept of publishing information, to make money?

Here's one example: let's say you're particularly skilled at using a certain kind of software. As you know, most software isn't very easy to use, straight out-of-the-box. And as you also know, most of the standard manuals that come with software programs are horrible.

So how about if you produce an e-book or a DVD (or both) showing your customers how to use this software? Even if you only sell this product for $97 each, at almost 100% profit, it sure doesn't take long for this project to start lining your pockets with some serious extra cash, does it?

100 sales brings you in $9700 in revenue, and almost as much in profits. Not to mention, you'd probably pick up some consulting work and cross-sales to other goods and services from this.

And it's not like you need to do a ton of research to write the book or produce the DVD either. That's the beauty of this.

What if you're a massage therapist?

A book about the "Top 10 Ways To Keep Your Back Nimble And Pain-Free" would be something your customers would want, right?

Maybe you could couple it with "5 Ways To Make Sure Your Golfing Game Doesn't Cripple You: How To Completely Eliminate Back Pain While Golfing!"

Collect flowers as a hobby? How about a book identifying different flowers in different areas of the world? Or maybe you can reveal "The Secret Locations Of The World's Rarest And Highly Sought-After Wild Flowers!"

What if you sell industrial-sized turbine motors? I bet a good DVD showing your customers how to use those motors, and how to keep them running maintenance-free, would be a big hit, right?

Maybe this is the way to go with it: "3 Ways To Avoid Costly Repairs To Your Turbine And How To Extend Its Life By As Much As 7 Years!"

You can come up with a useful information product for almost any hobby or business you have.

What's that you say -- you've got a land-based dry cleaners so you can't use this idea?

Not true!

How about a book that explains how to remove certain stains from a variety of materials and carpeting, or maybe a video that explains the care and storage of high-end wedding dresses?

Or maybe you just give these booklets away to all your new customers. That should be incentive for someone to do business with you, right?

Or perhaps, you can create a book along with some software, for the dry-cleaning industry about how to increase profits and streamline losses, for other people who own dry-cleaning businesses, just like you?

You see, the possibilities are endless!

And remember, nothing is out of bounds here. Even if you can't sell information products, you can definitely give them away as premiums to your customers, to enhance the value of your goods and services, so you can...

Make Your Offers Irresistible!

For example, don't you think if you owned a pet shop, you'd have a better chance of selling your kitty litter if you gave away a FREE report along with every single purchase, called "7 Ways To Eliminate Cat Odor!"

And how about you give away a free offline or online course and a couple of DVD's on how to train your dog? Or information about how to care for and groom your dog, or preventive health care information? Or maybe you give all of this away with every new puppy you sell.

Every new dog owner desperately wants this kind of information, and they'd be glued to those videos, along with their kids.

Or let's say you're an accountant -- wouldn't your clients love to know "How To Beat The IRS At Their Own Game!"

You could even use this technique if you're doing something that really makes everyone nervous and uncomfortable, like, what if you sell cemetery plots?

I bet you're customers would love to know, "Everything You Must Know About Buying Cemetery Plots!"

Can you start seeing all the incredible possibilities here?

Great, so before we wrap up, let's recap what you learned:

1. **First, the most profitable product to sell is information.**

2. Second, you can sell information directly or *indirectly* related to what you do. And you can also give it away to your customers and to new prospects, as incentives to work with you.

3. **And lastly, another thing you can do with information products is to start using them as premiums or bonuses to make your offers irresistible. Or you can bundle them along with your conventional goods and services to increase sales or generate new leads.** This entices new people into doing business with you, and gives you the "edge" in selling more, and in selling your items for higher prices.

When it comes down to it, "information" is the easiest product to create, and there's no product that's worth as much to your customers and clients, either.

Remember, if you are perceived as a problem solver, you will be the authority people want to deal with. But if you're perceived as a salesman only, well... you probably know how people feel about you in this situation, already.

P.S. There's also no "limit" on what people will pay for your information. And the truth is, the more "niched" your information is, the more it's worth!

***

O.K., so now you can probably start thinking of a few ways you can improve the current offers you're making to your prospects, by adding an information component to your core products, right?

Good. Because I want to share some business statistics with you. In an information publishing business, you can realistically expect your net profits to be somewhere between 50% to 70% of your gross profits, depending on your other expenses like marketing and advertising, employee salaries, and things like rent and other overhead.

I used to be a practicing CPA, and I can't recall ANY other business that's going to consistently crank out these kind of margins. Can you?

So if you're not in the publishing or information business, get into it. My offline Seductive Selling newsletter happens to be the bedrock of my entire business, and if I take this one step further, my free online e-zine is the lead generation funnel for my offline newsletter business.

In both of these, I give out tons of great information. Obviously, in the paid newsletter we talk in detail about more solutions to specific marketing problems, we cover the implementation steps more specifically... and the information is much more turnkey and easy to use. In other words, my free newsletter tells you *what* to do, the paid for newsletter tells you *how* to do it.

Money-Making Action Steps Checklist

☐ **Figure out the most pressing needs of your current customer or client base.** The information you want to sell them addresses these needs and solves their biggest problems. Some of the easiest ways you can find out this information are by answering any of the following questions:

✓ **What do your customers thank you for, most of all?**

✓ What do your suppliers tell you are some of the hottest selling items in the marketplace today?

✓ **What are some of the most common continuing education or trade association topics talked about?**

✓ What are some of the most common continuing education or trade association topics NOT being talked about that people wish they had more information on?

✓ **Think about the most common questions your customers ask you, over and over again.**

✓ **What would make your business life easier?** This is a great way to develop a new business by selling information to your peers.

✓ **What kind of information do you wish your customers had that would make your customer support (and your life), much easier?**

✓ **What kind of information will enhance the experience of certain hobbyists?**
For instance, catching more fish... or knowing more about needlepoint patterns would make the participants in both of those hobbies very happy.

☐ What kind of information products do you already own or are you familiar with, that are incomplete or being marketed poorly?

☐ **What are the people in your industry belly-aching about most, at trade shows or online in forums and discussion groups?**

Chapter References

As I said, everything starts with my online newsletter. You can subscribe to it as follows:

• My free daily e-zine is right here on my homepage at kingofcopy.com, or you can also subscribe on the upper left-hand corner of my blog at http://blog.kingofcopy.com and you can also use my RSS feed on my blog as well.

Strategy # 3

My Secret Weapon Finally Revealed

In this Chapter I am going to spill the beans about literally the most important secret weapon I know in marketing, so pay very close attention to what you are about to hear. Almost no one uses this, but if you use it, and you use it correctly… you will make a small fortune, faster than you could ever imagine. **Ignore it, and you ignore what in my experience, is the best-kept secret in business.**

This secret weapon is the foundation that's allowed me to make a hair over $578,000 dollars with a small online list of less than 5,000 subscribers, which is unheard of, so listen, and listen good.

One of the members of my Mavericks Coaching Group, Bob Maunsell, from Worcester, Massachusetts, who runs a security business and who is a guru to others in the security industry, recently landed a $75,000 account using this secret weapon. He has now leveraged this strategy to the members of his own "herd" of followers so that they can now use it as well.

I encouraged Patrick Precourt (a long-time member of my Mastermind Group) to use it, and listen to what happened to him: Patrick, who runs the largest Pre-foreclosure business in Connecticut, recently started a business using this strategy, and if he gets no more additional business other than what he's done in the first month, it will yield Pat an additional $300,000 dollars in income this year alone. This doesn't include any other back-end business that comes up, either. (In Pat's case, since he is an active and prolific coach in his industry, he is very likely to get one to two times this base amount in additional consulting and referral business.)

What's this strategy?

The answer is simple: it is a good old-fashioned offline printed newsletter, sent out monthly, through the United States Postal service.

Here, listen to another success story: Chris Hurn, CEO of Mercantile Commercial Capital, LLC, is a long-time Seductive Selling Newsletter member and a coaching group member of mine as well. He is also a member of the 2007 Inc. 500 list of the fastest-growing companies in the U.S. Chris sends his monthly newsletter out to over 80,000 business advisors and entrepreneurs around the country. Having published one newsletter every month for nearly four years, Chris attributes 3 to 4 closed commercial loans (his core business) per month, to leads generated from his newsletter. Each of these loans is worth over $50,000 to his company, and this year, he's expecting his business to grow another 50% to just under $9 million in revenue, with a net profit margin that would shame Warren Buffet's Berkshire Hathaway.

So how is it that a printed newsletter can be responsible for generating so much money, and for creating so much business?

The answer is simple. See, this isn't the kind of newsletter you may be thinking about, I can promise you that. This is an information newsletter that people will pay a small fortune to get their hands on. Or, it's a topical, Readers Digest-like pop-culture newsletter you mail out for free, to people who have raised their hands up and responded to your lead generation ads.

In the first case, your newsletter is both a revenue generator, a relationship builder, and a way to talk about and generate enthusiasm for you and for your other goods and services. In the second case, your newsletter converts your leads into paying customers and clients.

Here's another example: 26 year old whiz kid Dustin Mathews from Tampa, FL (a former member of my Mastermind group) took the highly competitive real estate speaking and information industry by storm in a little over one year's time (that's only 12 issues) with his edgy newsletter, Dirty Talk.

Originally he started off with a back office copier machine, a roll of stamps and some plain old-fashioned sweat, to get his first few editions out. Now advertisers cover the complete cost of his newsletter while he gets to talk to large list owners each and every month in this lucrative field.

By targeting centers of influence in the industry (Dirty Talk is a free newsletter), he has been able to generate over $100,000 in speaking gigs and joint ventures, and has become the "go to" guy who's now responsible for the planning and execution behind many of the million dollar plus product launches, in his industry.

A printed newsletter is the biggest secret weapon behind the most rapid successes of all the entrepreneurs I know, especially those folks who publish information. Meaning those people who publish or sell "How To" information.

And here's why: first of all, people who consume information, can't get enough of it. Golfers who buy "How to shave a few strokes off your golf game" information, will go to the end of the world to buy an unlimited amount of this kind of knowledge and insight.

Same thing with fitness buffs (that's why there's an endless amount of supplements, books, magazines, DVDs and how-to courses), marketing aficionados, bass-fishing buffs, real estate investors, bird watchers, and so on. You name it -- there's a market for it, and the more rabid and passionate the market, the more rabid the buyer of the information in that marketplace.

For instance, on the next page is a picture of less-than one-third of my own home library. I'd say close to 90% of the information in it, is business-related.

You're very likely to find similar situations with anyone who is passionate and devoted to their craft, hobby, art or business.

So if printed newsletters are so powerful, then why doesn't every business-owner write one? There are a number of reasons, so let's go over them. You may not necessarily like some of these answers, but that doesn't mean they aren't true:

1. **Laziness.** It takes time and effort to put together a monthly newsletter. My newsletter takes two to three full days to compile, write and edit, and that's after three years of getting the formula down and having some kind of a template to work through. And that doesn't include the time in between when I'm clipping out ads and articles and writing down thoughts to discuss in my newsletter each month.

   But there again, Seductive Selling is twelve pages long, uses small font (9 to 11 points), and usually contains 3 to 8 pages of additional examples as inserts. These inserts often include re-writes of ads and sales letters sent in by subscribers.

   However, the good news is, you don't need to do *nearly* as much work to create an effective newsletter. Nevertheless, most folks are still too lazy to even do *half* as much.

2. **Discipline.** Even more difficult than #1 is discipline! See, you can find loads of people who are willing to put together ONE issue of a newsletter, but that number drains down dramatically when you ask them to repeat the same task every single

month, like clockwork. Not surprisingly, scientific studies show that "discipline" is the #1 determinant of success or failure.

"Here's just a very small portion of my library!"

3. **Inability to deliver good content.** Many people feel overwhelmed with the task and responsibility of being able to inform and entertain their audience every month.

However, this is something you must stay on top of, religiously, if you want your newsletter to make you money, and if you want your paid subscribers to stick around. It's also why, if you don't know your audience very well, you are better off hiring freelancers to write your articles. Many times, you can even find these writers within your subscriber base itself.

Consistently delivering compelling content allows me to maintain my subscriber base for over twice as long as industry standards.

4. **Inability to meet deadlines.** Whether your newsletter is a paid subscription model, or even if it's a free lead-generation tool, you'd better be able to deliver it on time, every time. My newsletter gets shipped out every month, around the 20th. I suppose if I had a glitch once or twice, my subscribers would cut me some slack, but I don't want the kind of internal headaches or stress this would bring me. I've been publishing my newsletter for over 4 years now, and we haven't missed a deadline yet. I feel a very strong sense of commitment to my members and I'm very particular about this. And from all the feedback I get, they appreciate this and it doesn't go unnoticed.

5. **Inability to write.** We'll talk more about writing later on, in the Chapter about writing copy, but appreciate all you need to do here, is to turn your normal conversations into print. Newsletter and newspaper writing is conversational in style. Rules of grammar pretty much get thrown out the window. Clarity of communication, and quality of content reigns supreme. As a student in school, I NEVER did well in English or writing. I was always more of a math and science geek. To think I'd make a small fortune from sitting down and plunking away at the keyboard of my computer, was never even a thought, and it still amazes me sometimes.

6. **Lack of entertain-ability.** Look, let me make myself perfectly clear. It really doesn't matter what your newsletter is about, but if you aren't "entertaining" your readers, having even the best content in the world won't matter. People can only handle "so much" information about butterflies, marketing, real estate, or whatever your topic is. Your newsletter should also be a source of entertainment, controversy, and personal growth. It should challenge your readers to elevate and expand their thinking, and you should definitely be able to make them laugh every once in a while.

I'm lucky. I'm fairly quick-witted and never shy away from controversy. I've also been aggressive and had a number of somewhat controversial headlines in my newsletter, like this:

"There's A Reason Why People Are Broke"

"Imagine Me, A Virgin... Again!"

"D... Is For Dysfunctional, Right?"

"How Long Does It REALLY Take To Make A Million Dollars? Just ask me."

"What Is Peter North's Secret?" (It's NOT what you're thinking!)

I can tell you now that each of these headlines were tied to critical marketing concepts, and I can also tell you that my office received loads of e-mails on each one, about how entertaining these issues were, and how much they made people laugh.

And the truth is, if you can teach people something, tell them compelling stories, *and* make them laugh, all at the same time... this is just about the best kind of learning experience you could provide.

There's something else a newsletter offers. Something intangible most people fail to grasp, and yet it is vital to cultivating and nurturing your relationships with your subscribers.

See, the reason why it's so difficult to cultivate new personal relationships the older you get, is simply because you have less time to spare. What with marriage and raising a family, and add to that the time and mental commitment it takes to run a business, any time left over for a business-owner is usually reserved for your family, or for yourself if you can grab a few moments of peace.

And reality is, to develop friendships, you need time. You can't see someone once a year at an association or trade show meeting, and really be good friends with them, can you?

Well, it works the same way with your business relationships. You need multiple contacts to connect and build a relationship, and **this is the primary function your newsletter serves**.

Who else, besides me, gets to come into your home and spend one or more hours with you, one-on-one, in quiet contemplation, every month?

Probably no one.

This, by the way, is also the reason you want your newsletter mailed out, and not distributed online. Your readers consider it more valuable and important when they get it in the mail. Not to mention, if you take a look at all the .pdf files lying around your hard drive, you've downloaded onto your computer over the years... there are probably more of them than you could ever possibly get to, even if you wanted to.

Plus, if you sell a paid newsletter subscription and distribute it online, you are guaranteed it will be bootlegged and widely passed around for free. When this happens -- and I say "when" and not "if," because it is as certain to happen as the sun rising in the east tomorrow morning -- you are being ripped off, and your paying subscribers are also being ripped off.

I'm not saying that technology may change in the future to make this practical, but for now, an offline mailed newsletter creates the most value and forges the deepest relationships with your prospects and your customers.

Other Reasons You Want To Have A Newsletter:

- **Client or customer acquisition tool / great vehicle for lead generation conversions and for upsells** - This is why I pack so much information into Seductive Selling! People read it, and over several months, they get to know me fairly intimately. They get insight into the wisdom, knowledge and experience I have and they get exposure to my personality. And most important, they get to benefit from the ideas and strategies I'm giving them and they turn these ideas into money for themselves.

Once they profit from this information, many of them want more of it, and more access to me. For these folks, their next move is usually to order one or more of my products (which you can find online at kingofcopy.com/products). From here, many continue escalating through my goods and services funnel, higher and higher.

They go into one of my Coaching or Mastermind groups, they book a day of consulting with me, or they hire me to write copy for them. This is the second most important reason you want a written newsletter, with "relationship-building" being the first.

- **Addict your following.** This is part of your relationship-building. How many times have you renewed a membership or subscription, simply out of habit? Probably quite often, and this is another reason to have a newsletter. Your readers get used to their monthly consumption, and therefore they get used to you being in their lives. At some point in time, even if they aren't reading every issue, the pain of not having you in their lives, becomes greater than the slight inconvenience of having you in their lives, even if they can't necessarily get their money's worth out of you, *every* month. In this case, "addiction" is good.

- **Pass-along value.** A newsletter has tremendous pass-along value, and in my case since there is also an Audio Success CD with each newsletter, and a separate packet of examples, there's even more to pass along. I can't tell you how many members have told me they subscribed after reading an issue or two on loan from someone else.

- **To tease or give early notice for your future business ideas.** Your newsletter is a great place to test out new ideas and get priceless feedback on them. I often ask for feedback or interest in an idea I have about developing a new product or program, and my members readily let me know their interest -- or disinterest, as it may be.

- **Sponsors.** If you want to sell advertising, a newsletter is a great place to do it.

You want to be careful here, though, not to start looking like a magazine or newspaper, that only costs a few dollars! Remember, **content is King**.

- **Continuity Income.** If you offer a paid newsletter subscription, it is a great source of continuity income. For me, a guy with a wife and three children, this is very important. I sleep well knowing that with very good predictability, when I wake up on the first of the month, every month, I can count on "X" number of dollars coming in from my various continuity programs. And believe me, I've had my share of sleepless nights over money in the past, so this is important.

Who should you be writing to:

Don't try to be People Magazine. You don't want to try and appeal to a broad swath of consumers here, because it is much more difficult to sell information like this. You want to go deep into a specific field or niche. In fact, the deeper the better.

Don't just write about fish tanks, write about caring for tropical fish living in giant-sized tanks. Don't write about cars, write about Ford Muscle Cars issued from 1959 - 1969. In my case, I don't just talk about marketing, I talk about emotional direct-response marketing and copywriting, and to a lesser extent, successful thinking.

I also share stream-of-consciousness experiences in the daily life of a busy entrepreneur, and how these experiences often impact your business and your personal life.

Each issue, every month, is an idea bank filled with case studies and strategies, and actual live marketing examples. These are topics my members are very interested in and excited about, since the newsletter is geared primarily towards entrepreneurs, business-owners, and independent sales people.

The more specific your topic, the better your newsletter. And so, the deeper you go into a niche, the more passionate people are about it, the more valuable your information is... and the more you can charge for it.

What should your newsletter look like:

With the purchase of this book, you should have received one issue of my newsletter, so you can see my layout. I have changed this layout once or twice, and I've also added one or two new columns along the way. (You can actually buy a copy of the very first issue of my newsletter and other back-issues to see how it's evolved over time at kingofcopy.com/backissues.)

The thing is, you want your newsletter to be easy to figure out, easy to follow, and easy to read. Use serif fonts (like this one, which is "Times," `or this one which is "Courier"`) because they are easier to read offline. (Newspapers all use serif fonts.)

Keep things focused on the content by avoiding big, colored graphics and photos, and write just like you speak (we'll cover writing later on, in a big giant Chapter of its own). Feel free to talk about almost anything, as long as your core message revolves around the topic you've promised to educate, entertain and inform your readers about.

Biggest and most common newsletter mistakes:

- **Making your newsletter "pretty."** Two reasons why you shouldn't do this. One, people are reading your newsletter for content, not aesthetics. If it's too pretty they forget this and start focusing on the pictures and that's no good. Two, a pretty newsletter looks like a magazine -- and last time I checked, magazines cost around $5 bucks, not $20 to $99, like most niched newsletters.

- **Charging too little.** Your newsletter is worth a lot more than you think it is! My personal strategy with pricing of almost everything, is to go into the marketplace and see what people are charging top-dollar for, for similar products. Then I price my goods and services higher than that, knowing I have superior marketing and superior quality products and services. So far I haven't had a problem, but I maintain a sense of healthy paranoia about delivering superior quality, and I never lose sight of this. I am also *always* looking to raise my own bar a little higher.

- **Comparing your newsletter to a book.** Your newsletter can, and should be contemporary. If there is something going on in the news that's on everybody's mind, then by all means discuss it. Feel free to discuss whatever makes sense and whatever your audience tells you they want to hear about -- even if it's not directly related to your main topic. Your newsletter is *not* a book! You *can* go off-topic with it. And don't worry -- if you make a mistake you'll get another shot at it next month, so take advantage of this and have fun with it!

- **Not getting personal.** Your newsletter is, and will become, from a professional standpoint, the centerpiece of who you are and what you do. This is the perfect forum to open up and share things about yourself, and your readers will love hearing it. In my column called "The Back End," I've discussed everything including the abusive home life I suffered through as a child, my first marriage, my custody fight over my sons, our struggles raising teenagers, and in one issue I even revealed a personal quirk I have.

  Now while you may not be as outgoing as I am, my point is that you should open up and develop rapport with your subscribers. This is Reality TV, only it's in print. And last time I checked, the public has an insatiable demand for Reality TV.

- **Not taking risks.** Listen, the biggest breakthroughs you're going to make in life, happen during those times when you've laid it all on the line and taken some risks.

  And the truth is, if you want to have a breakthrough, you generally have to "break" something. And usually, that something is some sort of a perceived mental barrier or limitation. Nothing explosive happens out of conservative plans, so get out of your comfort zone if you want to grow. Remember, you are in control here!

  The good news is, you get almost *immediate* feedback on your results and you can quickly make adjustments for the next time. Say the outlandish -- say what people are afraid to say themselves, but are thinking. Most of the time you'll be rewarded handsomely for it.

- **Towing the party line.** This goes hand-in-hand with what I said about not taking risks. Your newsletter should be the perfect *escape* for your readers. It should take them to a happy place they don't get to go very often, especially if your newsletter is relevant to their business world.

  Towing the party line is easy -- it takes no imagination, no guts, and little effort. Being creative and authentic, however, takes savvy and courage. Think about which one of these traits you want to be known for, and then decide which way you want to go. I know where I'm headed, do you?

Another thing I do in my newsletter is, once in a blue moon, I toss in some goodies.

For example, the last two Januarys I gave my readers a listing of all the books I read in the prior year, along with a mini-critique of them. This was very well received. (I now post most of these book reviews on my facebook page under the "We Read" section. You can friend me on facebook at kingofcopy.com/facebook.)

I'll also toss in a bonus CD every once in a while, or a special report or something else that's interesting and enhances my members' experience.

As I said, a good newsletter in the right marketplace, will literally be like a fountain of money for you.

For more information about how to put together an offline monthly newsletter, I have a program coming out soon called Offline Newsletter Profits, which you can find at kingofcopy.com/newsletter. Inside this program, you learn how to actually write your newsletter, how to sell it, and there is also expanded information on everything else discussed in this Chapter. Contact my office for more information.

Money-Making Action Steps Checklist

☐ **In the last Chapter you figured out what kind of information your marketplace wants.** Now figure out how you can offer this information to them in a newsletter format.

☐ **Think about whether or not it makes sense, in your particular business, to use your newsletter as a free lead generation tool, or as a paid membership newsletter.** As you're thinking this through, consider what your real needs are, and don't be fooled into thinking transaction size is related, at all, to whether or not you should have a paid newsletter or a free one. For instance, if you're a retail consumer dry cleaner, it probably makes more sense to have a free newsletter to hand out and pass around. But, if you remember the example of Chris Hurn, who's a commercial banker with an average transaction value of $50,000 per loan -- he's also using a free newsletter to generate leads as well.

☐ **DON'T commit to doing a newsletter unless you're serious about it.** Nothing's going to sabotage your current (and presumably, good) relationship with your customers or clients, faster than making commitments you can't keep. Remember the old adage, "Rome wasn't built in a day, but it burned in less than a day!"

☐ **If you're going to start a newsletter, don't worry about making it "perfect,"**

otherwise it'll never get done. Remember, if it's free, no one's going to hold you to any kind of strict literary or aesthetic standards anyway, and if it's a paid newsletter, your readers are concerned about content, not aesthetics. Besides, your newsletter (whether free or paid for) is going to change and evolve over time, just like you and your customers. My newsletter today looks *nothing* like my first few issues did. In fact, the name isn't even the same!

☐ **Just do it!**

Chapter References

- For information about my Seductive Selling Newsletter, and to take a free 30-day test drive of it (and receive 18 Free gifts worth $3,632), watch the video at kingofcopy.com/ssnl

- For more information about how to put together an offline monthly newsletter, I have a program coming out soon called Offline Newsletter Profits, which you can find at kingofcopy.com/newsletter. Inside this program, you learn how to actually write your newsletter, how to sell it, and there is also expanded information on everything else discussed in this Chapter.

Strategy # 4

How To Create Continuous Streams Of Income

This is going to be somewhat difficult for some people to swallow, which is why most people won't do it. And this, of course, is why most people never make big gobs of money. But remember, if something sounds uncomfortable, it's probably because it's stretching you a little bit. And when something stretches you, you're making progress! So let's get on with this, right now.

First, let me tell you that I was broke for many years. I declared personal bankruptcy in 1997, and because I grew up with no money, and had parents who were incredibly pessimistic about money, I had loads of negative "scarcity" messages implanted into my head.

I never really had the emotional freedom or attitude that allows you to make big money until probably 2003, when I turned 40. And this was only after a lot of soul-searching, lots of personal therapy to overcome violence and childhood abuse, and finally getting comfortable with the fact that, **"Yes, I do deserve to be rich."** (And so do you, by the way.)

Because of these experiences, and because of spending many years in sales always hunting for my "next kill," just to eat... today I won't take on any new business, or start a new business, unless there's some sort of a continuity component to it.

In a nutshell, a continuity business is one where you get paid on a continuous and regular basis, for services rendered over time. So for example, I run a coaching and a Mastermind program, and members pay monthly to belong to them. My Seductive Selling Newsletter is published monthly, and obviously my members pay monthly for this service as well.

But there are many other kinds of continuity models out there -- some of which you may already be familiar with, others perhaps not.

- **Book of the month clubs, and all its spin-offs including, Audio CD's, Audio CD books, and DVD's... cigars, lingerie, and beer of the month clubs.**

- Online membership sites and forums

- **Dues and subscriptions to social and professional clubs or industry and trade association magazines.**

- Heath club memberships

- **Car wash VIP membership programs**

- Any installment loan or leasing payments (boats, furniture, whatever)

- **Informational subscriptions for CD's and DVD's**

- Memberships to martial arts schools

- **Music lessons or other hobbyist programs (sewing, scrapbooking, art clubs or memberships)**

- Vitamins and supplements

- **Training and educational programs (fitness, photography, drawing, hunting, marketing, fishing, online stock trading, etc.)**

The list is virtually endless!

For me, the continuity business is a no-brainer. I'm not interested in working every single time I need to sell something to someone. I'd rather have one selling process that delivers some kind of ongoing top-quality goods or services, that allows me to get *paid* for this delivery on an ongoing basis as well.

This is much better than having to repeat my selling process over and over again, looking for new customers all the time.

Isn't it?

I also prefer monthly payments over any other periodic stream for several reasons:

1. **Like I said, I like waking up on the first of every month, knowing with relative certainty, how much I'll earn if I did nothing else.**

2. **When I was selling life insurance, I learned quarterly payments had the lowest policy persistence.** Meaning, people canceled policies they had to pay quarterly, more than any other kind of payment. Further observation has shown me similar results in other subscription types of businesses.

3. **I don't want to commit to doing something for more than 6 months or so.** I love being an entrepreneur because of the freedom I have. Forcing myself to "lock in" to a long-term commitment to anyone other than my wife and kids, makes me uncomfortable.

   The pace of life is so fast today. You never know what kinds of opportunities may present themselves to you, and I like to be flexible enough with my scheduling to take on new projects or new studies, or to spend time with my wife and kids if I want to.

   It's also harder to get your customers to commit to this, for the same reason. And obviously, more people are willing to commit to smaller chunks of money than bigger chunks.

   So for all these reasons, monthly works just fine for me.

As a result, all of my businesses, and most of my products for that matter, have continuity models attached to them.

Some of these continuity programs are "forced" continuity programs. Meaning, when you buy a bigger product, smaller-priced ongoing services or subscriptions come attached to it.

For example, when you order my Lead Generation Explosion system or Lead Generation Explosion for Accountants... my Seductive Selling System... or my ABC's of Real Estate Investor Marketing, you also get a free 30-day trial of my offline Seductive Selling Newsletter.

If you want to stay a member and keep the newsletter, you don't have to do a thing -- it automatically gets sent to you every 30 days. If you don't like it, you simply call or fax my office within 30 days from the time you placed your order, and your subscription gets canceled, no problem.

This is what "forced" continuity means. It means you can't order the main product, without getting the continuity product attached to it.

One thing I've done, which I've never seen before, is I used to have TWO forced continuity items on one of my products. I recently terminated a program called my Seductive Selling Coaching Program, simply because after close to 3 years, I lost interest in it.

This program was sold as a forced continuity program, along with The Seductive Selling Newsletter, when you ordered my Seductive Selling System.

I've never seen **anyone** offer two forced continuity programs at once - this was groundbreaking, as far as I can tell.

Let me explain why it worked, though, along with something you need to know before you make your own forced continuity offers.

In marketing, there are no black-and-white absolutes. You're dealing with human behavior, and you never really know how people are going to behave in any given situation.

So you make your decisions and you work with what's most likely to happen. For example, someone who spends $997 dollars with you (which is what my Seductive Selling System costs) is very likely to be able to afford to participate in monthly continuity programs of $49.95 (ongoing Seductive Selling Newsletter membership) and $197 (what the Seductive Selling Coaching program cost).

Not that someone who makes a smaller purchase from you can't or won't pay money for a larger continuity program, but you want to set up your continuity so that the price point of your monthly program is the same or less than the price point of the initial purchase it's attached to.

This is important, so please pay attention.

So for instance, when people join online membership sites, it's common to see an initial offer where you get a bunch of introductory information for one price -- say... $29.95. Along with this, you also get a 30-day free trial of the membership site as well. After that, if you want to continue being a member of the site, you pay that same $29.95 per month.

And in fact, I am currently in the process of setting up a few niched businesses like this with a partner of mine in a variety of hobbyist topics.

Bottom line is, it is much easier to get someone to agree to a lesser purchase, than it is to get them to agree to extra additional ongoing continuity programs that are more expensive.

Let me also point out that forced continuity works best when your buyer gets a free trial of the program. Think about it, when there's no risk to you, you're much more likely to want to get involved in something, as opposed to just committing and signing up straight from the get-go.

Make sense?

So don't be afraid of continuity, or of forced continuity. The lion's share of the money I earn is based on this model. And in fact, my friend Christian Godefroy who has one of the most brilliant marketing minds I've ever encountered, at my insistence, recently adopted continuity into his business.

He works primarily in the French speaking marketplace and has a massive list of over three hundred thousand names. This continuity promotion generated in excess of $307,000 in ongoing revenue, in one week's worth of sales alone! This couldn't have happened to a nicer or more deserving guy, but my point is that if you plan your strategy right, the continuity business will make you a lot of money, and it also allows you to forge one of the strongest relationships possible, with your customers.

As we discussed in the last Chapter about running a monthly newsletter, few people get to interact with their customers every month. You, as an ongoing service or product provider, however... get to do this regularly. This is why the continuity business is such a *great* way to maintain long-term and meaningful relationships with your customers.

You'll find this model is widespread in niche publishing and consulting industries, where the provider is also a good marketer.

Here are a few things that are *very* important with respect to continuity programs, and especially with "forced" continuity programs. Oh, and make sure you consult with a legal expert before you get your continuity-based business going. (**I am NOT a legal expert!**) O.K., here you go:

☞ **You want to make sure you're giving full disclosure about all aspects of your offer (length of trial period, costs, shipping charges, all of it!).** On my web pages and my offline material, I disclose fully, that these trial subscriptions are continuity based, especially when it's forced continuity. I also disclose this a second time on the order forms, again, both online and offline, and in your shopping cart when you order online.

Don't overlook this. We *rarely* have problems with people who've said they didn't know they were going to be signing up for an ongoing service, simply because of our complete and consistent disclosure. However, I've heard horror stories where people have gone the other way -- they've gone out of their way to *hide* the fact that they are going to be signing their customers up for something ongoing.

This is called deception, and that's *not* a way to build a business. On the other hand, it's my firm belief that consistently offering full disclosure is one of the reasons why I've been able to do so well. Remember, making almost $600K with less than 5,000 list members is unheard of. **What I'm telling you here is VERY important, so pay close attention to it.**

☞ **When someone lets you know they want to cancel their participation in your program, cancel them *immediately*.** I never realized this was such a problem until I myself tried canceling a few different subscriptions over the last few years. In 3 out of 4 situations, not only was my subscription not canceled, but I was continually billed until my assistant contacted the customer service department. In one case, she had to contact them three times over a three month period.

Take care of cancels right away, or else you'll be saddled with chargebacks, a bad reputation, and lots of wasted time trying to clean up this whole mess.

Lastly, here's something that might help you. It's a snippet of an article from the October 2008 issue of my Seductive Selling Newsletter. The article talks about current FTC rules and regulations related to ongoing continuity, "negative option," or "till forbid" programs.

Make sure you consult current rules and regulations before putting any kind of program like this into action, and make sure you offer full disclosure.

FTC Watch: This past summer, the FTC began cracking down on "Free Trial" offers, so listen up.

One of the best ways to introduce your goods or services to your prospects, is through a free trial offer. With many of these offers (my Seductive Selling newsletter included), when you accept the free trial, you may also be agreeing to buy additional and ongoing products and services.

Basically the FTC is trying to guard against a deceptive "negative option." A negative option means "unless you proactively do something to cancel, you're going to be charged moving forward." Or, "if you do nothing, you'll be charged."

The FTC ruling says you can't misrepresent something as "free" if it's not.

Sounds fair, no?

You have to disclose all the terms and conditions of any negative option offer, clearly and prominently. You have to include:

1. **The fact that if you accept the trial offer, you're actually agreeing to be enrolled in a membership, subscription or service contract... or that you're paying for additional services if you don't cancel within the trial period.**

2. The length of your trial period.

3. **The cost of the goods and services you'll incur, if you don't cancel during the trial period.**

4. How to cancel during the trial period.

5. **Whether or not you will be charged a non-refundable membership fee if you don't cancel within the trial period.**

6. Whether some kind of fee will be charged automatically to a credit card you used to buy other goods and services.

Let me just say you simply *cannot* disclose your negative options, enough. And just so I can be fair to both of us, let me tell you up front *again*, this is NOT legal advice and that you need to seek appropriate guidance on this from an appropriate advisor, or from the FTC's website, which is at ftc.gov.

***

Money-Making Action Steps Checklist

☐ **In the last Chapter you figured out what kind of newsletter you can sell to your marketplace.** If you plan on selling a paid subscription newsletter, then you now need to figure out the kind of offer you're going to need to make, to attract as many people as possible. Will you sell it standalone, or will you sell it as a forced continuity product add-on with another, higher-priced item, or... will you offer it both ways?

☐ **Another thing you need to consider, is that *you* don't have to provide all the**

actual content of whatever it is you're selling. For instance, there are *loads* of continuity subscription services that simply consist of a monthly interview on audio CD, or a monthly interview with a transcript included. This can easily be done if you're in an industry where there are many experts out there, especially when your marketplace is hungry for information -- which is almost any industry or hobby where the members are passionate. Keep this in mind, in case you're stressing out about creating content by yourself. (You can have others write or compile your printed media for you, but you *will* dilute the "personality" component of your content.)

☐ **Put a lot of effort into systematizing your monthly or periodic deliverable.** You want to have a cookie-cutter system you can easily replicate each and every month, and you want to be able to have quality, reliable and dependable sources of content you can plug into your products or deliverables, regularly.

☐ **Once you have a systematic program in place -- one your customers clearly enjoy -- you don't want to change it too often or too radically.** Your continuity product will become as familiar to your customers as your local daily newspaper. And you wouldn't want to open up your local newspaper one day and suddenly find the sports section and the business section have been swapped around, right? So keep this in mind, and create a system you can replicate both for your best interests, and for your customers' ongoing best interests.

Chapter References

- Current programs I have for sale which offer forced continuity to my Seductive Selling Newsletter include, Lead Generation Explosion (kingofcopy.com/leads), Lead Generation Explosion for Accountants (kingofcopy.com/accountant), the Seductive Selling System (kingofcopy.com/seductive), and the ABC's Of Real Estate Investor Marketing (kingofcopy.com/abcre). Review each of these web pages to see how the continuity component is added.

- One of the smartest and most effective ways of selling ongoing continuity items, is to offer them on a trial basis and make a "big bribe" compelling offer, up front, along with your free trial. To see how my newsletter is sold on a "free trial" continuity basis, with a "big bribe" offer, go to kingofcopy.com/ssnl

- Coaching is also a big part of my continuity business and for this I have two programs: My Mastermind Program (by application only at kingofcopy.com/mastermind) and Mavericks Coaching Group (kingofcopy.com/mavericks)

- And lastly, to see an example the kind of content that can make up a coaching program, you can look at the subject listing of my old Seductive Selling Coaching Program at kingofcopy.com/seductivecalls

Strategy # 5

Why Most Ads (And Most Marketing) Fails

Okey dokey. I've given you my one big secret weapon, and now we're going to move straight into some more proven direct-marketing strategies. For starters, if you want to attract a specific audience, you're going to have to attract them for a reason. You're going to need to cultivate some sort of specialty. And then, within that specialty, you need to identify something different or unique about yourself in your marketing.

You want to specialize in "something," or specialize in catering to one particular demographic of your customer or client base. And here's why: being a generalist doesn't allow you to charge a lot of money... it's not a particularly compelling reason for someone to work with you... and it's very difficult to separate yourself from your competition and answer the one big question your prospects have, which is... "Why should I work with you over someone else?"

Now here's a little secret: you can actually target *many* different kinds of customers, and you can be proficient in multiple skill-sets. But what should be kept separate, is your **marketing** for each of these different customers or skill-sets.

Meaning, use separate marketing pieces to attract your prospects within each market segment you want to work with.

So for instance, if you're a financial planner, the very WORST thing you can do is come up with an ad or a website like this:

CG Financial Planning*

- Investments
- Retirement Planning
- Annuities
- College Planning
- Life Insurance
- IRA's and 401(k)
- Estate Planning
- Mutual Funds
- Stocks and Bonds
- REITs

Call Craig Garber at 813-909-2214 for an appointment.

* Licensed and insured

This kind of ad is an absolute waste of space, yet unfortunately it's what 99.9% of all ads look like. It is nothing more than a big business card, and I don't need to tell you what happens to most business cards, right?

Yep, they wind up hitting the circular file (the trash can), much sooner than later.

See, most people are preoccupied with trying to cast as wide a net as possible, so they can (supposedly) attract everyone. But when you're trying so hard to attract everyone, in reality what winds up happening is... you wind up attracting no one, simply because your message isn't strong enough to resonate with *anyone* in particular.

Just think, would you rather have your knees operated on by a surgeon who removes tumors, performs gastric bypass surgery, and does cardiovascular work as well, or would you rather see a top orthopedist who specializes in knee injuries?

Chances are you want to work with the knee specialist, right?

Well, your prospects are feeling the same way. So what happens is, in trying to appeal to everyone, you wind up appealing to no one in particular. No one can make any kind of a connection with you, because you're not speaking to **their individual needs.**

What you want to do instead, is create multiple marketing campaigns, or multiple websites, and perhaps even multiple "identities" that address one or two specific and related needs (perhaps like Estate Planning and Life Insurance... or Retirement planning and Annuities) and then talk to those prospects who are specifically interested in handling these issues, only.

Then of course, if you're doing a good job, once you get your foot in the door with your customer in one of these areas, they're going to want you to help them with other goods and services. But you must initially attract them to you for *one specific reason*, first.

You simply cannot be all things to all people. This is a huge mistake people make not only in their marketing, but also in their business.

Remember, good marketing gets your foot in the door. Good service, good ethics and technical savvy, keeps that door open.

Most entrepreneurs don't ever learn this and they focus solely on the "doing" aspect of their business (the technical stuff). Frankly, if you're the best "whatever" in the world, but you have no customers to work with, then all you've done is waste your time and effort becoming "the best."

This is why most businesses fail and why few entrepreneurs really make big money.

Being specific allows you not only to define yourself, but most important, it allows your prospect to put trust and confidence in you. They feel you understand their specific needs and you (more than anyone else) know how to make their specific frustrations and pains go away. And because of this, they will take your recommendations and your suggestions seriously, since you're speaking to them directly. They will also happily pay you more for your expertise.

As I said earlier -- in my business, I'm not just a "direct-marketing consultant." I'm a very skilled copywriter (which is a very specific specialty in and of itself), with a particular expertise in creating lead generation strategies, and emotionally compelling direct-response sales copy.

Oh, and by the way, here's the kind of ad I might put together if I was going to create something for a financial planner who wanted to attract high-net worth business-owners and retirees who are interested in getting their estate planning handled correctly.

Contrast this to the small business card type of ad we looked at in the beginning of this Chapter:

Retirees And Entrepreneurs Worth Over $10 Million Dollars: FREE Report Reveals What The Government Doesn't Want You To Know!

Are you a retiree or entrepreneur with a net worth of $10 Million dollars or more? And if so, are you sick-and-tired of hearing nothing but legal mumbo-jumbo from every supposed estate planning "professional" out there?

Are you frustrated by lawyers who are jumping at the chance to shove hundreds of pages of pre-made trust documents under your nose, every time you even mention a will?

And have you had it "up to here" with financial planners and life insurance agents looking to line their pockets with your hard-earned dollars by trying to sell you a billion dollars worth of life insurance policies before they even finish shaking your hand?

Instead, wouldn't you just love to know, in plain and simple English, how to prevent Uncle Sam from ripping your life's savings out of your family's hands at the worst possible time?

If so, then you *MUST* get your hands on this **FREE** Report that's just been released, called...

"How To Completely Eliminate Paying ANY Taxes At Death!"

This report is not available in stores and reveals 7 little-known secrets used by the wealthiest families in America, to pass money down from generation to generation, regardless of how much you're worth.

Inside this free report, you'll discover:

- **How to make sure your spouse can't pass any of *your* hard-earned money over to a second (or third) spouse, or even worse -- to that spouse's children!**

- How to *guarantee* your deadbeat son, daughter, or other dysfunctional family member, won't get their grubby little fingers on your assets at your death or even *years* later! (This is actually much easier than you think.)

- **And... if you own a business or real estate and you have partners, you'll also discover how to prevent an untimely death or accident from ruining your business, in a New York minute!** (This is THE most often overlooked and costliest problem for many businesses. And you'd better be careful here -- the IRS has *several* sneaky traps you must be aware of!)

To get your **FREE Report**, call the toll-free Estate Planning Hotline at xxx-xxx-xxxx, any time, 24 hours a day, 7 days a week. No one will be on the telephone to hassle you, and no one will try and sell you anything.

Your **FREE Report** will then be rushed out to you *immediately*!

P.S. Don't forget, in a case like this, it's what you *don't* know that ultimately *destroys* you -- so act now!

You could also modify the layout of this ad and edit or shorten some of the copy so that you can wind up using something similar to this as the front page of your lead-generation website, as well.

Money-Making Action Steps Checklist

☐ **In order to figure out what field you should be specializing in within your existing business, ask yourself these questions:**

   ✓ **What kinds of customers do you currently work with?**

   ✓ What kinds of customers or clients do you like working with, or would you like to work with more often?

   ✓ **Are there services you're not providing that you should be offering, because customers have asked for them?**

   ✓ Is there a certain demographic or line of business that's highly profitable?

   ✓ **Are there others in your field who have a unique specialization you'd like to have?**

   ✓ Is there a new line of service, or a new trend that's going to be popular soon, based on everything you're hearing from your peers and from trade or industry magazines, or as a result of an economic, pop culture, or market shift?

☐ **Once you've nailed down the area or demographic you'd like to specialize in, focus your marketing on addressing how to eliminate this specific market's biggest problems, fears, concerns, or worries.** Then figure out how to satisfy their strongest hopes, dreams and desires, and use all of these items as benefits that make up the centerpiece of your marketing.

☐ **Remember, you're in the problem solving business, not the "I want to sell you something" business.** So if you want to be effective in your marketing, focus on solving problems first, not selling things.

Chapter References

• If you want to see other examples of display ads and sales letters I've written, besides the ones for my own product pages at kingofcopy.com/products, go to kingofcopy.com/writingsamples

Strategy # 6

The REAL Secret
Behind All Great Business Relationships

Talking about business relationships may sound boring and old-fashioned, but the truth is, it's a big reason why many people fail in business. And it's also why they make far less than they could be making, for sure.

See, your income will always be directly proportional to the strength of your relationship with your list -- both your prospect list, and your buyers' list. And the strength of *any* relationship is based on two things: the frequency of your interaction, and the intensity of it as well.

So for example, I'm sure you're much closer with your spouse or significant other, today, then you were after you knew them for a week, right?

Well, business relationships are no different. Most entrepreneurs mistakenly believe someone is going to stumble across your website and just start buying from you right away. Yet nothing could be further from the truth

It doesn't work like that in the real world, and it doesn't work like that in the virtual or business world, either. In fact, when it comes to the internet, because the barrier to entry online is so low, you have to work even harder at this online than you do offline.

At least in person, your prospects can size you up much easier. At least they know you are real. Online, no one has a clue who you are or if you're even for real.

No one's going to give you money because you have the best-looking website, or because you've been in business for 50 years or because of any of the other standard clichés you can go through. You see, the reality is...

No one cares how much you know...

until they know how much you care.

This is true for absolutely every single relationship you will ever get involved with, and it is *especially* true in business.

This means, if you're looking to show your list of prospects how much you care, you need to contact them as much as possible. E-mail them or send them offline information -- in other words, speak with them as frequently as you possibly can.

I realize this is going to horrify some people reading this. Most people feel uncomfortable e-mailing their list too often, but that's probably because all you're doing is e-mailing your list with nothing but sales pitches. Or, fake attempts at offering something, or pitching some product from a friend or joint venture partner of yours. In reality, all you're trying to do is sell them something.

Don't get me wrong -- I love selling! But "selling something" alone is *not* a relationship!

Imagine if the only time you and your wife connected was when you sat down once a week for family dinner on Sundays. Think you'd have a real romantic relationship as well, if this was the entire extent of your personal connection?

Probably not, right?

Well guess what? It's the same way with everyone in your life, even your prospects. You need to contact them frequently and the nature of your contact has to be meaningful and valuable, if you want to have a meaningful and valuable relationship with them.

I e-mail my list during the week, daily -- and we have a very low unsubscribe rate, and obviously a high buying rate. I've even e-mailed my list two and three times a day during a rare time when I'm running a special promotion, with no side effect or increase in the number of people who unsubscribe. I usually don't e-mail my list on the weekend, but that's because I don't want to.

If truth be told, however, I'd probably make even more money if I did this. But I need some mental down-time and a chance to energize my batteries as well, so I take weekends off.

In the next Chapter I'm going to explain what you should be talking about with your list when you do contact them. Then I'm going to give you a few live examples of how I do it, in the Chapter after that. This way you can start developing your own identity and your own style of communicating with your list of prospects.

But my point is, the only way you're going to develop a strong relationship with your list, or with anyone for that matter, is by increasing the frequency and intensity of your interaction with them. After all, the bottom line is, people are simply much more inclined to buy things from those folks they trust and have a strong relationship with.

So communicate often, and be real.

Oh, and by the way, don't worry, you're not alone in being concerned about contacting your list too often. Most people are *terrified* of doing this! But this is a very significant component of my success, and it will be a significant component of your success, if you follow my advice and do the same thing.

In fact, communicating with my list so frequently is second nature for me, to the point where I almost take it for granted.

Here's a quick story about this: at my last Mastermind meeting, one of my members was frustrated because he'd built his list up to a sizeable group and was wondering why he wasn't getting the results he expected.

He asked how my relationship with my list was so good, and before he even finished his sentence, another member shouted out, "He e-mails his list daily and he sends them good stuff."

So please keep in mind, the two factors that determine the quality of your relationships: frequency of contact, and intensity of interaction.

We covered frequency here, and in the next Chapter we'll cover the intensity or depth of your communication.

I put creating sincere and lasting relationships above every other strategy when it comes to marketing. This... is what brings home the bacon!

Money-Making Action Steps Checklist

☐ **Begin thinking about how you can show your prospects and customers you "care" about them more, and that you're interested in forming meaningful relationships first, before selling them something.**

☐ **Most business-owners and entrepreneurs communicate with their list W-A-A-Y too infrequently.** Are you guilty of doing this?

✓ If so, why?

✓ If it's because you don't know what to say, other than trying to sell them something, don't worry -- in the next Chapter I'll give you some compelling suggestions.

☐ **How often do you think you need to communicate with your list, and... what kinds of things do you think they'd like to hear about?** Start paying close attention to this and begin implementing and testing your ideas. There's never a better time to do this than right NOW!

☐ **If you still don't know exactly what your list members are interested in, run a survey asking them questions about the kind of information they want.** A tool I have used for this that works very effectively and is easy to use, is surveymonkey.com, but there are others out there as well.

Chapter References

- To learn more about communicating with your prospects on an emotional "gut" level, check out the Seductive Selling System. It is my flagship marketing system and the only product I know of, that gives you real-life and practical examples of emotional marketing and sales copy to model. You can find it at kingofcopy.com/seductive.

Strategy # 7

How To Establish Unshakable Trust And Rapport

Let me tell you something you may find strange. As I said, I e-mail my online list daily, and... in every single e-mail I'm sending out, I'm also selling something.

And yet, very few people unsubscribe from my e-mail list.

Why is that?

The answer is simple: it's all about the content. Let's talk about this by looking at the **8 Reasons Why People Unsubscribe From Your List:**

People unsubscribe from your list because of these eight things. They are very important so pay close attention to them, because **this is where your money is made or lost:**

1. They aren't interested in what you're talking about and they made a mistake by signing up in the first place. This has nothing to do with you.

2. **What you promised them when you invited them into your site, isn't being delivered to them.** This is important. One thing you need to evaluate is whether the offer you're making to people that invites them to subscribe to your online e-zine, is consistent with the information they're actually getting once they sign up. If your offer isn't congruent with your deliverable, then no one's going to stick around very long, and no one's going to buy from you, either

3. **Your list isn't hearing from you often enough, and then when they do hear from you, all you're trying to do is sell them something.** This is just selfish and rude, so don't do this.

4. **You don't have any kind of personality or identity of your own.** People have relationships with people, not with "e-mails."

5. **There are so many different people sending and writing your e-mails, your list doesn't know who they're forming a relationship with, or what's going on.** This happens a lot on websites where there are multiple contributors.

6. **Sending e-mails from someone that wasn't identified when your prospects signed up.** This happens often in big faceless corporations. You sign up with a company for some kind of information, and your e-mails suddenly begin coming from a person you don't know (perhaps a corporate employee, or even several different employees or departments).

   For example, you sign up on a company website, and then "Julie" the director of human resources, keeps mailing you. Most people won't open up "Julie's" e-mail because they don't know who Julie is. This is called "you are oblivious" syndrome.

7. **You are committing the cardinal sin of wasting your prospect's time by being boring.** This is the bulk of why people unsubscribe from lists, so be very sensitive to this. You will *not* get a second chance if you make this mistake, for sure.

8. **You stay on topic too much.** At first blush, you might not think this is a mistake -- but it is. Your job is to entertain, educate and inform. And you can't do all three of these things if all you're ever doing is talking about the one topic your website or business revolves around.

   This is no different than running into someone who's always talking about one thing -- their kids, for example, or their job. They aren't very interesting, no matter how important that one subject they focus on, may be. Just the same way people need to be multi-dimensional to be attractive, so do you, when you're communicating with your list.

The best way to develop your relationship with your list, is to consistently educate, inform and entertain them in a compelling manner. I'll assume you know how to educate them -- this is simple. You just cover a wide range of topics and subjects within your own "main" topic.

We'll cover informing your list in this Chapter, and entertaining them in the next Chapter.

So, what do you want to inform them about?

Good question.

You want to be viewed as an authority in your area of expertise, and depending on your target market, almost as a consumer resource. You should be giving out as much information as you can possibly offer, about your subject matter.

Don't worry about, "If you do this, then they won't have anything to buy from you." There are several reasons why this won't happen:

First, in life, you really *do* get what you pay for. If someone's going to invest in whatever kind of information or goods and services you're selling, *that's* when they're getting your really good stuff.

And second, this has to do with reciprocity. Those prospects who can relate to you and who appreciate what you're doing and what you're offering, will ultimately buy from you as a result. Yes, you're going to have loads of freeloaders on your list who will never buy a thing, but those folks *aren't* your customers anyway, so who cares?

You e-mail often and you give out good information to those people who *want* to hear from you and eventually buy from you. Not for the people who don't want to buy from you. A retail store lets everyone in to browse and sample and touch the merchandise, whether they're buyers or not, right?

You need to do the same thing.

I also have loads of free interviews and videos on my site, so people can get to know me through a variety of different media sources, and so they can learn as much as possible about me. Trying to figure out whether or not to trust someone in today's day and age, isn't easy, and you need to make yourself as available as possible - without actually being available.

Using different forms of media is important, since everyone takes in information differently. Some folks prefer learning visually, and others are auditories (they like to hear things), so why not offer a little bit to everyone?

I also have social media accounts on twitter and on facebook. Although it is a great way of getting messages out there, en masse, in its current format, I see twitter as nothing more than a wasteland of useless and unproductive chatter. Just look around at the lion's share of the twits and you'll see what I mean. (No one really cares if you think your cat is the most adorable pet in the world. Honestly.)

But I see facebook as a much more mature, more rabid way of creating and expanding your relationships, primarily due to the more diverse exchanges and supplies of information you can have (by sharing photos, videos, stories, background, etc.)

Just focus on and care about your potential customers. Those are the folks you're trying to inform, educate, and entertain, and those are the ones you want to have a relationship with.

The third reason why you want to do this, is because it positions you as an expert. Anyone who's ballsy enough to have all this knowledge and share it, is automatically presumed to be an expert (as long as you're making sense). **And the more often you share it, the more of an expert you're perceived to be.**

Just make sure you know what you're talking about. If you don't, you'll be outed as soon as someone buys something from you, and you don't deliver on the claims and promises you made.

Now let me show you a few examples of some of the e-mails I send. You'll see they are consistently content-rich and filled with great information. I'll put these e-mails in a different font so you can see when I go back to speaking to you about them, afterwards.

`e-mail #1`

`Subject: Large One?`

`Here's a proven, and truly easy way to start increasing your sales, immediately.`

`All you need to do is add these 2 words to your selling system, and you're good to go.`

`In fact, this trick's so good, I wish I could take credit for coming up with it, but the truth is, it comes from a little-known marketing legend.`

`Here's the deal: In 1947, Elmer Wheeler was one of the best-known salesmen of his time. His "Wheeler Institute of Words" developed a "best practices" of selling, by testing a variety of words in over 19 million selling situations.`

`I'm right in the middle of reading one of Elmer's most famous books,` *`Tested Sentences That Sell.`*

And here's a great little selling trick that comes straight out of this book:

Ever go into a restaurant and order a drink?

Of course you have.

And what does your server usually ask you, right after you place your drink order?

They usually say "Small or large?", right?

Well, imagine for a moment... you're the owner of this restaurant.

Do you have any idea how much your sales would increase over time, if... instead of saying "Small or large?" after your customers ordered their drinks ... you told your servers to instead, say...

"Large one?"

Let me take the guess-work out of this and make your job easier for you.

Elmer Wheeler tested this experiment in five-thousand separate selling situations. And the results showed, when your server asked "Large one?"...

7 out of every 10 people... answered "Yes!"

So, let's say a large soda costs you 35¢ more than a small soda -- are you with me on this? This means, simply by saying "Large one?"... 7 out of every 10 customers that walk through your door, end up giving you an extra 35 cents!

Now you may be thinking, "So what?... It's only 35 cents."

A-h-h-h, but remember....

Little Hinges Swing Big Doors Open!

Follow me here for a minute: If you've got 5 servers... and each of them does this with 100 customers a day, this means each of them will be serving large sodas to an extra 70 people a day.

That's an extra 350 large soda sales a day. (5 servers x 70 large sodas each).

350 extra sales, at 35¢ each, is $122.50 a day in extra gross sales for you... which translates into $857.50 extra a week, and over 52 weeks, this turns into...

$44,590 Dollars A Year...
With ZERO Extra Marketing Costs Involved!

Not bad, hey?

And if your large sodas cost 50¢ more than your small sodas, in that case, you wind up making an extra $63,700 dollars!

70¢ more? O.K., that one's easy -- just double the 35¢ figure -- now you're selling $89,180 Dollars more!

See how easy this stuff is?

It's insane, isn't it?

But what if you don't have a restaurant?

How can you use this trick in your business?

Well, let's say you own a photography store. How about, when people are filling out their envelopes to get their pictures developed, instead of saying "Singles or doubles?", you just say "Doubles?".

If you own a landscaping company, instead of asking "Shrubs and lawn?", you'd say "Whole yard?"

And if you're a hairdresser, instead of asking "Cut and shampoo?", you just say "Full Treatment?"

Make sense?

When it comes down to it, the basic premise of this selling trick, is...

If You Don't Ask... You Don't Get!

And polishing your request up so it's "benefit-oriented" for your prospect, makes this process work smoothly, effectively, and without looking like you're trying to "sell more".

Notice how you're not asking "Do you want a large soda?" -- you're just saying "Large one?"

See, you'll have to experiment a little bit to find out what works best in your situation, but now at least you've got one helluva head start on things, no?

And can you think of any easier way to make this kind of extra money?

Elmer Wheeler really was a "selling genius" and you'll pick up quite a bit from him.

And from the excitement and enthusiasm he comes across with, you know he enjoyed his work.

Here are a few of Elmer's famous quotes:

"Your first 10 words are more important than your next 10,000."

"People seldom want to walk over you until you lie down." And...

"Don't sell the steak, sell the sizzle."

Remember, little hinges really DO swing big doors open --

and success lies in the margins, not in the vast open
spaces. So keep your mind open to finding the small things
that others let slip through the cracks.

   Unfortunately, Wheeler's books are all out of print.
You'll find them showing up pretty consistently on e-bay
though, and, you can also find some of them on
www.abebooks.com and on www.alibris.com.

   P.S. If you think Wheeler's onto something, inside my
Seductive Selling System, you'll find 47 different
emotional buy-buttons to push, and the exact words to use
to push them. Make sure you check it out at
http://www.kingofcopy.com/seductive

You can see how, in this tip, I covered the following topics: selling, persuasion,
marketing, and copywriting. You can also see how I inject a ton of enthusiasm and
personality into my message.

This is a great tip almost anyone can use, to make more money.

You'll also see how I gently promoted my Seductive Selling System in the P.S. See,
when you're consistently giving away good content like this, no one objects to you trying
to sell them something. And those who do object, will simply unsubscribe -- but like I
said, those folks aren't your customers anyway, so you shouldn't really be concerned
yourself with what they think.

Make sense?

Good, let's go on to the next e-mail.

e-mail #2

Subject: Does your sales copy "stammer?"

When you're selling something -- especially in print --
you'd better be smooth and you'd better make sure you're
giving everything you've got. Because you don't get a
second chance to make a first impression, especially when
you're selling in print.

For instance, a big problem for many people, is that they "stammer" in their sales copy. Not literally, but figuratively, meaning... your copy doesn't flow smoothly.

See, compelling sales copy reads NO different from how you'd talk. It's one of the ways you get to engage your prospect, and remove any sense of "selling" from the equation. By writing the way you speak, you're able to lull them into a conversation they don't even realize they're having.

And once they get to a certain point in that conversation, they become vested in it, and they can't get out.

Right?

So your job is to get them to this point, using as many different strategies as you possibly can.

Anyway, when you don't speak in print, the same way you'd speak in person, things get sloppy.

You sort of "stammer," and you wind up reminding your prospect they really ARE just reading a sales letter and not having a conversation.

And that's not good.

"Conversation" is good, "sales letter" is bad.

One DEAD giveaway of this is when you use the word "that." "That" is a word which is often used in print, but almost NEVER used in conversation the same way. It's one of those words your 2nd grade grammar teacher taught you to use when you write, but has almost no value at all when you're selling something in print.

So for example, I might normally see a sales letter with something like this in it:

"I am telling you that this is the real deal."

Now if you say this out loud, it's going to sound strange, because if you were talking to someone and making this comment, you'd never say it like this, would you?

Go ahead, say "I am telling you that this is the real deal, "out loud. Not "out loud" inside your head, but actually "out loud" as in "sounds and words coming out of your mouth."

Something's missing, right?

Of course.

That's because what you'd normally say in this instance, is "I'm telling you, this is the real deal."

See, when you get rid of the useless "that," what you're saying is much more conversational.

Look at another example. Watch how the word "that" makes this sentence stammer:

"We were told that every time we exercised, miracles would happen"... is nowhere near as clean as "We were told, every time we exercised, a miracle would happen."

Right?

So keep in mind, one of the ways you're going to be able to smooth out your sales copy and make it read like the proverbial greased slide you want, is by getting rid of all the useless "that's" lying around.

So get going on this first, and next...

Go sell something, Craig Garber

P.S. Because of MULTIPLE requests for more information like this, I've created a new column in my offline newsletter, to discuss specific sales copy issues like this one. It's called "Little-Known Copywriting Secrets From

81

The King's Treasure Chest," and in this month's column, we
talk about making your letters speak directly to your
prospect, heart-to-heart. Make SURE you check it out by
taking your free 30-day test drive, and claim your 18 free
gifts (now including TWO free sales copy critiques), right
now at: http://www.kingofcopy.com/ssnl

In this tip, the content revolves around copywriting and selling. So the natural sales pitch here in my P.S. was to talk about the new column in my offline newsletter that deals specifically with copywriting.

What you're going to find, is once you get good at this, you may wind up writing your tips around what you want to promote. You don't have to do this -- meaning, your tip doesn't necessarily have to relate to what you're promoting -- but I like to, because if your reader enjoyed the tip... they are sort of "primed" to buy a product that is related to the information they just read.

Also, I usually start my tips with things like "Hey (first name)" or "Hi (first name)" or even just "first name." And then once in a while I'll throw in "Good morning (first name)" (most of my list is here in the US, but about 20% is outside, so I don't do this all the time)... or even "Hey (first name), check this out."

You do this because that's probably how you'd start a personal conversation with them. You wouldn't say "Dear (first name)" in a conversation.

Sometimes I'll use first caps in my subject line (first letter of each word capitalized, like the headline of a sales letter), and other times I won't.

I've tested e-mail open rates on this and first caps is *slightly* higher. But sometimes, depending on your subject matter, it's more compelling and curiosity-provoking to use a regular (non first-caps) subject line that's more of a one-to-one e-mail.

Also, I usually format my daily e-mails to be no more than 60 characters wide. To do this I use a simple free script program located at http://www.formatit.com/index.html. There are other programs like this around the web -- some even more simple to use (one that comes to mind is EZ Text Formatter, for Windows), this is just the one I happen to use.

You format your e-mails to "X" number of characters across, because it's aesthetically easier to read and doesn't appear as long. Also since many people get their e-mail on mobile devices, this helps make it smoother for them to read, as well.

Now some people will say, "Yes, but your e-mails are quite long, content-wise. Who's going to read that much?"

And the answer is simple: If someone is interested in what you have to say, they will read that much. It's no different than reading a book or watching a movie. You'll read a long book or sit through a 3-hour movie if it's interesting, but you'll ignore even the shortest articles if they're boring, right?

Your prospects will handle your e-mails the same way. **As long as you're not boring, they'll read it.**

Remember this, always.

e-mail #3

Subject: The essence of "crisp" copywriting.

Hi Craig,

One of the things you want to keep in mind when you're writing, is clarity. I don't mean grammatical clarity, that's another issue, but what I mean is, visual and sensual clarity. And not sensual as in "horizontal bop" sensual, "sensual" as in appealing or being tangible by as many of your five senses (smell, touch, hearing, vision, taste) as possible.

You want your prospects to "feel" what you're saying, and you also want them to have a vivid image of what you're talking about, right there in front of them, smack dab in the center of their mind.

Kind of like those old cartoons you probably watched when you were a kid, when Elmer Fudd was chasing Bugs Bunny and all Elmer could think about was rabbit stew.

Remember those?

Inside his mind, not only was chubby little Elmer picturing a nice healthy meal, he was actually envisioning the smell of the roasted rabbit, surrounded by carrots, parsnips, and other vegetables, all sitting there on a big round silver platter, with piping hot steam rising up from the little bunny. This was so "real" to Fudd, his mouth would actually be watering.

Remember that?

Good, now let's get back to work: The very best way to be crystal-clear in your communication, is by being detailed and specific. In fact, this is what separates the really good writers of anything (fiction, science-fiction, copywriters, whatever), from the rest of the pack.

But there's a fine line you need to walk here, when you're doing this. Too much or too little detail *isn't* really the issue -- relevancy is the issue.

Kind of like when you're writing a sales letter. You know, the age-old question of "How much is enough?"... "How long is too long?"

The answer really isn't any "number" of pages or words... it's "when you've said everything you need to say," that's when you've said enough. And of course, as long as you're being relevant and not boring, you can pretty much say as much as you want.

So with respect to being "crisp" and being able to create imagery, the best way to do this is to be detailed and descriptive. And here are three things to remember about this:

* To create vivid imagery, stimulate experiences: See how, a few minutes ago, I was talking about the Bugs Bunny thing? I tapped into your own prior experiences and your own sense of nostalgia. That's a good thing to do.

Nostalgia is a very powerful emotional buy-button.

* Use emotional triggers. So for instance, the other day I was in the gym and I saw a guy around my age, working out with his son, who was around 12 or 13 years old. It made

me a little sad because my sons are now old enough that we
don't work out together as often as we used to. It's
amazing how fast the time flies by. I used to hear that
all the time, but it doesn't mean anything until you live
it.

You need to understand what your prospects are thinking
about, and then... make then feel "something." This is the
biggest way to strike up an affinity with your prospect --
yet everyone seems to focus on the hype and on the sizzle.

Rest assured, the sizzle doesn't matter if your prospects
don't trust you. Which is exactly why really good sales
letters are far less hypey than most.

Keep this in mind.

* And lastly, use story-telling action words. For
instance, don't say you put "a border around your yard so
all the bugs and beetles can't get in." Instead, say you
put an "unassailable wall around your yard."

See, when you do that, your prospect can't HELP but
create all sorts of sensual experiences and visual imagery
that locks them into your message -- and into you.

This... is the essence of "crisp" copywriting.

That's all f-f-f-olks!

Now go sell something, Craig Garber

P.S. Look, this month I made a HUGE mistake. In my
offline newsletter, which is normally 12-pages long and
printed in sized 9 or 10 font, I had SOO much to say, that
the lion's share of it is now printed in 8 to 9 point font,
effectively adding another 25% to it.

One critical issue is on page 5, where I reveal a number
of different terms people normally use to describe the
"supposed" benefit of what they do, and I show you why
these terms are completely ineffective, and why they don't

work.

Do NOT miss this, or you will surely lose out on MANY
future sales. Test-drive it free, right here, AND get 18
free gifts, to boot. Make sure you watch the goofy video
about all these bonuses at: http://www.kingofcopy.com/ssnl

This e-mail, too, covers information about marketing and copywriting, but you'll
notice it also has humor and entertainment in it. I'll talk more about this in the next
Chapter, but what you want to do, most important, is sprinkle bits and pieces of your own
personality into your sales copy. This is what your readers use to make judgments about
you, your attitude, and your work ethic and your creativity (more on this later).

You'll also notice I seem to promote my offline newsletter most often.

That's because prior to this book, my offline Seductive Selling newsletter was the
"entry point" into my product "funnel." And once people get exposed to me through my
newsletter, there's usually a rapid ascension up this funnel to my other products and to
my coaching programs.

Oh, and by the way, here's an important tip. The reason I use the full url in each e-
mail, with the "http://www" included, is because you want your link to be "live" when
your prospects get them in their e-mail's inbox.

You want it so all your readers have to do is "click" on the link and it sends them
directly to the web page. Many e-mail clients (programs you use to read e-mail) won't
display an active "live" link unless the http://www" part of the web address is included.
Just saying kingofcopy.com/ssnl isn't enough in this situation.

e-mail #4

Subject: How to "breathe life" into your
copywriting.

Hi Craig,

The more vivid you can make whatever it is you're
selling, the more people will buy. See, the more lifelike
something is, the more someone can picture themselves using
and owning it.

So for example, if you're a wedding photographer, don't sell the pictures, sell the memories.

Sell the lifetime of joy and warmth, husband and wife will have... sharing these moments with their children and grandchildren, for years to come.

Talk about how proud they'll be every time they walk by their wedding photo in the hall, and how their friends will chuckle at it years later, because Craig had so much more hair back then.

And most important, let them know how important this day is to you. Because people don't care how much you know, until they know how much you care.

Make sense?

Good, so how do you do this?

Well, there are three things you need to know.

One, put your goods and services to use! Don't leave them collecting dust up on your prospects mental shelf, put them IN your prospects mental shelf, by placing them in their hands, eyes, and whatever else they need to experience things.

Two, think of the end benefits. People don't take pictures to take pictures, they take pictures to make memories. And they don't plant flowers so they can sweat out in the yard for four hours in the middle of August, either.

Describe the impact of these end benefits on a "gut" level. You know, what are the real meaningful and beneficial results?

And lastly, let your prospects have fun with whatever they're doing. When you can put a big smile across their face, you become their hero -- and... they become your customer.

Now go sell something, Craig Garber

P.S. Discover how to use GUARANTEES in your headlines in
Example 6 of this month's Seductive Selling Newsletter.
Try it free and find out why people in 12 countries read it
at: http://www.kingofcopy.com/ssnl

***

Check out ALL the King's products at
http://www.kingofcopy.com/products

Follow me on Facebook: http://www.kingofcopy.com/facebook

Comments? Leave them here on my blog -- let me know what
you're thinking: http://blog.kingofcopy.com

***

The topics in this e-mail include copywriting, marketing, positioning, explaining how to define and promote benefits, human nature, and emotional selling.

I give away a wealth of information like this, all specific to my area of expertise, which is emotional direct-response copywriting, and direct-marketing strategies revolving around selling and lead generation.

Remember what I said -- you need to be concerned with your **relationship** first and foremost, above everything else. And what better way for your list to think highly of you, then by giving them free resources and proven strategies they can use to make their lives better or more enlightening?

You want your readers to always be looking forward to the *experience* they're going to have with you. **People remember experiences far more than they remember things.** Give information, but create an experience in doing this, and you'll have a lifetime of rabid fans.

e-mail #5

Subject: The story of the beautiful old woman by
the bay.

88

An elderly woman sat gently on the couch in the middle of her living room, overlooking beautiful Nantucket bay.

It was now, in her last hours, she was having one final connection with those she loved so much. On the one hand, she was filled with sadness over all the memories and loved ones she was leaving behind, but on the other hand, she knew she'd be joining her loving husband of 39 years, who'd passed just 6 months earlier.

And in this, she took comfort...

When you looked at the woman, even at her advanced age, and now close to passing, you could still see the vestiges of her beauty. Her once long blonde hair, was now grey, but still thick and strong.

And her eyes, although they now squinted, were the same shiny blue, sparkling in the sun. They were so lucid it was as if you could see the reflection of the waves splashing up against the rocks outside her window, when you looked at them.

And her figure, once the envy of many women, although now demure... was just as thin and lithe as it had always been.

Yes, she'd lived a great life, and now it was time to say goodbye to her sons and daughters, her grandchildren and even her friends and neighbors.

In her hushed but lovely voice, she spoke out one final time as she drew her last breath. Gently measuring her words, she said, "I have lived a long life, and I love you all so much. And if you want the best advice I can give you, listen to an old lady when she says, 'Regret nothing.'"

"See, you are not your mistakes. And there are few mistakes you will ever make, that truly have any long-term effects. However, the regret of not doing something will haunt you forever, and this is a mistake you can never fix."

And with that, she was gone.

***

A valuable lesson, hopefully one you won't forget.

Also, appreciate that you can be the best copywriter in the world, but if you can't make your prospect feel something in just a few paragraphs like I just did, then all your talent and any sales skills you have, are meaningless.

That's because people buy based on emotion, period.

Remember that.

Now go sell something, Craig Garber

P.S. The Holiday Issue of this month's Seductive Selling Newsletter has 16 pages of marketing examples, and a holiday lesson for us all. Discover why it's now being read in 12 countries world-wide, and test-drive it free at: http://www.kingofcopy.com/ssnl

***

Check out ALL the King's products at http://www.kingofcopy.com/products

Follow me on Facebook: http://www.kingofcopy.com/facebook

Comments? Leave them here on my blog -- let me know what you're thinking: http://blog.kingofcopy.com

***

This was a very emotionally moving piece I wrote to show the importance of being able to move your prospects.

Several weeks later I had a few people ask me where I heard this story from. I didn't hear it anywhere, I wrote it myself. It was inspired, actually by a movie I got to watching late one night, called *Evening*, starring Claire Danes.

I often tell stories or parables in my e-mails. Some of them I will read, and then re-write or twist or add my own characters in there, and others I'll just create, like this one.

Telling stories is a wonderful way to bond with your prospects. It's also a great way to learn things, since there is usually a lesson involved somewhere, and the story anchors that lesson in your prospect's mind, very effectively.

e-mail #6

Subject: How to make your prospects buy? The answer is simple.

"Just tell 'em what they want to hear."

Here's the deal: If you're like most entrepreneurs I know, you probably spend incredible amounts of time trying to be the best at whatever it is you do.

And the time, effort, commitment and passion it takes to be the best, is absolutely overwhelming sometimes. Few people realize exactly how much success extracts out of you.

That's why I often say, "Success isn't for the weak or timid."

The problem is, what we think about most, is what we usually do. And what we do most is who we are. Unfortunately, this becomes a big marketing issue for most people.

See, your prospects aren't interested in what you do. They could care less how you spend your time and how long it took you to become a master "whatever."

When you go out and buy a CD off of iTunes, for example, you don't sit and consider which guitarist practiced harder before you make your purchase, right?

Of course not.

All you think about is which one sounds better to you.
Which one makes you feel whatever kind of mood you're
looking to feel.

Right?

Do you ask your doctor what his grades were on his final
exams, before you let him slice you open?

I don't think so.

And see, your prospects aren't interested in that about
you, either. They're interested in the same thing you're
interested in. They're interested in the benefits of what
you do. They're interested in RESULTS.

They want to know this: if they give you money, what are
the results they can expect... how long will it take them
to get these results... and how will their lives be
different AFTER they give you money.

No one cares that you had to stay up all night long to
finish making your batch of doughnuts, or your wicker
furniture.

So often, I see marketers -- and especially copywriters
or someone trying to pass themselves off as a copywriting
expert -- talking about in their sales letter, how many
books they've read or whose courses they took.

This is almost laughable. It's like telling someone in an
online dating ad that you've tried on loads of different
clothing at Neiman Marcus, so you'll be presentable when
you go out on a date.

Who cares!

Remember, when you're selling, focus on results,
benefits, and experiences. Not how long it took you to

become the whiz-bang you are.

That was your choice and your problem, and you should never make your problems... someone else's problems.

Especially your prospects.

Now go sell something, Craig Garber

P.S. Just finished December's year-end Seductive Selling Newsletter. If you're ready for a marketing and copywriting journey back in time, in "The Nostalgia Issue," then take a test-drive of it today, and get 18 Free bonus gifts just for saying "maybe!" at http://www.kingofcopy.com/ssnl

* * *

Check out ALL the King's products at http://www.kingofcopy.com/products

Follow me on Facebook: http://www.kingofcopy.com/facebook

Comments? Leave them here on my blog -- let me know what you're thinking: http://blog.kingofcopy.com

* * *

It is very important to be blunt and offer opinions and eye-opening information to your readers. Push your personality to the edge. I'm fortunate in that I can be myself, but if you're shy or bashful, then push yourself or develop a likeable character you can be.

People relate to people, not to robots who drone on about nothing. I don't care if people don't like what I have to say or if they don't like me, and you should feel the same way -- let them unsubscribe.

These people aren't your buyers, anyway. You're not doing this for them, you're doing this for those folks who *do* like you, and who *do* resonate with what you have to say, and who *do* want to buy stuff from you.

It's your business -- build it the way you want to, and attract those people you want to attract as your customers. It's not only your right to do this, but it's your obligation to yourself to do this.

<u>e-mail #7</u>

Subject: This is going to be too deep for some people. How about you?

Hey Craig,

This past weekend my family and I went out to the Plant City Strawberry Festival. Plant City is a small town along the path of progress, about 20 miles east of Tampa. I'm not sure where Plant City ranks as far as Strawberry production nation-wide, but I believe it's one of the biggest producers of strawberries on the east coast.

Funny, a lot of people think tourism is Florida's number one industry economically (think "Mickey Mouse"), but it's actually agriculture and farming. Tourism is number two.

It's always strange for me going out to a place where there are so many people, since I spend most of my time working at home up in my office. Outside of the gym, I'm really not around too many "crowds" at any given time.

What's also funny is how I feel totally at ease walking through Times Square or Washington Square Park in the heart of New York City, but not quite as at ease in the crowds at the Plant City Strawberry Festival, which is clearly nowhere near as chaotic and hectic as Manhattan.

Which just goes to show you, it's all about what you're used to.

THIS is your norm, and this is your comfort zone, even if it's not as good for you as other choices you can make. In other words, people will sooner stay in a bad situation (fill in the blanks: relationship, job, friendship, marriage, whatever), than get out of their comfort zone to "fix" things, even when they know it's good for them.

It's almost like, better the devil known, than the devil unknown -- but in this case, the unknown devil isn't unknown, it's just un-comfortable.

In fact, I was talking about this with a good friend of mine over the weekend. See, the thing is, we're ALL afraid of something, no matter what level you're at.

The only thing that separates successful people from the rest, is that we consistently DO these things we're afraid of, and of course, like most things in life -- you ultimately do get through them.

We know the ONLY way to achieve something, is to become comfortable in the "doing" of the uncomfortable. Then, once you get through it, your comfort zone sort of gets "re-set" to this new level, letting you tackle the next "big thing" on your scale up the mountain. (I told you this was going to be too deep for some folks.)

I'm not immune to any of these fears, anxieties, or doubts, either. The only difference is, I expect, and actually welcome them, because I know once I kick down the door in front of me, the next door after this, is going to be even better.

The unsuccessful person rationalizes their unwillingness to make progress, by accepting the current status quo as being "good enough" for them. The problem with this is, "good" is a relative term based only on what you know.

Success is about being good at the next big thing -- the benefits of which you CAN'T actually "know," until you're there.

Make sense?

So promise yourself you'll do just ONE thing you weren't planning on doing this week, because it's been making you feel uncomfortable or awkward. And then reward yourself with the benefits of whatever breakthrough it leads you to.

Then tell me what you did so I can publish it in the next
offline issue of my Seductive Selling Newsletter -
http://www.kingofcopy.com/ssnl

Tomorrow I won't be so deep. I'll be very shallow since
I'm anxiously awaiting for Borat to be released on DVD and
I've already ordered my copy from Amazon.com.

Now go sell something, Craig Garber

* * *

Check out ALL the King's products at
http://www.kingofcopy.com/products

Follow me on Facebook: http://www.kingofcopy.com/facebook

Comments? Leave them here on my blog -- let me know what
you're thinking: http://blog.kingofcopy.com

* * *

In this e-mail I talk about success and human nature. I wanted to close this Chapter
out with this one because as you can see, we're now straying from the initial subject
matter people came to me for, which was emotional direct-response copywriting and
marketing information. And we'll cover "straying" more in the next Chapter.

You'll also see I'm encouraging people to respond and leave comments, which
people do, on my blog, and by replying to my daily tips. I recently switched my blog
over from blogger to wordpress, because it is much easier for your readers to leave you
feedback and because this feedback is displayed openly for everyone to read.

Plus, my computer guy tells me wordpress has a lot more bells and whistles, and I'm
game for that, for sure.

A few other final comments about writing your e-mails and about communicating
with your list.

From time to time, I will point out free resources outside of my website because they
can help my readers. Frankly I don't do this too often because I'm not looking to be an
encyclopedia. I want my prospects and customers becoming very dependent on me and
my resources, within this small realm of my expertise. I want to train my list to buy from

me, not to rely on me as a general wealth of knowledge.

Also, you'll notice I said, "I want my *prospects and customers* becoming very dependent on me," and not "I want my *readers* becoming very dependent on me." Make no mistake, these are prospects and customers first.

In other words, don't forget why you're doing all this. Yes you're a good person, but you're running a business. **And the point of your business is to make you money.**

Your goal is to convert prospects to customers by selling them stuff. Yes, they are also your readers, but if you're looking at them like readers, you'll be concerned with "entertainment" and journalism, before selling. If you're looking at them like prospects and customers, you'll be concerned with developing meaningful relationships and selling and making money.

Subtle difference, but very critical in your ability to make money and to keep your eye on the ball and focused on the important things.

Regarding the length of your message -- look, I write a lot. The likelihood of someone either wanting to write as much as I do, or being skilled enough to do it consistently and efficiently, isn't very likely. But the good news is, you don't have to write this much if you don't want to.

200 to 250 words is good enough, and if you can say something important in less than that, then go for it. **Buy yourself a good book of quotes, or look online for them, and use some of them as a starting point for topics of conversation.**

In the beginning, it might seem hard for you to do this, or the thought that you're writing to "X" number of people may seem intimidating. Just say "Screw it." Throw caution to the wind. Once you get started, its no different than driving a car, riding a bicycle, ice-skating, or kissing a woman (or whoever it is you like to kiss).

Chances are, the first time you got behind the wheel to drive, or the first time you did *any* of these things, you were scared to death, and today you don't even think about it.

The first time you do this is going to be the most difficult time, and then after that, it gets easier and easier to do. And you get better at it as well, which is really nice.

Lastly, when you're writing your daily (or weekly, or twice-weekly, or whatever) e-mails, don't put so much pressure on yourself that you start thinking every single person on your list should like every single e-mail you put out. That's simply not practical or realistic.

Even your husband, wife or your children doesn't like everything you do, all the time. So how can a bunch of business contacts and strangers possibly feel otherwise?

All you need to do, is consistently do your best, and people will love what you're saying, as long as you're being genuine and delivering good content to them. That's what's most important -- the quality of your content, and **being real**.

Money-Making Action Steps Checklist

☐ **Start figuring out what kind of information would be most beneficial to your list.** As I said earlier, sometimes sending them a simple survey works great (I use surveymonkey.com).

☐ **The easiest way to have an abundant and ever-ready bank of reference material to use as fodder for your follow-up tips online, or for your offline newsletter, is to tap into the following resources:**

✓ Google and yahoo.com keyword alerts

✓ **New York Times and other newspaper keyword alerts**

✓ Industry and trade association magazine articles online and offline

✓ **Industry and trade or peer-group forums, discussion groups, and membership sites online**

✓ E-mails and queries you receive from your list

✓ **Other news or tips you subscribe to that will either provoke controversy (people love controversy) or stimulate the brains of your readers**

✓ Personal goals and journals

✓ **Customer or client experiences you have, or that you read about**

✓ Customer complaints

✓ **Legal issues facing your marketplace**

✓ Economic issues impacting your trade or business, or the economy as a whole

✓ **Conversations you have with friends, family or customers**

✓ Your travels

✓ **Stories from your youth**

✓ Conversations you overheard on line at the grocery store or at the coffee shop

✓ **Funny and self-deprecating experiences you have**

✓ Dysfunctional family gatherings and other chaotic "slices of life"

☐ **Don't forget to run all your e-mails through a spam filter before you send them out!** Most autoresponders probably have them available, but there should be many others online if you search for them or ask around. I just switched to a more advanced spam filter that checks content as well as the spam list, but because so many words are spam words (words that will trigger spam filters in e-mail programs, or even in ISP's themselves), I sometimes intentionally misspell words in my e-mails. This way my e-mails will get through these filters.

Here are some examples of these words and how I try and get around the spam filters by misspelling them:

Spam Word	**Mis-spelled to get around spam filters**
Money	Munney
million, billion	millyun, billuyun
Free	Fre.e
Guarantee	Guar-un-tee
Loan	Lone
Opportunity	Oppor-too-nity

☐ **Don't forget video!** This year I am using video as well as print, to communicate with my list. I'd encourage you to do the same thing. Video is a readily accessible media today and you should be using it.

Chapter References

- If you want to listen to and watch the free interviews and videos I have on my website, go to kingofcopy.com/media

- Check out my facebook profile and become a friend of mine at kingofcopy.com/facebook. I don't pretend to be any kind of a social media expert, but facebook appears to be a more natural place that encourages more normal interaction.

- As I said, to me, in its present format, twitter is nothing but useless chatter. Every desperate peddler of some kind of service is on there trying to get your attention. I find twitter to be a classic example of sociology at work.

  If you're not familiar with sociology, let me explain it to you. One of the principles of sociology states that people give up their sense of personal responsibility to the members of a group they belong to.

  This is why, for example, you might be more inclined to help a homeless person or someone in trouble, when you're walking down the street on your own, as opposed to when you're walking down the street in the middle of midtown Manhattan, surrounded by hundreds or thousands of people. In a group, some of your personal responsibility simply gets surrendered to the group.

  To me, this is how I look at twitter. People say the most incredibly stupid and insipid things, because they have no personal accountability for what's coming out of their mouth. They've abdicated all sense of responsibility and common sense, over to the millions of people who are also screaming as loud as possible, and saying nothing.

  I've tried, several times, to have some sort of thought-provoking "anything," but it's been a complete waste.

  Here's an example of what I mean. I once posted on there something like, "My son's thinking of joining the Marines, and with the war going on, that scares me."

  Out of close to eight hundred followers, not one of them said a peep. However, when some idiot said, "Who likes chicken?," it prompted dozens of responses.

I just have ZERO patience for things like this.

I see twitter as a potential gateway to new and much more rewarding forms of social media, and maybe I'll wind up eating my words, but I also see twitter fading into obscurity very soon, unless it changes its current format.

Anyway, having said all that, if you still want to follow me on twitter, you can find me at twitter.com/kingofcopy

- I am now answering your questions, LIVE via video, every Friday in a segment called "Ask Me, Baby." To send your questions in, simply complete the form at kingofcopy.com/AskMeBaby, and to watch all the previous "Ask Me, Baby" videos, go to kingofcopy.com/videos or to youtube.com/seductiveselling

Strategy # 8

How To Entertain Your List

Here's something few people know: Your prospects actually want to know as much about you, as they want to know about whatever it is you're selling or whatever area of specialized knowledge you possess.

And here's something else most people don't realize, which I first mentioned in the last Chapter: you will initially attract your prospects and build your list because they came to you for topical content related to your business. But you will *keep* them around, as prospects and as customers, because of your consistent ability to *entertain* them *and* your ability to make them think.

In this Chapter I'm going to show you how to keep your readers entertained by sharing some "entertainment-style" e-mails I've sent over the years.

In general, I'd say, the topical breakdown of the e-mails I send out is as follows:

* **Copywriting and marketing 40 - 45%**

* Success, achievement, personal productivity and other mindset issues **30%**

* **Personal stories or opinions, pop culture types of issues 20%**

* Pure promotional e-mails **5 - 10%**

The second category (success, etc.) is a spinoff of the primary category, and frankly, you can't discuss marketing or copywriting, unless you're willing to include most of these subjects as well. Otherwise it's like trying to discuss cooking without discussing spices. The two of them are synergistic, and combined they make a much better whole.

You entertain your audience several ways. Using humor is effective, as long as *other* people think you're funny too, and as long as your humor is appropriate, not too juvenile, and not discriminatory in any way.

That's why self-deprecating humor is the best kind of humor to use. You can't offend anyone when you're making fun of yourself, plus it shows you're human and good-natured and that you're not pretending to be perfect.

You *will* offend people once you insert your personality into your marketing, but who cares? Like I said, if someone's offended by your character, they're not going to be a customer of yours anyway, so get over it and move on. Remember, not everyone is going to like you, and frankly that's not why you're in business and it's not why you're here on this earth. Being liked by everyone is impossible for even the *most* likable person.

Lastly -- and I touched on this last Chapter -- you also entertain people by telling stories.

Let me share a few of the "entertainment-style" e-mails I've sent out:

e-mail #1

Her Sweaty Curls In The Palm Of My Hand

Hi Craig,

Here's a little piece I wrote for my daughter a few years ago. It's her birthday today, and I hope you enjoy this as much as I enjoyed writing it.

Let me know what you think:

I love putting my daughter to bed. It's one of the few times I get to disconnect and simply enjoy being right there in the moment.

We usually spend a lot of time talking about what went on during her day... we make a bunch of jokes and get each other laughing... and then I cuddle her and she falls asleep cuddling her little doll.

Last night, I thought she was asleep and when I started getting out of her bed, she said softly... with her eyes closed, "Don't go daddy. Hold my hand."

As long as I live, I will never forget this. It was as pure as life could be.

So I laid back down with her and I let her curl her little fingers around my thumb, while I gently cupped the rest of my hand around the back of hers.

You know, there are certain distinct facial features that babies, infants, and young children have, that get lost as they get older.

For example, her lips.

The thin line between your lips and the skin immediately around your lips, is very defined when you're young. But this line loses its sharpness as you grow up. It's as if fine sandpaper somehow slightly smoothes the edges down, as you go from being an infant to a young child.

And her eyelashes.

You can see each individual long dark eyelash as if it was a slim rod growing up out of her eyelids, slightly thinner than a narrow pencil lead you slide into an automatic pencil, but nowhere near as stiff.

And as she's falling asleep, I'm lucky enough to rub my course fingers back through her silky fine damp blonde curls, and over her perfectly smooth round head. I can feel each of her hairs brush over my clumsy calloused hands, which, for some reason... don't seem to be so clumsy at this moment.

As I'm looking down at her face and at her tiny little body, I'm hoping -- hoping with all the might I can muster up -- that somehow I will never ever lose this feeling, or these memories. That I can somehow permanently etch this image into my mind like an artist burns the edge of a soldering iron into a wooden block, creating a permanent design.

It would be great if I could recall images like this one,
that are buried away inside my memory banks,
"automatically," the same way your elbow "automatically"
twitches when you bang the spot right behind it. This
would be the perfect pick-me-up whenever your get down or
frustrated about something -- whenever life's momentarily
kicked you in the gut.

Although as I'm here in this moment with her, it seems
hard to think that life could be anything but perfect. Her
little spirit is so warm, nothing could possibly diminish
it.

She is only the second woman in my life I've ever gotten
close to -- her mom (my wife) being the first. And both of
them have a very soothing effect on me.

As I'm sitting here, I am reminded again of what's
important. The truth is, sitting in front of your computer
yields few, if ANY "memorable" experiences. And it's the
memories in life you carry around that make you or break
you. That fill you up or leave you feeling empty.

On second thought, I don't think I'll have too much
trouble recalling something this powerful. At least... not
for a good long while, anyway.

Now go make some memories, Craig Garber

P.S.: Make feeling good about yourself, your business,
and your life... a PERMANENT state of mind. Discover what
turned things around for me at:
http://www.kingofcopy.com/science

***
If you enjoyed this, forward it on to a few of your
friends and business associates. And if you have any
comments, just leave them here on my blog at:
http://blog.kingofcopy.com

Got a difficult question? Just ask me, baby!

```
http://www.kingofcopy.com/askmebaby

    Check out ALL the King's products at
http://www.kingofcopy.com/products

    Friend me on Facebook at:
http://www.kingofcopy.com/facebook

    If this message was forwarded to you and you'd like to
start getting this in your Inbox, just sign up on my home
page at http://www.kingofcopy.com


    ***
```

This is actually a piece I send out every year on my daughter's birthday, and I always get lots of great feedback on it. Educating your list is one thing, but making them FEEL something -- that's an experience they're going to remember you for.

This is just one kind of entertainment you can provide.

In this next e-mail, oddly enough, I happen to talk about sociology again.


```
e-mail #2

Subject: Forgiveness is on every corner.

Hi Craig,

    You know, a lot of people feel I'm a hardass about some
things.  And frankly, when it comes to business, I am.  The
truth is, you need to be a hardass in business, because in
business, "soft" and "successful"... don't necessarily mix
well, any more than chocolate and pizza mix well.

    On the other hand, I get a lot of feedback from offline
newsletter subscribers of mine about how this is an
interesting dichotomy.  They get to see another side of me
-- with my family -- and obviously, I'm not such a hardass
with them.

    That's because "hardass" and "family" also doesn't mix
```

well, either.

Now what I'm going to tell you today is something that may throw you off, so sit tight. I'm going to tell you about something I feel VERY badly about, and hopefully, in the process, I'll be able to forgive myself a little bit.

Monday, my younger son Casey (he's 15) and I went to the gym. We were about halfway through our workout when there was a loud commotion over by the treadmills. Apparently, a man had fallen off the treadmill, and he was now lying on the floor, shaking in convulsion-like twitches.

This isn't something you typically see, and as a result, there's no "normal" way to react to it. It's one of those moments when things seem to "slow down" right in front of you, simply because it's so out of your typical context of daily living.

The man was around my age, somewhat overweight but not gigantic or anything like that, and he was just lying there on the ground.

The first thing you do in a situation like that is, of course, you grab your kid and hold on to him. When mortality is flashed so closely in front of you, it's only natural to hold on to your own, and... to hold on to them as tightly as you can.

Now when I was a kid, I studied sociology for one year, back in high school. If I recall, sociology is the study of group dynamics, and one of the founding principles of sociology is that individual responsibility is surrendered to a group when you are part of this group.

So for example, this is the reason why it's easier for a group of people to ignore a homeless person, en masse -- or to NOT stop and help someone in need on a busy street. Everyone in the group has surrendered their personal responsibility to the group as a whole.

And here's where I screwed up.

You see, I KNOW this principle, and I've always prided
myself on my ability to "rise above" conventional human
behavior. I expect myself to do the right thing, even when
most others march in silent compliance, unaware why.

Now back to the gym.

Shortly after that man had, what some folks feel was a
fatal heart attack, they swiftly closed the gym and asked
all the members to leave. On the way out, I saw two young
children -- an older sister, perhaps 12 or 13, and her
younger brother, perhaps 9 or 10 -- sitting down and
sobbing near the front exit of the gym.

I wanted to go over to them and see if they were O.K.,
but... I didn't.

I wanted to give them a hug because I'm sure they needed
it.

I wanted to help them somehow and do a million other
things that flashed through my mind at that particular
moment.

But... I didn't do any of these things.

I thought, "Surely they aren't the children of the man
who was lying on the floor inside -- they'd be by his side,
right?"... and then I thought, "Where's Casey?"... and
then, "If these were my kids I'd want someone there for
them."... then, "I need to help those kids and make them
feel safe so they will stop crying."

But in the end, I did absolutely nothing.

And I have felt sick about this, ever since. In the end,
I surrendered my responsibility to the rest of the group,
just like every other person on the assembly line that was
there, and now I can't go back and fix it.

When I saw those kids crying, I thought of my own

```
children crying, and then I thought of myself crying as a
little kid... and then... I simply froze.

I don't have all the answers, that's for sure.  And
sometimes... I just don't have any.

Now go sell something, Craig Garber

P.S. Only 2 Days LEFT to get your hands on this month's
Seductive Selling Newsletter & Audio Success CD Of The
Month!  Discover how I TRIPLED a client's business on page
3, and get $3,632 worth free gifts when you test-drive it
here: http://www.kingofcopy.com/ssnl
```

You'll notice how, in this tip, not only did I share some intimate feelings with you, as well as a very moving and somewhat disturbing experience I had, but I also showed you, plain as day, how I'm FAR from perfect.

Let me give you my theory about this. Since *no one* is perfect, trying to pretend you *are*, by "positioning" yourself above everyone else, just makes you very difficult to relate to, and it doesn't endear you to anyone.

Also, smart people who've been around the block (which thankfully, happens to make up the lion's share of my customers and clients), also know you're completely full of crap if you're trying to come off like this.

In fact, a good portion of my customers and the people I attract tend to be grizzled veterans of life, not much different from me, in that respect. So why should I try and be someone I'm not. Why would I try and lie to them?

I'm me, and I'm O.K. with that, and I encourage you to be the same way.

Revealing your flaws and your wrinkles just lets your readers know you're still human and you're not pretending to be perfect.

I've been through personal bankruptcy (1997)... divorce (1993)... had a brutal custody battle for my sons -- and lost (1995 - 1998)... and then finally got custody of my kids in 2000 when their biological mom was arrested for child abuse.

I grew up in an abusive home with a violent and misguided father, and a fragile mother who sat around watching the show. And all this means is...

I'm as nutty... as... the next guy!

So why try and hide anything?

<u>e-mail #3</u>

Subject: "He's not my son? No way..." (Happy Birthday)

Hey Craig,

I have never ever done this before. Today I am publishing an article that was in my offline Seductive Selling Newsletter, about a year ago. It's in honor of my younger son, Casey, who's a great kid with an incredible work ethic and sense of commitment. Today's his 17th birthday.

This article comes from a column called "Tales From The Back-End," which is a two-page editorial column that starts on the last page of the newsletter. Here goes:

Casey was 9 months old when I split up with his biological mother. When he was very young, he looked so dissimilar to me, I questioned whether or not he was even my biological son. Someone had suggested to me at the time, that I go for some sort of genetic testing to determine whether or not he was my son.

After all, why keep paying child support if he's not even my kid?

However, I decided not to do this because I couldn't bear with the emotional fallout of what might happen if he wasn't my son. I loved him and I wasn't about to give him up -- mine or not. Today, of course, everyone tells us he's the spitting image of me (except he's good-looking), so it's not even a question.

Turns out I made a good decision in more ways than one.

The other day, Casey, who's probably at around 6% body
fat, came to me and was frustrated because the kids in his
class assume his abs look great and he's so defined,
because he's skinny.

This isn't true at all. In fact, while Casey's always
been thin, he wasn't particularly shapely until he started
working out about 3 years ago. At the same time he did
this, he also began a strict dieting regime, and through
all the training he does, he now looks great.

He's chiseled as a matter of fact.

But here's what he does to look like this. First off, he
watches what he eats, like a hawk. He trains literally
every weekday and usually one day on the weekend. He's on
his high school swimming team in the fall, the wrestling
team in the winter, and he runs track in the spring.

So he trains in whatever sport he's in, 5 days a week, he
goes to the gym and lifts weights at least three days a
week, and once in a while, he'll train in one or more
sports on Saturday.

Sundays he usually plays touch football with his friends
at the Middle School field nearby. Obviously, his ripped
abs aren't a gift, they're a hard-earned prize he is well
deserving of.

Now here's some more interesting stuff about Casey. He
pinned someone once in a wrestling match, but in the last
two years he's never actually won a match. He comes in
dead last in every single swimming meet he's in, and he is
usually so far behind in his road races (he runs cross
country), that the other runners have all lapped him at
least once by the time Casey finishes.

Sounds weird, doesn't it?

No, not really. You see, Casey was born 10 weeks early,
and weighed 3 pounds, 6 ounces at birth. I held him in the

palm of my hand the first few days, like a small furry baby macaque monkey.

He was in the hospital for 5 five weeks, living in an incubator, and had a heart monitor attached to him for the first year of his life. And because of his prematurity, he was born with a mild case of Cerebral Palsy.

He had issues with his fine motor skills as a young child, he walked late, and today, because he's walked on his tippy toes for his entire life, his walking gait is basically all out of whack. He's got a limp, and so when he runs and does any other physical activity, there's just no way he can compete with kids who've developed "normally."

We'll get back to that word "normal" in just a minute, because it's a real stinger, from time-to-time.

In reality, Casey (who's pretty much been on the honor roll his entire school career) is quite lucky. As you'd imagine, we've taken him to a number of different physical and occupational therapists during his lifetime, and what we've seen, as far as kids being born with Cerebral Palsy, is nothing shy of devastating.

Many children are either confined to a wheelchair for their entire lifetime, not in control over their own movements, unable to speak or properly communicate, and have other troubles that, to be honest with you, are too overwhelming for me to confront.

Yet, Casey has always been athletic. Anne and I both coached him in soccer when he was 5 and 6 years old, and from age 7 to 10, I coached him in basketball. He's always played all kinds of sports - t-ball, baseball, tennis, martial arts -- you name it, he's done it -- and we've always encouraged and supported him in all of these endeavors.

And he's always competed fairly and hung in there. As he's gotten older however, the distance between him and his peers, physically -- especially in competitive team sports -- has distanced, simply because of his physical limitations.

However, what hasn't changed is that Casey's still hanging in there, going toe to toe with whoever he needs to, sweating, fighting, digging out that last ounce of energy.

Now let's get back to that word, "normal." It is one thing to be "different" mentally. We can all sit and feel good, and even sometimes smug, because we pride ourselves on being different from everyone else. Knowing "being different" is one of the reasons we're successful.

But this is voluntary "abnormality."

Whether you're driven to success, or driven to be the best at whatever it is you enjoy, this is a *voluntary* departure from the norm. No different to the teenager who dresses in goth clothes, or the martial artist who follows what they believe is the "true" style of their art, or the designer who goes against the grain of conventional design, on purpose.

But there's a big difference between choosing to be different, and being forced to be different. Being forced to do anything, stinks. Being forced to be physically different, is a HUGE challenge.

I've discussed this with Casey, especially lately. He's getting well-known around his school campus, and I'm sure one of the reasons why is simply the fact that he is so determined, and the fact that he is different.

(In fact, a few articles have since been written about him in our local papers. If you want to check them out, they are here: http://tinyurl.com/ad3lqb and here: http://tinyurl.com/cxcl9u)

In his mind, he doesn't see himself as being handicapped or limited. He knows he has limitations, but he also knows it's up to him how far he goes in life, and that if he allows his limitations to define how far he goes, he loses as soon as the race starts.

He'd rather focus on his abilities than on his disabilities.

I well up with tears every time I see him run a race, because I would like him to not be different. And I always stick out in the crowd because I get up in the stands and start cheering him on like crazy, even though he's the last one in line.

But he is far stronger than I am about this -- see, he doesn't feel powerless at all.

Where I just want to take away any kind of disability or unfair advantage he has, and make it easier for him, he doesn't see this -- he just thinks he needs to work a little harder than the other kids, that's all.

A few weeks ago, Casey's wrestling coach told Anne candidly, that Casey may never win a wrestling match in his entire high school career, but he also told her that at the same time, he wishes all the kids on his team had half Casey's attitude and work ethic. Apparently he's the first one to get to practice, and the last one to leave, and he never ever tries to ditch out on any chores or take any short-cuts.

(Note: Casey won his first wrestling match this season. This article was originally written last season.)

Last week at his first track meet, his Cross Country coach told me virtually the same thing.

Casey just went for his first job interview -- he'll be working at the YMCA this summer in their camp, as a counselor. He will soon be eligible to get his drivers license in late September, and he wants to make sure he'll have enough money to buy a car as soon as he can drive.

(Note: Casey bought his own car about a month ago, and loves the freedom of driving, and he's now in his second track season. In his first race of this season, the one mile, he beat his personal best from last year.)

He's also well-liked at work and gets more hours than any of the other kids.

Casey is not only a champion, he's also one of the most gentle and forgiving people I know. Unlike his dad, he rarely flies off the handle but like his dad, he's pretty much the same person all the time. He isn't moody at all and has an even temperament.

If you look at the quadrant of personality styles, he's pretty much an "amiable" -- doesn't get pissed off too often, and doesn't piss others off, either.

Don't get me wrong, he's far from perfect -- after all, he is a "normal" teenaged boy and he drives us nuts like all teenagers do.

But he's running his life the way he wants to, and he doesn't let society decide what's right, what's wrong, and most important -- what kind of limits he has and doesn't have.

And overall, he makes good decisions. Each of my children, in some way or another, has inspired me. I think, in Casey's case, he's probably going to be a hero and an inspiration to loads of different people throughout his life. And they, like me, will be lucky to have met such a gentle and successful person.

One of the best decisions I ever made -- and really, it was a no-brainer at the time -- was to ignore the possibility Casey wasn't my son, biologically. I know he now is, but maybe even more important, he and I have shared a lifetime of love and growth in our relationship and will continue doing so. And, he's the kind of person I'd want to have in my world, whether he was related to me or not.

Life sometimes throws us all curve balls. Some health wise, some relationship wise, and some business-wise.

Very few of us however, are able to persevere with the same sense of tenacity my son has. He's truly made lemonade out of lemons, and he drinks it daily.

Happy 17th Birthday Casey. I love you every day. YOU are the true "man in the arena."

"It is not the critic who counts; not the man who points out how the strong man stumbles, or where the doer of deeds could have done them better. The credit belongs to the man who is actually in the arena, whose face is marred by dust and sweat and blood; who strives valiantly; who errs, who comes short again and again, because there is no effort without error and shortcoming; but who does actually strive to do the deeds; who knows great enthusiasms, the great devotions; who spends himself in a worthy cause; who at the best knows in the end the triumph of high achievement, and who at the worst, if he fails, at least fails while daring greatly, so that his place shall never be with those cold and timid souls who neither know victory nor defeat." Theodore Roosevelt, Paris France, April 23,

Now go sell something, Craig Garber

P.S.: In this month's "Tales From The Back-End," you can look forward to reading why "In many ways, he's my hero." Test-drive it free and get 18 (Real) bonus gifts (WATCH the silly video) at http://www.kingofcopy.com/ssnl

***

Check out ALL the King's products at http://www.kingofcopy.com/products

Got a difficult question? Just ask me, baby! http://www.kingofcopy.com/askmebaby

Friend me on Facebook at: http://www.kingofcopy.com/facebook

If you enjoyed this, forward it on to a few of your
friends and business associates. And if you have any
comments, just leave them here on my blog:
http://blog.kingofcopy.com

If this message was forwarded to you and you'd like to
start getting this in your Inbox, just sign up on my home
page at http://www.kingofcopy.com

* * *

Casey is an amazing person and I have lots of respect for his determination and
persistence.

Last season, at Casey's annual awards ceremony for his high school wrestling team,
he was presented with the commitment award in wrestling and a special framed plaque
for track and field. He's a wonderful kid and we're ever so lucky to have his positive
attitude and easy-going manner around the house.

He's also got the patience and tolerance of a saint. At 17, he's already accomplished
more than most adults will ever do, and he's done it with a great attitude and tremendous
perseverance. And he done all this in the face of what some people might consider to be
overwhelming obstacles.

Sharing things like this are priceless in building a relationship with your list.

Here's a copy of one of the articles about Casey, along with the picture of him that I
recently snapped at one of his races. The article was written by Joey Knight, for the St.
Petersburg Times.

***

Gaither's Garber leaves his disability in the dust

TAMPA — It was meteorological irony at its finest. Amid rain, wind and an early
March chill, Casey Garber had his day in the sun.

In the 1,600-meter run at the Wildcat Fast Times Invitational at Wesley Chapel,
Garber passed two others to avoid last place. One was caught on the backstretch of
the second lap, the other between Laps 2 and 3.

"It felt good," the Gaither sophomore said softly, the words sifting through his orthodontic retainer. "I was going faster on the fourth lap than I was before."

If you were among the brave souls who weathered the entirety of that waterlogged meet, Garber might have caught your eye. His knees were bent slightly inward as he ran, and his strides were abbreviated. From a distance, it might have appeared as if he were running on tiptoe.

That mild case of cerebral palsy, his dad explains, has resulted in some nerve damage.

Funny, it never damaged his nerve.

Instead of wrestling with his condition, Casey James Garber just, well, wrestles. He also runs track and swims for Gaither.

"I want to make new friends," he said. "I like competing, and I just want to stay active. That's it."

Well, not entirely. Casey wakeboards, maintains a 3.2 grade point average, works at a local supermarket and YMCA, and periodically inspires.

"Even though he's got some kind of disability — I'm not sure what he has — he's still out here trying, doing everything," Cowboys senior sprinter Brian Tabor said.

"He still works out with us in practice. ... He's out here every day. He'll go out on mile runs with the distance guys and he'll be one of the last people to come (back), but he goes out and still does it."

In an obstetrical sense, the skinny kid with the brown bangs emerged from the blocks early. Too early, in fact.

Casey weighed 3 pounds, 10 ounces when he arrived 10 weeks prematurely at Plantation General Hospital on March 19, 1992. He remained hospitalized roughly five weeks, his dad says, and was diagnosed with a mild case of cerebral palsy, which is caused by damage to the motor control centers of a young, developing brain.

"Ironically, of our three kids, he's definitely got the strongest immune system and strongest resistance to being sick," Craig Garber said.

What he doesn't have are nerves that fire in the same sequence to certain parts

118

of his body as a non-CP person, Craig said. The result: an abnormal style of walking and running (mostly on tiptoe) and a lower musculature that hasn't been allowed to evolve fully.

"In fact, to be honest, we got a bad diagnosis when he was a kid," said Craig, who, with wife Anne, has an older son and younger daughter.

"We took him to a doctor who was a specialist, and he said he had mild CP but would get better, but you can't get better. It's nerve damage. Fortunately, you don't get worse, but you don't get better."

Saddled with that prospect, the Garbers adopted a creed -- "no limitations" -- as defiant as it was succinct. In the process, Casey adopted a passion for sports.

"He always kicked a ball, threw a ball," said Craig, who publishes a monthly business/marketing newsletter from his Lutz home. "He watches SportsCenter. He's a typical jock."

Pushing to the limit

Casey has played tennis and soccer and even earned a brown belt in martial arts while still living in South Florida. Although he responds well to occupational therapy, his dad says, he essentially blows off physical therapy because he'd rather do sports.

This school year, he has earned letters in swimming, wrestling and track.

Key word: earned.

Although Casey is unlikely to compete in Thursday's Class 4A, District 6 meet, Cowboys track coach Ladd Baldwin said he has run in a handful of races this season. Last fall, he placed 20th in the 100-yard backstroke at the 3A-4 district meet. Wrestling coach Mike Santos confirms Casey won at least two matches this year, maybe more.

"I never held him back. On the contrary, I try to push him to the limit every time to see where his limit is," said Santos, who watched several prospective wrestlers quit the torturous preseason conditioning Casey finished.

"I don't think in his mind there's any limitations to what he can do. He'll try at least. That's incredible in itself."

Casey grinding it out during a race, giving 110% as usual.

Athletically, Casey's weaknesses fluctuate with the seasons. In swimming and track, he struggles to generate speed and power with his legs. Craig says his son "wants his legs to go, but they won't go because of that maladaptation of his body."

In wrestling, "his big struggle comes on top because when you're in the neutral position, he lacks a little bit of balance in comparison to other guys," said Santos, who won a 103-pound state title at Leto in 1995. "Even if he doesn't get the takedowns, he'll fight the whole six minutes. ... That's half the battle right there."

Thing is, Casey wants to wage the other half. Otherwise, finishing last wouldn't encourage him to get faster, as he says it does. Today, he persists. Tomorrow, he'd like to prevail.

Coaches say he can.

"I was not the most physically talented guy in the world. I just worked harder. That's what I see Casey being able to do," said Gaither distance coach Bill Jenkins, a former standout runner at the University of Alabama. "He'll get out there and he'll work his butt off, and it's going to pay off."

To mom and dad, that still might not top the emotional dividends.

"There's a big difference between being different voluntarily and being different non-voluntarily. (The latter) doesn't feel so good," Craig said.

"So to see he goes out there and doesn't not feel so good ... makes us feel wonderful. It brings tears to my eyes every time I see him finish a race, because he's dead last and he's always kicking butt, giving 110 percent."

***

Casey was also profiled for his accomplishments in the Tampa Tribune, and both of those articles are framed and hang proudly up on my office walls.

I'm hoping you're starting to see the wonderful benefits of sharing a part of you with your list, and the passion and intensity of all the great relationships you can create.

You can also entertain your list by being controversial, by commenting on current events and pop culture items, and by just having something creative and different to say. And if you can create or prompt shifts in thinking, on top of that, you'll be a real winner here.

Don't be afraid, and don't be bashful. The world is waiting to hear your story -- now all you have to do is tell it!

Oh, and as a side note, Casey won his first wrestling match recently. In some ways, this was a small miracle... but in others, I'm not surprised at all.

Money-Making Action Steps Checklist

☐ **I've been fortunate to live a life filled with many different experiences -- some good, and some not so good.** But isn't this true for all of us? Start going through your mind and clearing the cobwebs about who you are and what's allowed you to get to this point. Here are a few ways you can do this:

   ✓ **Start going through old photographs and picture albums.** This is one of the most effective ways of jogging your memory.

✓ **There are now loads of different kinds of "fill in the blanks" biography books you can buy in bookstores or on amazon.com.** One I have here, for example, is called "My Life, A Collection Of Memories." These books have questions that are great prompts.

✓ **Keep in mind that almost anything you've experienced can be relevant and interesting, as long as you don't commit the Cardinal Sin of marketing when you're telling your story.** (Don't be boring!)

✓ **Always be optimistic in what you're saying.** No one wants to hear from someone who's a downer, let alone hear from them on a regular basis.

✓ **Don't be afraid to share your mistakes, foibles, and regrets, but remember... this isn't a therapy session.** (Be positive -- see above.) Don't make your problems, everybody else's problems.

✓ **If you're just shy, by nature, you have three alternatives here:**

1. **Go for the gusto and slowly come out of your shell.** Think back about all the big breakthroughs you've had -- this may be another one for you! Often, forced breakthroughs are the best ones.

2. **Adopt a character or a persona you'd like to be.** Be careful though, you're going to have to be that person for a long, long time. Many people do this -- they actually even call the person who's writing, some kind of a comic-like character, like "Pirate Pete" or something like that. For someone like me who's naturally outgoing, I can just be myself. But many people who are much more bashful, use this technique VERY effectively.

3. **Starve.** Let me tell you, if you're not willing to establish genuine rapport with your list, by sharing your story, you're falling into the trap of being just another nameless, faceless big and dumb (or small and insignificant) company. Don't do this -- you deserve better, and so does your list.

Chapter References

• You can see more of my background in my biography online at kingofcopy.com/whois.html

• And here are ALL the tips I've ever written:

Tips Archive 1: kingofcopy.com/tips/tiparchives.html

Tips Archive 2: kingofcopy.com/tips2/tiparchives2.html

All blog archives (post website): http://blog.kingofcopy.com

Strategy # 9

The Best Way To Communicate And Sell

In case you haven't noticed, this isn't our parent's world we're living in. Things are changing and moving so fast, it's literally impossible to keep up with them. In fact, the world today isn't even the same world we were living in 6 months ago!

And of course, the world will never be the same since 9/11.

For instance, can you guess which country is expected to be the number one English-speaking country in the next 10 years?

China!

And "No," I'm not kidding!

And did you know, India has 3 times as many people graduating from college as we do here in America?

It's true! It is any wonder competition for jobs, work, business, and space, is getting fiercer?

There's a great video about change you should check out sometime, on this web page: http://youville.blogspot.com/2007/07/world-is-changing-fast.html.

And with all this change, sometimes it's hard to keep up, so let me tell you exactly what you want to be focusing on -- today, right now.

For starters, it's been my experience that there is absolutely *nothing* as powerful as the printed word. Believe me, I could not have accomplished making the outrageous amount of money I did, with such a small list size, if the printed word wasn't so powerful.

So if you're going to focus on anything, focus on your ability to constantly improve and become more creative and skilled in your ability to communicate in print.

And when I say "print," I mean both online and offline. Don't think my selling has been limited to online only. I send out direct mail offers to my customer list regularly, and in fact, I plan on doing that even more this year.

In fact, NEVER rely on e-mail alone to communicate with your list. You would be foolish to ignore using other forms of media and technology to communicate with, and ultimately sell to, your list. Especially nowadays, when technology makes this so easy to do, and so accessible to anyone with an internet connection.

Relying solely on one form of media is like relying on one customer. Eventually, the mule's going to break down and you're going to be out of luck.

You simply MUST use alternative forms of media to sell, and communicate.

The *primary* reason why you want to do this, is because people learn, and take in information best, through a variety of ways. (You can read more about this in Kerry Johnson's excellent book called *Subliminal Selling Skills*, if you can find it.)

In a nutshell, people typically learn best, and are categorized into one of these three primary types of processors:

- **Visuals** - Visuals typically take in information best when they can see what's happening. These folks like to read, watch presentations, and review books and reports. Showing them graphs and charts is also effective. You can sometimes predict a person is a visual, from their occupation. For example, artists, architects, pilots, and writers are often visuals. If you know you're selling or presenting to a visual, you want to use visual tools and express yourself in terms they will relate to. For example, "Can you <u>see</u> how this will help you?"

- **Auditories** - A person who is an auditory, takes in and processes information best when they can hear it. They'd rather listen to an audio CD or a presentation, than read it. Auditories are often musicians, speakers, and telephone sales people. When selling to auditories you'll want to use phrases like, "Does this <u>sound</u> like it makes sense for you?"

- **Kinesthetics** - Kinesthetics make decisions based on how they are feeling. They are very intuitive and use their "gut" to decide what to do. Typical occupations they may have are carpenters, creatives, preachers, and counselors. Selling to kinesthetics, you'd want to use a phrases like, "Do you <u>feel</u> this is something you'd benefit from?"

I'm kind of an odd duck. When I was younger I was almost exclusively an auditory. As I've gotten older and my time has become much more valuable (and much more scarce), I've become more of a visual, since I can read faster than I can listen. However, I am fairly intuitive as well.

In general, I'll use the sense that's going to allow me to process the most amount of information in the least amount of time. When it comes to evaluating character and integrity though, I'll almost always go with my ears before anything else.

So if you're trying to sell me something -- good luck!

Anyway, since you almost never know (100%, anyway) the kind of prospect you're dealing with, you want to make sure you're touching on all three of these senses, and this is why using various forms of media to communicate with your list, is important.

For example, I know MANY of my Seductive Selling offline newsletter members love my newsletter, but a significant percentage of them enjoy the Audio Success CD of the month even more, because they're auditories and prefer hearing information, over reading.

Let's talk about some of the other media you should be using besides print media, which includes... direct mail (sales letters, tearsheets and advertorials, postcards)... space or display advertising... online sales letters... and e-mails:

☞ **Photographs**

It is brain-dead easy to put pictures on your website, on your blog, and in your printed materials. Every digital camera comes with software to transfer your pictures onto your computer.

In my offline newsletter, every issue has 3 or 4 photos of things I'm involved with, clients I've met with, or current events related to my family. Many of my members have told me they enjoy watching my children grow up, and seeing some of the places I've traveled to. They feel like they know me better, and on a more personal level -- and *your* prospects and customers will feel the exact same way.

This is also one of the reasons I like facebook - they make posting pictures very easy and it's a great way to see people in their normal environments.

126

Remember some of the rules I told you earlier. Don't be negative. Don't show pictures of yourself when you're angry or piss drunk because you just caught your spouse cheating on you! Show happy moments people will appreciate, and laugh along with you.

Like this one, of my wife and I at Bahama Breeze, one evening:

Or... like this one of my kids, last Christmas:

Casey, Sam and Nick outside New York's Rockefeller Center

☞ **Audios**

People will relate to you more, and be able to make even better "gut" decisions about you, if they can hear your voice. Here are some of the things I do, audio-wise. Think about how you can do a version of them that would be most appropriate for your own business, and allow you the greatest depth of interaction with your customers and prospects.

✓ **CD Interviews:** Like I said, every month, my Seductive Selling Newsletter Subscribers get an Audio Success CD, where I interview unusual and interesting guests who are thrilled to discuss their marketing methods, the secrets to their success, how they've overcome obstacles, and their general

128

business practices and personal habits. These interviews usually last between 70 and 80 minutes, are filled with great information, and usually a ton of laughs as well. In fact, one thing you'll find with me, is that I really enjoy what I do and I don't take myself too seriously. If I can't laugh and have fun with whatever I'm doing, I usually don't do it. Life's too short to do otherwise.

Oh, and if you have an unusual or interesting story to tell, or if you're successfully using any of the techniques in this book to make a hefty profit, and you'd like to share your story with my Seductive Selling Newsletter members, let us know by faxing your story and your contact information to my office at 954-337-2369. Who knows, maybe you'll be my next interview?

✓ **Teleseminars**: I often run content rich teleseminars for my list and private teleseminars for my customers. In fact, many times I'll run a series of teleseminars on a specific topic, and then turn those teleseminars into a product to sell. Or, I've also sold products that consist of a series of teleseminars.

If you're going to do this, one thing you can do is offer the product to the people who are participating on your teleseminar, at a discount. This way you get testimonials and spread lots of goodwill around, and then you can sell it to the rest of your list at a higher price.

✓ **Interviews**: I am liberal with giving interviews, but I do have some parameters. For example, a while ago, someone asked me to do an interview. He doesn't sell anything to his list, and he told me he's having financial problems. This kind of an interview simply isn't worth my time. Why would I want to give out tons of quality information -- information I've spent a lifetime acquiring -- to a bunch of non-buyers?

This doesn't make sense and simply isn't a good use of your time, is it? However, on the other hand, I'll bend over backwards and work my butt off to give you the best experience of your life, if the people listening to my interview are potential buyers and qualified prospects.

I hope this doesn't sound cold, but at some point in time, if you're not there already... time *will* become the most precious commodity you have. And you're going to have to use it wisely and productively, or else you will never get *anything* done. Guilt or an unfounded sense of obligation to save the world and help the needy, isn't going to serve you well if you apply this philosophy to your business.

✓ **MP3's**: I also post mp3 recordings and interviews I've given, online on my site, from time to time. The collection of them is growing in the media section of my website. Again, I do this so my prospects can get a better sense of who I am and the quality of information I have to offer.

One problem I've had to overcome, believe it or not, is the fact that I'm an excellent copywriter. While most of the time, this is a blessing, people are also sometimes skeptical about whether or not the quality of what you're selling is as good as your sales copy says it is.

Posting up interviews and using other media like this, is a good way to show your prospects you're "for real." It gives them another way to get a feel for you and to make credibility and believability judgments about who you are and what you do. It allows your nonverbal communication to enter the equation, as a supplement to your print communication.

☞ **Webinars**

If you aren't familiar with them, a webinar is a combination of a teleseminar and a "live," on-screen presentation. It's like hosting a seminar on your computer. I have just started running webinars, using them as selling tools and as a way to pass good information along to my prospects, so they can get to know me. In fact, I plan on hosting at least 4 to 6 webinars per year. They are a great way to deliver audio and visual content *and* communicate with your listeners at the same time.

☞ **Publishing Articles**

One of the biggest sources of traffic for me, especially early on, was article publishing. The best way to do this, is to write an article and post it to one of the many article directories. The biggest one, I believe, is Chris Knight's ezinearticles.com, and if you go there and search for me, you'll find all the articles I've posted there, along with their rankings and other information.

I also believe there is software you can purchase, that will upload your articles to a number of different article directories at once, but we haven't done this for a while so I'd be reluctant to recommend one to you.

Article posting is another terrific way to position yourself as an authority on your subject. One warning though -- make sure you keep consistent with my "it's all about the content" ground rule. I've said it before and I'll say it again: **Good content is how I made all my money, and it's how you'll attract quality people to your site.**

If you put out garbage, that's all you're going to get back. You can't attract big bass if you put a little ball of stale bread on the end of your hook, and **you can't attract quality people (and they sure won't buy from you), if you don't consistently put out quality information and content.**

☞ **Online Television?**

Here's something new, one of my coaching group members just pointed out to me. Apparently, there is something called ustream.tv, that allows you to effectively, broadcast live, from your own computer, where ever you may be. I haven't used this yet, but I would like to be experimenting with it soon.

☞ **Online Videos**

This is something I've done a lot of, and again, some of these videos are available in the media area of my website.

✓ **Screen Shots**: You can easily make a video of whatever you want to go over on your computer screen using Camtasia (Windows) or iShowU or ScreenCast (both for Mac). I use screen shots often, to go over sales copy and do critiques on various marketing pieces.

✓ **Real Motion Video**: Nowadays, most digital cameras can create small video files which can be uploaded to your site or to YouTube.com. You want to make videos that are either fun to watch (but not stupid to watch), or informative and instructional. If you're making short videos, you can use either your digital camera, or even the new "Flip" video camera.

For lengthier videos, you're going to want to use a decent quality camera, for sure. And one thing you must be aware of is that people will put up with lesser quality video, but **they won't put up or enjoy lesser quality videos *and* poor quality audio on top of it.** So make sure your pricier camera comes with an exterior microphone jack for you to use.

As a Mac user, I use the iMovie software that comes with the iLife software bundle. It is really cool and very simple to learn to use. You can record and produce all your videos right there on your computer, with little effort and loads of bells and whistles. I do this regularly for my Ask Me Baby videos and for other messages I need to get out, straight from the comfort of my desk. You can also import videos from other sources and produce and edit them using iMovie.

There is also something called TubeMogul.com that allows you to upload and post to multiple video directory sites all at once. I've used it and it's a great resource, so check it out.

Here's some of the software you're going to need to upload and convert some of your videos, so they can be viewed online. I'm on a Mac, so my Windows references may now be outdated.

Mac

Visual Hub - to convert one format to another and make it in the "flash" format to upload and broadcast. (Sadly, I don't think Visual Hub is being supported any more.)

Also, buy a commercial license from Jeroen Wijering and then you get the right to use his wizard to create a wonderful viewer to play your videos. It is, by far, one of the easiest coding system templates I've seen (and I think it works on Mac AND Windows). You can find it at: http://www.jeroenwijering.com/

Windows

When I was on Windows, I used Flash Video Studio (http://www.flashvideostudio.com/) and this conversion was a very simple process.

And by the way, for all of this software, I'm only suggesting you check these out as resources because I've had positive personal experiences with these programs. I am NOT, by any stretch of the imagination, some kind of an expert in this area, nor do I have any kind of affiliation with these businesses, and your mileage may vary.

☞ **Special Reports, Worksheets, Hot Sheets or Checklists**

Each of these can be used to supplement or highlight certain content or concepts. People especially love checklists (5 Ways To... 7 Steps To...) that give them step-by-step instructions or strategies to use.

You can use each of these types of media to sell, educate, or promote your products, in addition to sales letters. And you can also use them as free "bonus" content to deepen your relationship with your list.

And of course, you can also bundle them up along with your existing goods and services to make new products or re-issue older products and have them updated with this new information.

Money-Making Action Steps Checklist

☐ **This one's simple: start using alternative forms of media to communicate and sell, with your list.** Remember, you're going to get better at this each time you try something. In fact, you should look at each time you do something -- anything, for that matter -- as an experiment or test, and nothing more. There are so many moving parts in direct-response marketing, it's impossible to nail all of them down, all at once. Each experience, or "test," however, brings you one step closer to success than you were before.

Chapter References

• Here's a link to the media section of my website. Check out all the audios and videos you want: kingofcopy.com/media

• I mentioned YouTube earlier. If you want to see my personal YouTube channel, check out YouTube.com/seductiveselling. Make sure you watch and comment on the videos on my channel!

• Feel free to submit questions for me to answer in the "Ask Me, Baby" section of my website at kingofcopy.com/AskMeBaby.

Strategy # 10

How To Become Number One In Your Industry

You want to be number one in your industry -- you want to be the best.

Why?

Because no one wants to work with the second best guy in town.

And how do you get to become the top dog? The answer is simple, but let me tell you how you don't get there, first: you don't get to take the top slot because someone let you have it... and you don't get it because someone's given you "permission."

The way you become the lead dog is simply: you righteously claim that spot.

This is called "positioning," and positioning has been a key component of my success as a copywriter and as a direct-response marketing consultant, right from the very beginning. Just think, anyone obnoxious and cocky enough to call themselves "The King Of Copy," is going to attract attention just on the merit of that moniker alone.

Thankfully, I deliver the goods and I never disappoint, but I wouldn't have had the balls to call myself that, otherwise.

But appreciate you don't need to literally be the best at what you do, you just have to believe you're one of the best, to call yourself the best. Besides, for most people, there's no way to "measure" how good you are anyway, any more than you can measure who's the best-looking or strongest person in your town.

Make sense?

Positioning is also one of the key strategies I put in place for my clients that lets them make a rapid ascent up the ladder in their industries, as well. And it's something you

134

must do if you want to be able to make as much money as possible, as rapidly as possible.

Positioning is the art of making yourself appear to be in-demand and one of the best, at whatever you do, and in whatever industry or trade you work in.

It's also the fine and subtle art of making yourself "scarce."

And why is this important?

Simple -- human nature.

There are two things you need to be aware of here. One, everyone wants to work with the best. And two, you always want more of those things you can't easily have.

And you don't need to be a Harvard economist to understand what happens when the demand for you goes up. Your value also goes up, and so does your ability to consistently charge and collect premium pricing.

Here's a very simple illustration of how human nature works: When we were dead-broke, I used to dream of being able to go strolling through the mall and buy whatever I want. Now that, pretty much, I *can* buy whatever I want, a trip through the mall is no big deal. It's usually just a relaxing afternoon out with my wife and children.

But when I couldn't afford to be there, my desire to be there, was much stronger. This is just a very simple example of how you always want more of those things that aren't so easily accessible.

If you're a coin, watch, or jewelry collector, or a collector of anything, for that matter... and a piece you want has been issued, but only in a "limited quantity," isn't the surge in demand (along with the surge in price) for that item, incredible?

Absolutely.

Here's a very primitive, but extremely effective way of looking at positioning: There's a reason the best-looking girl in your high school never had to search around for a date.

That reason was, because she had what all the guys wanted -- good looks, sweet personality, and usually, a sensual figure. And because of this, she was positioned at the top of her marketplace. In your business, you want to be the person who's perceived as having those skills or products **most desired** by your buyers.

135

Here's the secret about this, though: Many times, your buyers aren't necessarily aware of what those traits are. So it's your job to either inform them, or to create them.

And one of the ways of doing this -- or at least, one of the ways of creating the perception of this -- is by setting yourself up so you're taking advantage of the economic law of supply and demand as I just mentioned.

In case you don't remember, the economic law of supply and demand basically states that, as the demand for what you're offering increases, so must the price. And as the supply of what you're offering diminishes, the price of your goods and services must increase.

So you must "create" demand, by manipulating either the perceived supply, or the actual supply of whatever it is you're selling, including YOU.

O.K.? So say this out loud with me, s-l-o-w-l-y.

To increase my value and the amount of money I can charge for my goods and services, I must create demand by manipulating the perceived supply, or the actual supply of what I'm selling.

Alrighty then, I think you understand where I'm going here and how important it is.

Right?

Good.

So how do you do this? How do you manipulate the perceived supply of what you're selling?

One very effective way of doing this, is by doing something completely opposite to what most hard-working, hard-charging sales people do. You need to stop being so available to your clients, from a service perspective. Bear with me and I'll explain what I mean.

You want to *not* be available 24 hours a day... *not* chase people down so you can try and convince them to work with you... and you want to *stop* being a servant to your clients and customers.

See, there's a big difference between providing service, and being a servant. These two things are mutually exclusive, yet most people don't understand this.

Fortunately, it's up to you to decide how much access and hands-on service your customers have the right to expect. Unfortunately, most sales people and entrepreneurs make themselves far too available and do far more than necessary, simply because they don't know any better, and because they are usually too afraid of losing business.

Pay close attention to what I'm about to tell you next:

In any business relationship, being a slave is not a healthy way to "keep" your customers around, any more than in a personal or romantic relationship.

Think about it, aren't the highest paid professionals all inaccessible? You can't call up the President of the United States, and you can't call up the president of most companies, either.

Bill Gates doesn't answer the phone over at Microsoft, and I don't answer the phone (or take calls) here in my office, either.

Successful people are too busy doing what it is they do that makes them successful, to afford any kind of interruptions like telephone calls. **Accessibility doesn't have anything to do with your success, unless you make it that way**. There is no nobility in giving your cell phone number out to your clients. All you're doing is de-valuing your time and your ability to do what you want in your free time, and your privacy -- and in many cases, your dignity as well.

The other problem is, being too accessible is also a sign of neediness. Being too accessible makes your lack of business very apparent, and when this happens, your clients and customers simply don't value what you're offering as much.

See, the truth is, your customers can smell fear, the same way dogs can smell fear. When a dog smells fear, they attack. When your customers smell fear, they take advantage of you -- they call the shots in your business instead of you calling them.

And who wants to run a business where your customers are calling the shots? That's probably *NOT* why you went into business -- so someone *else* can dictate how you spend your time.

Not at all, right?

In fact, you probably went into business for just the opposite reason -- so *YOU* can run the show and call all the shots.

True?

Then why allow this to happen? Why let your clients control your life?

You wouldn't take crap from your boss as an employee -- which is probably one of the reasons why you went into business for yourself. But here you are, taking it from your clients, as a business-owner! When you're living like this, all you've done is set the price to sell a pound of your flesh, higher.

No matter how much you're making, what you're losing in terms of self-respect, simply isn't worth it.

I was once speaking up in Orlando at an event, and a cell phone kept going off. I admonished the young man for allowing that to happen. Not for his phone ringing, but for his submissive actions once it did ring. It was one of his clients and he "had" to leave the meeting to talk to the client on the phone, because they were in the middle of a deal.

I didn't ask this fellow, but I'd be willing to bet my house on the fact that he'd have had no problem ignoring the call if it was his wife, but he allowed a client to interrupt, ironically, his marketing education.

That's *not* customer service, it's slavery. Yes, you have an ethical duty to your clients to deliver the best service you possibly can. But you also have a duty to yourself first, to decide what kind of a lifestyle you want, and how you want to arrange your business to accommodate this lifestyle.

See, most people use their business as a governor for how they're then going to live their lifestyle. But who says it has to be this way? If all you do is continually model what most people are doing, then all you're going to get are the results most people get -- which, last time I checked, are mediocre at best.

The default option may work on your computer, but if you always choose the default option in life, I'm sure you'll agree, it's a life not fully lived. And who wants that?

Why not determine what kind of lifestyle you want to live, and then set up your business based on how it will let you maintain that lifestyle?

I know this sounds difficult, but it's not. It just requires you to shift your thinking and reprogram your business so it serves you first and your customers second. And the truth is, when you're feeling great about your business and your life, your customers are only going to benefit from this.

And ultimately, your customers will not only understand this, but they'll respect you for it. Maybe not the current ones you've been killing yourself for, for far less money than you deserve, but your new customers and clients will respect your parameters and they won't know any different.

For example, I dare you to try and get me on the phone. It just isn't going to happen. Even my clients know better than to call me without a pre-arranged appointment. After all, if all I'm doing all day long is answering the phone, then how on God's green earth am I going to make any money for myself?

And isn't that the point of going into business -- making money for yourself and living a healthier lifestyle?

When are you supposed to get your work done, if you're always available to "help?" And most importantly, how are you supposed to be taking care of yourself and all your existing business and clients and projects you're working on, if all you're doing is fielding phone calls and being interrupted all day long?

The truth is, you can't get anything done if you're constantly jumping every time the phone rings, and every time your customer asks you a question. But people do, and that's why most entrepreneurs don't get any work done until "after hours" -- when they should be home with their families.

The best way to position yourself -- the best way to increase your value to your customers -- is by doing just the opposite. The best way to position yourself is by letting your prospects know you *don't* just jump at the drop of a hat, and you *don't* work with just anyone.

You'll get more respect from them, and Lord knows you'll have a lot more self-respect and pride in yourself and in your business.

Plus, when a client knows your decision to work with them means they must have more than just a pulse, -- not only does *your* value go up in their eyes, as we just mentioned -- but so does *their* own value. They feel flattered you were willing to accept them as a client and let them into your funnel.

So right away the experience and relationship is enhanced for everyone.

In reality, you may actually have some sort of a qualification process like this, right now, but because you're not articulating this to your clients, this has no value for positioning purposes. And therefore, no impact towards your bottom line financially or towards your own emotional freedom.

So before we go, let me just give you a few different examples of how you might want to make someone qualify to work with you:

If you're in the service business, you can let people know the following:

You're only interested in working with those clients who are willing to pay a little more money for far better service.

One very simple way of doing this is by "flagging" your ad, right at the beginning, in your headline. A "flag" is when you specifically call out someone's attention you want to attract.

So for instance, I was recently running an ad that said, **"Real Estate Investors: Why Most Investors Never REALLY Make The Kind Of Money They Deserve!"** The flag in this headline is the phrase "Real Estate Investors."

Getting back to our service business example, you can flag your ad by saying something simple like, **"Do not read this unless you are willing to pay a few dollars more for much better service."** This immediately positions you as a top-quality provider of services.

Examples from my own business:

First, I never ever give away, or even offer, free consultations. There is well over 1,000 pages of content between my website and my blog. I also have a facebook page with more comments and information on it, and a facebook group called "Emotionally compelling copywriting = more sales." (which frankly, I don't do much posting on)

Add to this, literally over 100 testimonials on all the sales letters listed on my products pages along with the 4 or 5 content-filled e-mails I send out each week... if you can't figure out whether you and I are meant to be from all this, then we *aren't* meant to be.

If someone needs to talk with me, they book an hour of consulting time with me, plain and simple. I guarantee the time, so if you feel it hasn't been time well spent, no worries -- it's a risk-free deal for you.

And you get one hour, only.

Why?

Because if you need more, you book a full day of consulting, instead.

If you want to hire me to write copy, you book a full day of consulting and you get a 100% credit of that day towards your copywriting project.

Why do I do things this way?

Because I like it and because it makes sense for me.

And ultimately, because of my work ethic, what makes the most sense for me, *always* makes the most sense for, and is in the best interests of, my clients. See, when your own business is built on integrity, then what you offer others is just an extension of that, plain and simple.

And if this didn't work, there'd be no way I'd have all these testimonials all over the place and no way I'd be able to do the things I'm doing, so consistently.

So these are the rules I follow. Remember how I just got finished telling you how you should set your business up the way you want it?

Well, I'm a firm believer in practicing what I preach, and this is what I've done.

This model suits me fine for now. It makes sure I'm not wasting my time with tire-kickers and looky-loos, and it makes my clients pre-qualify themselves.

And this is important because you simply can NOT make big money if you're wasting your time.

Also, I take on very few copywriting projects simply because I don't have time for them, and I only take on those projects I strongly believe have a chance of being successful. And since part of my compensation is tied to ongoing royalties based on the success of the project, my compensation plan backs this up. This means once I agree to work with someone, they can be extremely confident about the work we're going to be doing together, and optimistic about the results they can expect.

I have turned down loads of copywriting projects for this reason, and I've refused consulting days as well, simply because the people weren't ready for it, or they couldn't make good use of the time.

The fact that I have turned down large sums of money before, lends even more to my credibility, and to your likelihood of success when working with me. I also let people know about this, as often as I can. In fact, you can read a true story about me turning down $50,000 dollars at kingofcopy.com/leads.

Another thing that's now become legendary in my circle, is the fact that I threw three people out of my Mastermind Group, some time ago. These folks were paying $18,000 dollars a year to belong to my group, but because they weren't, for lack of a better phrase, behaving properly -- I canceled their membership and then I let everyone know, publicly.

After this incident, I implemented an extensive membership application and interview process you must now complete, before being accepted into this group.

And what do you think *that* did for me, as far as positioning goes?

Don't you think clients and Mastermind members are more confident about working with me? Don't you think people in general, are more flattered to be "accepted" into this group? (As a side note, the quality of people in this group also went up, dramatically, when I implemented an application process. The application in and of itself, is a filter.)

Don't get me wrong -- you don't need to intimidate people. That's not what this is about and it's certainly now what I'm about. But you do need to establish ground rules about what you expect from your clients and customers, and then, when someone violates these rules, you must have some sort of consequences.

If you're a parent, you should be thinking, "Hey, this isn't any different from how I'm supposed to be teaching my kids!"

And if this is what you're thinking, then pat yourself on the back, because you're 100% right. And just like when you're disciplining your children, for any of it to be effective, you must follow through with the implementation of your consequences, which is always the hardest part.

But in business, the same way it works in your personal life, these consequences lend even more credibility to your positioning.

If you are a realtor:

You'd want to let your clients know you will only present offers to your sellers, from those buyers who have already been pre-qualified, or who have already shown some sort of verifiable way they can afford to buy the property. This minimizes any wasted time and manages false expectations far more effectively.

It also positions you as someone who values your time (and your clients time) and isn't interested in wasting it.

Also, making your clients sign exclusivity agreements for a certain length of time, before you're willing to accept them as clients in the first place, lets them know you don't just work with anyone -- you need your clients to show you they're serious about working with you, before you accept them as clients.

This is strong positioning.

There's a fine line between confidence and arrogance, but your ability to consistently walk along that line, creates your positioning and increases demand for you in the marketplace.

In general:

You want to keep in mind, the simplest and most effective way of making your prospects pre-qualify, is by using a 2-step lead generation process to attract them in the first place.

Once your prospects have gone through this process and have qualified to become your clients, it is very easy for them to now appreciate, understand and abide by your rules, since they've pursued you and not the other way around. Again, this is all about positioning.

Here's another example of this. I recently developed a turn-key two-step lead generation product for the pre-foreclosure industry, called the Pre-Foreclosure Success System. This has completely changed the way people in the pre-foreclosure investment business work. (This was developed long before the housing bubble burst and market conditions changed.)

Here's the usual process: An investor gets a list of names and mails a letter or a postcard to someone who's about to go into foreclosure. The basic message in this letter is something like "You are going to be kicked out of your home any day now, but I can help you. I can buy your home... I can prevent the banks from foreclosing on you..." or any one of a number of variations on this theme -- most not very eloquently stated, and many downright offensive and blatantly parasitical.

Now the problem with this is, depending on where you live, this poor homeowner who's about to get foreclosed on, is getting anywhere from 25 to 300 letters just like this! And the real estate investor's most common marketing answer to this, is to try and be as accessible as possible, so the letters wind up saying something like this: "Contact me

143

NOW! I will help you! Here is my office number... my cell phone number... my fax number... here's my wife's number in case I'm busy... here's my son's emergency cell phone -- he's only in third grade but tell him you want to talk to his dad about buying your home, and he'll get through to me."

Of course I'm exaggerating, but you get the gist of what I'm saying, right?

Instead of appearing caring, the investor winds up looking incredibly needy and desperate. And the way to help someone, especially someone who's in dire straits, *isn't* by being desperate, it's by being strong and confident, so they feel safe and secure working with you. This way they feel confident about your ability to lead them out of the scary place they've been living in for so long.

Also, the typical conventional pitch from the investor, is to get a "free consultation." And we all know what that means, right?

It means "sales pitch." Never call your initial meeting a "free consultation." It creates stress and anxiety for your client right from the get-go. A free consultation is just an opportunity for you to try and sell yourself to your client. It's where you "convince" the client they should hire you. Nothing strips you of your dignity, more than this.

Anyway, the investor ultimately wants to buy the prospect's house at a deep discount. In many cases this is the best deal the homeowner is going to get, and has short and long-term consequences that are far better than what happens if the property goes into foreclosure.

And because there are big dollars involved, and because most real estate investors are living deal to deal, these investors are generally pretty desperate to get these appointments for "free consultations," and that's exactly how they come off.

I completely changed the way investors approach prospects and turned the tables around significantly, by changing the positioning of the investors. With my system, the homeowner/seller is the one calling the investor, and is *thrilled* the investor is even willing to meet with them! And once they do meet, the homeowner is relieved to have found someone who's professional and sharp enough to handle their problems from that point moving forward.

This is not very difficult to do when you know how to position yourself. So what winds up happening in this situation, is that instead of begging for appointments, the investor has more people lined up and waiting to work with them, so they get to be more selective about who they work with in the first place.

I did the same thing with the ARMs (Adjustable Rate Mortgages) Loan Officer Marketing system - and this worked like gangbusters as well, simply by changing the positioning of the loan officer. Most loan officers are nothing more than interest rate peddlers, however using the positioning strategies we talked about in this Chapter, I turned them into highly valued consumer consultants.

At this point, we've covered a number of different ways of positioning yourself at the top of the mountain, so you can consistently charge more money and command the highest prices, but let's talk about just a few more.

See, like most things in life, there isn't just one secret to doing anything. It's the aggregate impact of consistently using a number of different strategies, all working together at the same time. For example...

Guarantees:

Other ways of positioning yourself are to offer the strongest risk-free guarantees in your industry. After all, who wouldn't be willing to pay more for guaranteed results, or for guaranteed service. And I don't care what you do -- there has to be some aspect of your business that's typically a bone of contention amongst your customers, which you can guarantee.

For instance, if you're an attorney, you obviously can't guarantee the outcome of your work, but you can guarantee you will return all your calls within 2 businesses days... resolve all billing inquiries within 48 hours... complete and file documents within a certain amount of time... explain all documents in plain and simple English... and promise (in writing) not to do anything that will needlessly run up the bills.

Doctors can guarantee waiting room times not to exceed a certain number of minutes... phone calls getting returned timely... prescriptions filed timely and insurance approvals processed within a certain amount of time as well.

Price Point:

When it comes to pricing, most people position themselves as the cheapest date in town. But when you do this, all you get are cheap or dirt-broke people as customers who are attracted to your price point, not to you. Always remember, the bait you put out, dictates the fish you catch.

The other problem with this is, unless you can *always* offer the lowest price (like Wal-Mart can), your customers will have absolutely no loyalty to you, ever. Customers like this are loyal to your pricing, not to you or to what you do for them.

This doesn't let you make a lot of money from a few people, this lets you make virtually no money from loads of people.

And maybe I'm missing something, but this doesn't seem to be a good model to follow, now does it?

So let's look at how I position myself with respect to price.

Not surprisingly, the way I position myself is by charging the most money!

Of course, you'd better be able to deliver one hell of a service, or else your ability to consistently charge (and collect) high prices will be short-lived. But often, simply by charging a lot of money, you're automatically perceived as being a leader in your field.

Think about it: no one puts BMW and Mercedes in the same class as Kia, do they?

For me, charging top-dollar, and using personality-driven marketing, has been a big part of my success. Call it the "WOW" factor that attracts people to me, if you will. Add to this, the success my clients have experienced has been so dramatic and effective (as evidenced by the dozens of performance-based testimonials I continuously make public), positioning myself as the top-dog has actually been very easy from the start.

Think about charging top-dollar like this: If you needed heart surgery, and you didn't have any information about the cardiologist who was going to save your life, outside of how much they charged... which one would you want to work with, the doctor who charges $5,000 dollars for the procedure, or the one who charges $15,000 dollars for the same procedure?

Chances are you aren't looking for the cheapest doctor in town, and you also don't want to put the cheapest tires on your car, either. Chances are, you also don't know too much about cardiology or tires.

Which means, if you're like most people, you're automatically gravitating towards the most expensive doctor and certainly *not* the cheapest tires, right?

That's because high pricing is a very powerful positioning strategy! (Think BMW and Mercedes versus Kia!) And since price is only a problem in the absence of value, all you need to do in your marketing is show value (using long-form copy, covering specific descriptions of your processes and the benefits of working with you over your competition, and providing loads of testimonials and guarantees), and you're good to go here. You've solved your positioning problem.

Who you are:

Oh, one more thing you should know about positioning. Lots of your positioning can be accomplished simply by how you refer to yourself in your marketing. This is where having a first-class moniker comes in.

Remember, people want to associate with the best, regardless of what you do. I don't care if you're a butcher, a baker, or a candlestick maker, no one wants to deal with the bottom performers in any of these categories.

No one wants an average mechanic working on their air conditioning unit, and no one wants an average contractor building their new house.

As I said earlier, when I took my copywriting and marketing consulting business online, I needed a name for my website. After a few days of thinking through a variety of different names, brainstorming with my older son Nick, he came up with a brilliant name: The King Of Copy.

We modeled it after the late Gary Halbert, who referred to himself as "The Prince Of Print."

Sure enough, the domain name was available, and from then on in, it was smooth sailing, and it's turned out to be very effective. Usually, people look at it simply because of the sheer arrogance someone has to have, to call themselves the "King" of anything.

But I'm *not* arrogant -- far from it, in fact -- but what I am, is a very smart marketer.

I want to reemphasize this point, because I know lots of folks reading this will feel uncomfortable blowing their own horn. But if you're thinking that doing something like this in your own business will turn people off, you're dead wrong. Again, do you think your customers would rather work with, or lean from someone who is mediocre, or do they want the best?

Do you want a mediocre person managing your finances, developing your marketing plan, operating on you, or fixing your brakes?

Of course not. **You want the best and so do your customers and clients.** And if your clients want the best, and you're as good as you feel you are, then letting them know you're the best is not only your right, but it's your duty and your obligation. To yourself, *and* to your marketplace.

One client of mine, Chet Rowland, from Tampa calls himself the PCO Millionaire. (PCO stands for Pest Control Operator.) Another, Brian Deacon from Asheville, North Carolina, calls himself the "GC's Secret Weapon." I came up with both of these proprietary names to position each of these entrepreneurs at the top of each of their respective industries. In fact, when I work with clients, one of the first things I do is come up with proprietary names and proprietary processes, that position them right at the top of their industry. This also "bullet-proofs" them from competition, almost *immediately*.

I don't do this to "brand" my clients, although branding is a side-effect of this. I do it so they can begin to dominate their industry or marketplace, and to establish effective and strong positioning for them, which is far more important.

Also, there can only be *one* PCO Millionaire, *one* GC's Secret Weapon, *one* King Of Copy. And when your marketing becomes proprietary, that's just another way of bullet-proofing yourself against your competition.

The only thing you need to make sure of here, is while you don't have to be perfect, don't ever lie about your competence and your abilities. Make sure you can deliver on all the promises you're making. There is nothing worse than faking competence and then letting your clients and customers down. Blown expectations linger for a long time. Remember, Rome wasn't built in a day, but it burned in less than a day.

Even if you're new at what you're doing, think about the one or two aspects of what you can do for your customers, that sets you apart from everyone else.

This has been a very thorough and somewhat lengthy Chapter, but that's because it's incredibly important, and it's one of the major contributing factors to my success. Remember, everyone wants to work with and get involved with a winner. So if you can't come up with some sort of effective positioning for yourself -- something that differentiates you from your competition -- then you're in for a very long haul.

My own positioning in a very crowded sea of copywriters is as follows: **I am a very sharp strategist, and especially strong when it comes to two-step lead generation strategies. And when it comes to writing emotionally compelling sales copy and understanding what makes people tick, I am second to no one.**

148

Money-Making Action Steps Checklist

☐ **First, figure out what it really is, you need to be the best at.** What do your customers want (not need) most, that gives them the most incentive to work with you, over your competition. No sense in trying to position yourself, until you know exactly what you need to position yourself for -- and against.

☐ **Next, for each of these items, come up with a specific strategy that allows you to position yourself as an industry leader -- without seeming arrogant, pompous or shallow.** There's a fine line between confidence and arrogance. I walk it well, but that's because I'm really NOT arrogant at all. I'm probably one of the most grounded people you'll meet, which is why I have the tolerance of a gnat for most supposed "gurus."

And the truth is, I'm not really in control of any of this. While I'm certainly not a religious man, I do believe some kind of higher power is running the show, and I'm too smart to even *think* I can control things like health, the economy, the marketplace and technology. This Action Step is about *positioning*, nothing else.

☐ **Make SURE your message is congruent with who you are and with your abilities.** Far too often I see people trying to make themselves scarce, but the rest of their communication reeks of desperation. So for instance, you can't say something like, "I only take on a very select few clients," if somewhere else in your marketing, you're offering free consultations. These two messages aren't congruent with one another, at all. If you're doing this, you're positioning *and* your credibility is going to be weakened, *dramatically*.

Chapter References

- If you want to see the positioning I use with respect to all my products, you can see them listed at kingofcopy.com/products

- To become one of my friends on facebook, go here kingofcopy.com/facebook

- For information about consulting with me on an hourly basis, and to see the guarantee I give, go to kingofcopy.com/consulting

- To learn about booking a full day of consulting, go to kingofcopy.com/consultingday

- To learn more about hiring me to write copy, see kingofcopy.com/workingtogether

- For information about 2-step lead generation and how to write a long-form sales letter / FREE Report, go to the only comprehensive program that exists at kingofcopy.com/leads

- For information about my Mastermind Group or to apply: kingofcopy.com/mastermind

- For information about the ARMs Loan Officer Program, go to loturnaround.com/arms

- For information about the Pre-Foreclosure Success System, contact my office at 813-909-2214.

- And lastly, you can even learn a lot from my "Contact Me" form at kingofcopy.com/contact

Strategy # 11

Three Critical Selling Mistakes: Which One Of Them Are You Making Right Now?

Over the last few Chapters you've seen many of the ways I communicate with my list. And unless you've been in a coma, you've also seen that an e-mail message doesn't leave my little fingers and go out to my list, without some sort of a sales pitch in it. (Outside of holiday greetings and well-wishes.)

And that's because **nothing gets bought unless you sell it first**. No offer means no sale. And no sale means no money.

Yet few, if any ads you'll see, even *make* an offer, let alone make a good offer.

"Call 555-1212" is *not* an offer. "In business 25 years at the same location," is also *not* an offer.

Not selling something to a list of buyers is like not making passionate love to a beautiful sexy woman who's lying there naked in bed, right beside you...

You Miss... An Opportunity... To Enjoy An Incredible... Experience!

(Sorry ladies, I couldn't help myself.)

So let's talk about some of the problems people have with selling. Usually it's one of three things: Either they don't sell enough, they sell too much, or they don't sell at all.

Not selling enough:

Appreciate that when someone signs on to your mailing or online list, they're signing up because they **want** something. And when someone wants something from you, in order to get it, from a consumer standpoint, this means they may want to **consume and**

buy something from you as well.

This is what drives our economy. The urge and desire to consume goods and services is overwhelming, and frankly, for all intents and purposes, it's why qualified prospects sign up to be on your list in the first place. They want to know if you have something to offer them, that makes some aspect of their lives, better... easier... or more effective and enjoyable.

But what happens is, since most people feel awkward about selling, they wind up communicating with their list only once in a blue moon -- and then, whenever they do communicate -- the *only* thing they're doing is trying to sell them something.

Now if you are a big, dumb company, people actually expect this from you and it's probably not going to hurt you too much. But if you're an individual or if you're a company based around an individual personality, it will *cripple* you.

See, talking to someone once a month, and just trying to sell them something, isn't a relationship. And in fact, this'll generally winds up frustrating many of the people on your list, and many will unsubscribe.

Think about it. You sign up to be on someone's list today, and then you don't hear a thing from them at all. Then, three or four weeks later you hear something from them, and all it is, is an offer to buy something.

Then you experience this same pattern every month or so.

Is this a relationship *you* want to be in?

Of course not.

So if you are doing this, know that you're going to wind up alienating many, if not all of your list members, very rapidly.

For starters, most of them won't even remember signing up to your list because they haven't heard from you for so long. Remember, the world (especially online) is moving at an incredibly fast pace right now, and unless you go out of your way to get someone to remember you, and unless you go out of your way to be different and create a relationship with your subscribers, you are merely a blip on the radar screen. A momentary novelty that was never fully indulged.

And all because you didn't, in reality, give your prospects what they originally wanted: an opportunity to develop a relationship with you, and an opportunity to buy something from you.

Don't make this mistake. And keep in mind, when you're giving out loads of great content whenever you communicate, like I do, people won't mind if you want to sell them something.

After all, you've earned that right. See, intelligent people know there really is no such thing as a free lunch. And *these* are your prospects and your future potential buyers. Don't worry about everyone else on your list, they're not your prospects.

Right?

And in a few minutes I'll show you how to sell something in such a way that you won't ever offend anyone.

Selling too much:

Another problem you run into is when you sign on to someone's list thinking you're going to get some sort of an e-course or a series of e-mails that are going to teach you something, or explain the product they are selling, or entertain you in some way.

Then, in reality, all you get are hard-hitting sales pitches -- or worse, sales pitches that humiliate and degrade you, implying you can't do so-and-so or your life's not complete because you don't own the particular item this person's trying to sell.

This is also a big problem and all it's going to do is make the lion's share of your list frustrated and angry.

Now there is actually a large chunk of people who *will* buy stuff from bullies like this. I call them "sheeple" -- half sheep, looking for a shepherd to lead them -- and half person. Most of these sheeple are biz-opp buyers. They will NOT stick around long and most will not buy from you over and over again (on continuity), and a very large percentage of them will refund your product, simply because this is what they do with everyone.

This is obviously not my style, nor is it the crowd I want or attract. In fact, I try and repel the biz-opp marketplace because of its transience. I work W-A-A-Y too hard to get the one-offs. I want serious entrepreneurs, and people who are serious about their marketing. Those are the people I can help the most and who appreciate and can't get enough of my material, and these are the people who stay with me for *years*, not for a few fleeting weeks while they're interested in the latest flashy thing put in front of them.

The only time I want to use flashy things as bait is when I'm fishing for bass out here on my lake.

And in case you're not seeing the pattern here, let me spell it out for you in plain and simple English: **You MUST consistently give your list members <u>quality</u> <u>content.</u> You MUST entertain them... and you must contact them often and give them multiple opportunities to buy, if... you want to build a relationship and sell to them, over and over again.** (And these rules are the same whether you're marketing online or offline.)

Sales pitches alone, just won't cut it.

The only time I've seen this model, the endless sales pitches with no content or entertainment or customer involvement, work successfully... is in a business with a HUGE variety of inventory. Typically, this would be a known brand with a cult-like following, and the entire purpose of their e-mail communication is to let list members know what products they're putting on sale this week.

Typically, people are also coming to these sites through referrals and word of mouth, or through write-ups in magazines, and NOT just stumbling on to you "cold" from Google.

So for example, I love good coffee. There's a coffee store in New York City, on Bleecker Street in the West Village, just around the corner from New York University, called Porto Rico (http://www.portorico.com). They've been in business for over 105 years, and if you subscribe to their e-mail list, once a week, like clockwork, they'll send you an e-mail telling you what brands of coffee they have on sale this particular week. (Check out their House Blend, and the Organic French Peruvian FT & Bird Free, they're both awesome!)

They have no relationship with their list, other than the fact that their list members love their coffee and they signed up to get the weekly specials.

Other examples of this are companies like big office supply retailers, and other big retail chain stores.

Most entrepreneurs, however, do not have this kind of a rabid following, nor do they have this kind of inventory in their business, that turns over so rapidly.

Side note: Funny story about the Porto Rico shop on Bleecker Street. When I was a kid, I spent every free weekend and moment I could, walking up and down the streets of the East and West village (primarily the West Village), and I probably passed Porto Rico no less than 500 times. (By the way, a few stores east of Porto Rico, and across the street, is one of the best Pizza parlors in New York, at Pizza Box. I've been going there for years as well.)

I wasn't really a coffee drinker back then. In fact, I really didn't get into drinking good coffee until I started dating my wife. Anyway, one time, I took her up to New York City -- this is back in the mid-1990s -- and we happened to stumble into Porto Rico and buy a cup of coffee. We have been steady customers of theirs ever since.

Funny how you only notice those things you're open to noticing, and only when you're ready, isn't it?

Not selling at all:

Remember, in life... the squeaky wheel gets the grease, and in business, nothing gets bought until it gets sold first. If you feel awkward about selling, and you think you're going to make a living by waiting for someone to approach you and ask if they can buy something from you, here's my advice: "Good luck."

You *may* make the occasional sale of "something," if you're lucky. But you'll never have any kind of systematic sales system or predictable income this way.

This is foolish thinking that will get you in the poorhouse, quickly. Weak salespeople have skinny kids and are starved for affection and mostly they are starved for cash.

Plus, "luck" isn't a very good business strategy, is it?

There's a reason why you give your kids money, there's a reason why you get upgraded at hotels, and there's a reason why money exchanges hands for goods and services, every day. And that reason is because someone asked for something.

See, the squeaky wheel not only gets the grease, but it also gets the money as well. If there's any one skill you should always be working on and trying to improve, it's your selling skills.

Money-Making Action Steps Checklist

Earlier, I mentioned I'd give you a little secret to selling, that would change your perspective on things, and change the way you look at your prospects.

This is an incredible idea and it's one I wish I could take credit for, but it was given to me by a close personal friend of mine, Christian Godefroy. Christian runs a site called Club Positive, and you can find him and enjoy all the beautiful stories he tells at http://www.positive-club.com/

One time I was stuck on a project, and Christian, in his humble and warm voice, said to me so eloquently, with his French accent: **"Craig... why don't you think about what you want to bring into the world... instead of what you want to get out of it."**

After I heard this, I was never stuck for a sales message, , ever again.

When you think about what you want to give, the emphasis shifts from you, to your prospect. People can sense this and they are drawn to it, since most people do the total opposite -- they are always thinking about themselves and what they can get out of you.

So next time you're trying to sell something, try and put yourself into this state of mind. If you're truly genuine about this, and you really feel this way, it will pay off for you in spades.

☐ **Think about the frequency of your sales pitches.** Are you selling not enough, too much, or not at all?

☐ **If you're not selling enough, figure out how to pitch your list more often, without compromising the content you deliver.** (You *are* regularly delivering good content, right?) In fact, figure out how to improve your content so you can sell even more! More important, figure out WHY you are so timid when it comes to selling, and work on this reason inside your head!

☐ **If you're selling too much, figure out how to focus on your relationship first, and selling, second**. (Remember, think about what you want to bring into the world... instead of what you want to get out of it.)

☐ **And if you're not selling at all, begin focusing on how to sell, and how to sell effectively.**

Chapter References

- My Magic Marketing program (http://www.kingofcopy.com/magicmarketing) is like the "Consumer Reports" of direct-response marketing information. In it, are dozens of reviews of incredibly useful selling programs I've been through. You'll find out which ones to get your hands on, and... which ones to avoid at all costs.

- My Seductive Selling newsletter has literally dozens of new selling strategies revealed every month, and it takes you through detailed reviews of different ads and marketing pieces, so you can see how to apply each of these strategies in different situations. I also re-write loads of bad or mediocre ads and give you these re-writes along with live step-by-step critiques, so you can see what's wrong and how to fix it. Test-drive it free and get 18 REAL gifts, just for saying "Maybe," http://www.kingofcopy.com/ssnl

- There is NO product on the market that teaches you how to create and use emotionally compelling sales copy and strategies, and how to push your prospect's emotional buy-buttons, like my Seductive Selling System. This system is so effective it comes with not one, but TWO risk-free guarantees. You can find it online at http://www.kingofcopy.com/seductive

Lastly, if you are afraid of selling "too much," here's a testimonial I received that should both get you excited and put you at ease. Yes, it's a great endorsement for my Seductive Selling System, but it's also a true story you can probably relate to if you're not a "natural" salesperson, or if you're just uncomfortable selling:

"Hey Craig, I just wanted to drop you a line to let you know a couple of things. First, you are the man! **I will never forget the day I called you and shared with you how "scared" I was to communicate to my list on a regular basis. I told you I was simply afraid to ask for the sale.**

We talked for a few minutes and you assured me that's what my list wanted from me. You also told me there were 47 ways to push your prospects' emotional "Buy Buttons" and get rich along the way! I asked how I could achieve this and minutes later, I invested in your Seductive Selling System.

Craig, I was in the middle of a trying to fill a room for a seminar and struggling to do so. **Using your system,** I began implementing your methods for getting people to buy, but I only had 21 days left before the event. Each day I sent an email containing just one technique and each day someone registered for the event. **That's 21 additional people to my event. You came through for me with flying colors. But it gets better!...**

It wasn't until our post event briefing that my staff and I began discussing how those 21 people allowed us to fill our room block with the hotel, how they registered for future events and the profit that was generated from those 21 people.

Craig, I'm proud to say, your system netted me $42,176.00 in 25 days! It took me

4 days to get through the material (I'm kind of slow), and to begin implementing what I learned. Your course is kick-ass and simple to use. You should seriously triple the price.

You are instrumental to my business and I can't believe you didn't sell me this course when I met you a year ago. Shame on you! Please pass this note on to anyone who's on the fence about investing in your course. **If I can achieve this kind of result, anyone can.**

In closing, if someone doesn't own your course, they are LOSING OUT, big-time. Period! The price you'll pay by NOT owning The Seductive Selling System, is FAR greater than the small price you're going to pay to invest in it."

Mark Sumpter - Kansas City, MO

Strategy # 12

How To Make A LOT More Money With NO Extra Marketing Costs

This is an incredibly simple way to make a LOT more money, and it won't cost you anything extra to acquire new customers.

Here, check this out: In business, there are only three ways to make money:

1. **Get more customers.**

2. Charge more money for your goods and services. Or...

3. **Get your customers to buy more often, or spend more money with you each time they do buy.**

What I'm about to reveal now, is another one of my little secrets. In fact, it's an incredibly simple way of getting your customers to spend more money with you each time they buy.

See, every single "larger" product I sell, comes in two different levels -- call them a "basic" level, and an "advanced" level. The difference between these two levels is that the "larger" or more advanced package comes with more items, and therefore more benefits.

For example, my Seductive Selling System comes in a "Complete" and a "Light" package as follows (this is a summary listed on the Seductive Selling System form and on the website):

Here's What You're Getting Inside The Seductive Selling® System!	Value	COMPLETE System	"Light" System
✓ "47 Ways To Push Your Prospects Emotional 'Buy-Buttons' And Get Rich Along The Way"	$4,700 (47 x $100 each)	YES	YES

187-page manual			
✓ 5- DVD's containing 4 ½ hours of LIVE step-by-step detailed sales copy critiques and reviews of 20 Classic Direct-Response Ads	**$17,940** (20 x $897 each)	YES	YES
✓ **20 Classic Direct-Response Ads, including 2 ads I was paid $40,000 dollars to write**	**$40,000 +**	YES	YES
✓ 1-Hour Audio CD Interview, "The 3 Most Incredibly Powerful Selling Secrets, and The ONE Most Overlooked Selling Formula Consistently Used By The Wealthiest And Most Prosperous Maverick Marketing Millionaires On Earth, To Make A FORTUNE!	**$500**	YES	YES
✓ **Transcript of the Audio CD Interview**	**$47**	YES	YES
✓ 2004's Tales From The Throne	**$197**	YES	YES
✓ **Emotional "Buy-Button" Audit Certificate**	**$250**	YES	YES
✓ FREE Sales Copy Review Certificate	**$250**	YES	YES
✓ **FREE Test-Drive Of The Seductive Selling™ Offline Newsletter and Audio Success CD****	**$97**	YES	YES
✓ 18 FREE (REAL) Bonus Gifts!	**$3,632**	YES	YES
✓ **5 Audio CD's Containing the 4 ½ hours of LIVE step-by-step detailed sales copy reviews of 20 Classic Direct-Response Ads, straight from the DVD's**	**$485** (5 x $97 each)	YES	**NO**
✓ 5 Complete Transcripts from the Audio CD's	**$235** (5 x $47 each)	YES	**NO**
Total Value If Buying Each Item Separately...		**$68,333**	**$67,613**
Your Low Investment, But Only If You Order Now:		**$997**	**$797**
Or... EZ-Installment Program		4 at $255	3 at $277

You'll notice the difference between these two products in this case, is the extra Audio CD's with 4 ½ hours of content in them, and the 5 Audio Transcripts from these CD's. These products offers added value to nearly everyone since few people rely on DVD's ONLY to consume information, especially detailed information about marketing and writing sales copy.

Also, most people don't want the "cheaper" version of anything. **They want the best, and they want the best value.**

Want to know the sales stats on this?

O.K., here goes:

87.9% of all people buy the Deluxe System, which costs $200 more Now can you imagine how much money I'd have LOST if I only had the one basic system at $797?

Let's work through the math on this, over just 100 sales. Out of every 100 sales, 88 people will take the bigger package. **This means an extra $17,600 dollars!** ($200 x 88)

My question to you is...

Can You Afford To Walk Away From Money Like This In Your Business?

If the answer is "No," then you need to incorporate this model into your business, right away.

Regardless of whether you sell hard goods, or services, or if you publish information like I do, using this model makes you a TON of extra money with minimal extra work and literally ZERO extra marketing costs.

See, there's a very significant percentage of your buyers, who'd be thrilled to buy more things from you. All you have to do is ask them. (Remember, nothing gets bought unless you sell it, first.)

Let's look at the numbers on my Lead Generation System, because they are even *more* startling! First, let's look at the difference in these two packages, which are called the Deluxe and Standard options:

Here's What You're Getting Inside **Lead Generation Explosion!**	Value	DELUXE System	Standard System
✓ **ENTIRE Full Marketing Campaign That Generated A 42.7% Response!** Including... • **Front & back of all 3 Postcards in the sequence** • Website lead generation capture page • **Online thank-you / confirmation delivery page** • 6 e-mail follow-up conversion messages • **3 "set it and forget it" fax conversion messages** • Original notes and strategy discussion memo to client • **Teleseminar strategy, selling, and positioning memo to client**	$13,000	Included	Included
✓ **DVD1**: 49-minute sales copy and marketing strategy breakdown and detailed step-by-step explanation of initial actual postcard campaign.	$500	Included	Included
✓ **DVD2**: 47-minute sales copy and marketing strategy breakdown and detailed step-by-step explanation of the rest of the entire campaign.	$500	Included	Included
✓ **Audio CD1** - Audio Track from DVD1	$500	Included	Included
✓ **Audio CD2** - Audio Track from DVD2	$500	Included	Included

✓ Audio CD3 - Behind the scenes interview with Brian Deacon, The GC's Secret Weapon!	$500	**Included**	Included
✓ "Lead Generation Assessment" Certificate	$250	**Included**	Included
✓ Quick-Start "Cheat Sheet": 15 Steps To Get Your Lead Generation Campaign Up-And-Running, IMMEDIATELY!	$47	**Included**	Included
✓ FREE Test-Drive Of The Seductive Selling® Offline Newsletter and Audio Success CD**	$97	**Included**	Included
✓ 18 FREE Bonus Newsletter Gifts - $3,632 dollars!**	$3,632	**Included**	Included
✓ Bonus Audio CD4 - Sales copy and marketing strategy breakdown and detailed step-by-step explanation of another 3-step full-page tearsheet lead generation display ad campaign, that generated a 7.5% response rate!	$500	**Included**	No
✓ **Bonus CD5 - Lead Generation Explosion Swipe File!: Word documents and .pdf files from the FULL 42.7% Response Campaign, and the pdf's of the 3 full-page tear-sheet display ads from the 7.5% campaign!**	$997	**Included**	No
✓ Seductive Selling® Coaching Call - Lead Generation part 1 (Audio CD & Full Transcript)	$197	**Included**	No
✓ Seductive Selling® Coaching Call - Lead Generation part 2 (Audio CD & Full Transcript)	$197	**Included**	No
✓ **6 Bonus Audio CD's - FOUR HOUR Teleclinic, Q & A Lead Generation Explosion LIVE!**	$3,750	**Included**	No
✓ **Bonus: Transcripts From Live FOUR HOUR Teleclinic**	$282	**Included**	No
TOTAL VALUE		**$24,449**	**$18,526**
Your Low Investment, But Only When You Order NOW		$747	$497
Or... EZ-Installment Program		**3 at $257**	2 at $257

Since the basic package in this system is only $497, and I'm asking people to make a slightly bigger leap, both percentage wise (50%), and dollar wise ($250), up to the larger package which is priced at $747, there's *lots* of extra value added to the Deluxe System:

✓ **You get a bonus CD with another detailed review of another lead generation piece I created that pulled in a 7.5% response via direct mail.**

✓ You get all the original pieces of the main campaign on a Microsoft Word Document CD, so you don't have to waste time trying to figure out how to lay these ads out on your own.

✓ **You get TWO hour-long "plus" coaching calls I did, along with both of their transcripts.** These calls show you, step-by-step, how to create long-form "free reports" (sales letters) to use for lead generation. In a nutshell, they teach you how to write sales letters.

162

✓ **You get 6 Audio CD's of a Four-Hour Teleseminar on Lead Generation that I hosted, along with the transcripts for this tele-clinic.**

That's a TON of extra value, so the numbers I'm about to give you should make perfect sense.

Ready?

O.K., in this scenario...

98.4% of my customers have ordered the Deluxe System!

Again, can you afford to be walking away from numbers like this?

That's an extra $25,000 for every 100 orders!

Pretty profitable, isn't it?

Now there are three things you want to keep in mind whenever you're offering these different levels:

One: Make sure in your sales material you CLEARLY describe the differences and explain the added benefits and the extra value you're offering. Don't rely solely on a brief description like the charts I've shown you. These charts are summaries of all the benefits already presented in both the sales letter and on the order form.

Charts like this make it much easier for your customers to summarize what they're getting, and it's also a great way to get the attention of "skimmers" (people who just skim through your letter).

Remember, people have no problem paying you top-dollar for value, but if you don't have the common sense to explain and show them what this extra value is, then they're not going to have any way to assess it on their own.

Two, don't offer too many different levels! I've been in direct-response marketing since 2000, and I don't think I've ever offered more than two different levels of products in my own business. I have worked with clients who've created three different levels, but even with this, I'm uncomfortable. In fact, this book is the first product I've tiered in three different levels.

At the end of this Chapter, I've included an article about this specific topic, which you'll find helpful.

And three, make it brain-dead simple for your customers to take the bigger package by giving them tremendous value! As you can see, the more you're willing to include for the bigger package, the greater the percentage of your customers who will take this deal.

The good news is, if you are a "regular" business, meaning you sell hard goods or services (you're not a publisher of information), I will tell you now, the easiest way to add value to your products and create multiple levels, is by adding some kind of information to the mix of what you're selling.

Go back and re-read **Strategy #2** ("Want a HUGE net income? Become a publisher and sell information.") for more specifics on how to do this and for ideas about the kind of information you can offer your customers and clients.

Try this out and let me know how it works for you. I promise it will make you a small fortune over time.

Oh, one more thing about this, and it's VERY important, so listen, and listen good: **Always offer your most expensive program first, and your least expensive program second.**

Here's why: See, when you present your most expensive option first, your prospect has this as their frame of reference, and they'll have to convince themselves why it makes sense to get *less value* by choosing the less expensive item.

And who wants to get less value?

No one, right?

But when you present your least expensive item first, *this* is your frame of reference, and then you put your customer in the difficult position of having to "convince" themselves to spend more money, which is always a much more difficult thing to do.

No one wants less value. If you'll notice, my most expensive and best value propositions are always offered first, and I encourage you to do the same thing.

Now here's that article I promised you about offering too many choices:

"Enough Already!"

Last week I met up with an old friend of mine at one of

our local cigar retailers.

The store was having a little get together for their customers, which basically means they had a manufacturers rep stop by. The rep was offering a discount on his brand of cigars if you purchased them that evening.

I hadn't seen this friend in a long time -- we used to do a lot of business together years ago -- and even though he's a lawyer, it was still nice to get together with him, once again.

Anyway, when I walked into the store, I was immediately given a ticket for the evening's prize drawing, and then straight away, the guy at the door went into the sales pitch.

It went something like this:

"If you buy one La Gloria Cubana cigar, you get another one free, and then you'll get another ticket for the drawing. But if you buy a box, you get 10% off, and then you'll also get a discount on your next purchase, plus you'll get 8 or 9 coupons extra, depending on what box you buy. The free cigar isn't available here, you get it from the girl behind the counter over there when you pay... now if you buy one of these 3 boxes over here, you get 9 coupons and a..."

Ay..yai..yai!

At this point, I told the guy he needed to make things simpler for me, that he was giving me information overload.

I felt like a country boy who had just been dropped off in the middle of Times Square!

And this is exactly what happens when you give your prospects too many choices, instead of just offering them "This" or "That."

And when your prospect becomes overloaded with more information than they need, you know what happens?

Exactly -- they get put off and then wind up doing

nothing.

It's like going to a restaurant and you open the menu and there's 200 dinner items on it. When this happens, your night out goes from an enjoyable experience, to... "work!"

So whenever you're closing, remember to make it short...

And sweet.

Now go sell something.

Money-Making Action Steps Checklist

☐ **Start taking inventory of what you sell, and begin figuring out how to add more value to your goods and services.** Consider "bundling" different items together into "common sense" value packages. (Hint: Reread Strategy #2, this will REALLY help you figure out how to incorporate this into your business.)

☐ **Make the items you're adding things that will make your customer's experience more enjoyable and productive.** Don't add useless items with little value, just for the sake of "heft." This really turns people off and they will not buy from you again because you've shown them you're more fluff over substance.

Also, the bonuses you add in do NOT have to be related. Years ago, when Shell Oil was trying to market their credit cards, for example, they found the best bonus item was a set of steak knives -- go figure!

☐ **If you're not sure what else to add to your packages, split up existing "big" items into two smaller items and offer a basic and deluxe from these.** Or, survey your customers and clients and see what they'd like you to do for them, to make their experience with you even *better*. Also, check out your competition and see what they're doing and figure out how to apply some of their good ideas, to your business. Then, use better marketing and some of the strategies inside this book, to one-up them, by selling at a higher price, and by creating repeat buyers.

Chapter References

• To see how the Seductive Selling System is split up into two separate program levels, go to kingofcopy.com/seductive.

- To see how Lead Generation Explosion is split up into two separate program levels, go to kingofcopy.com/leads.

- For excellent information about bonuses and about using direct mail in general, read Richard Benson's book, *Secrets of Successful Direct Mail*.

Strategy # 13

Upselling: The Secret To Making Even MORE Money

In the last Chapter we talked about, how there are only three ways to make money in business:

1. **Get more customers.**

2. Charge more money for your goods and services. Or...

3. **Get your customers to buy more often, or spend more money with you each time they do buy.**

In the last Chapter we spent a lot of time going over how to increase the amount of money your customers spends with you each time they buy, by offering them different levels of your goods and services.

The reason why this works so well is because once someone commits to spending money with you, they are "all ears" and quite eager to now get the best values you have for them. And they will gladly pay you more money for this extra value.

Now we're going to go over another strategy I use, called upselling.

First, let me explain what upselling is and why it works, and then I'll show you how I use it.

I'll then explain my overall business philosophy, and how I structure upselling to fit into my business model, so you can do the same thing in your business.

Upselling is when you sell a customer something else, in addition to what they originally came to buy from you.

A basic example of this is when you go into the grocery store to buy a container of milk, and you also wind up buying the National Enquirer and a pack of gum at the counter. The National Enquirer and the pack of gum are the upsells.

Here's why this works: appreciate that the toughest sale to make is your first one.

Once your customer commits to making their first purchase, selling them something else is much easier.

In fact, upselling is so effective, to the point where some businesses have what's called "loss leaders," which are effectively, "ethical business bribes," just to get their prospects buying "something." These loss leader sales don't necessarily have any profit in them, and in fact, they may often create a loss for the business owner.

They do this though, because they know the toughest sale to make is the first one, and they just want to get the customer on board and buying something.

An example of a loss leader I have is the free 30-day trial to my offline Seductive Selling newsletter. I give away a EIGHTEEN free gifts for only $5.95 postage and handling, at a loss, because most of the people who take this trial, ultimately become long-term customers of mine. Once they are in my "funnel," they see the tremendous value and effectiveness of the information I have to offer. Many of these customers make additional purchases and begin ascending my sales funnel.

Here are some basic upsells you are no doubt familiar with.

If you've ever ordered something from amazon.com or from iTunes, or from almost any major retailer, right after you place something in your shopping cart, you'll see a web page that says, "Customers who bought (your product) also ordered (links to other products)." Or, "Here are some other items that people who've ordered this, also found useful."

This is very effective, because of what the late Gary Halbert used to call "The Porcupine In Heat Theory." See, porcupines only go into heat once a year, but when they *are* in heat....

Look Out, Momma!

They'll jump on almost anything at this point, and buyers are often no different. When someone is in a buying mood, they're usually in a buying mood to get loads of other things. Why do you think "a day of shopping at the mall" generally winds up being so costly?

It's because when you're in a buying mood... you're in a buying mood!

And it's the same way with almost any activity. Why is it when you're hungry, you'll sit down and eat the entire container of Ben and Jerry's Ice Cream and not just a few spoonfuls? Or the whole bag of chips or Oreo cookies?

That's just human nature, and while you can't alter it, as a marketer, you *can* take advantage of it. The same way you can encourage your prospects to order the biggest package with the most value, you can also sell them more "after the sale" simply by making them subsequent offers that makes sense.

For example, I have a few lower-priced "How To" products: my **Magic Marketing Guide**... **22 Ways To Completely Eliminate ALL Your Marketing Headaches**... **The ABC's of Real Estate Investor Marketing**... and **How To Make Your Dreams Come True.** These products both offer small one-off upsells, and almost 100% of everyone who orders, takes them.

You'll see on the web page, how this is done:

Magic Marketing: kingofcopy.com/magicmarketing/rapidresponseform.html

22 Ways: kingofcopy.com/22ways/order.html

ABC's of Real Estate Investor Marketing: kingofcopy.com/abcre/abcusa.html

How To Make Your Dreams Come True: kingofcopy.com/dreamscometrue/dreamscometrueusa.html

This is a simple way to execute this strategy, but frankly it's not the primary way I use it.

Let me explain what I mean and my overall business philosophy, some of which we've already covered.

One of the reasons I've been so successful is because I believe in having continuity business models. Continuity means selling something that gets delivered and consumed over and over again, like vitamins or newsletter subscriptions.

I like this model for several reasons. You only have to make ONE sale, yet you get paid over and over again for it. You also know, on the first of every month, you can expect a certain amount of predictable dollars coming into your bank account during that month.

For me, this is a REAL business. On the other hand, a business where you constantly have to kill "fresh meat" in order to eat, isn't one I want to be in. It's way too stressful and all your past efforts don't continue paying off for you in the future.

And I don't know about you, but I work w-a-a-y too hard for my past work not to pay off in my future. I've also had a number of very lean years where I worked like a dog and made nothing, early on, so I enjoy and prefer predictability. In fact, I am never interested in picking up a customer for the "quick hit" sale. I want them consuming from me forever, and I try and set up various mechanisms, including continuity businesses and upsells and back-end sales, to make this possible.

So with few exceptions, I rarely sell something that doesn't have a continuity component attached to it. In this case, the continuity component of the sale is in a sense, my upsell. And I also don't usually make that continuity product optional. I use "forced" continuity. Meaning, when you buy the original product, you are also buying the continuity product as well.

I mentioned earlier, that for a long time, on my Seductive Selling System (which is my biggest selling marketing system), I actually had **two** forced continuity items attached to it. There was the free 30-day test-drive of Seductive Selling, my offline newsletter, and you also got a free 30-day trial of my Seductive Selling Coaching Call program. This was a structured telephone coaching program which revolved around a different marketing topic every month. As a member of this program you got to participate on a live coaching call every month, you got to send in questions for me to answer on the call, and you also got to ask live questions on the call as well.

You also received an audio CD recording of the call, along with the transcript of the call, for only $197 a month.

As I said, I discontinued this program because after almost three years, I just got burned out on it, and the last thing I wanted to happen was for the quality of the information to slip.

And while we're talking about continuity and coaching, let me take a minute to say something about this. It is insulting to participate in a program or on a coaching call, where the call leader's objective is to get you to buy something else. It's disrespectful and it's an easy way to turn you members off.

This too, is yet another reason for my success. I cannot tell you how many programs I've been a member of, since 2000, where the sole purpose of the program leader, is to upsell you to the next program.

The truth is, if you're doing your job right, this will happen organically with a certain number of people, anyway.

Just focus on delivering a quality product, and on doing what you said you're going to do, and your customers will love you.

When people come to you for coaching or mentoring, they are looking for help and guidance. They're placing their trust in you, believing you'll give them the best information and content you can. If you deliver on the content part -- meaning, if you deliver on your end of the bargain -- your members will buy tons of stuff from you simply because you honored your commitment to them. You won't need to "sell" them into it.

I am proof of this, and I'm thrilled that my reputation is one of "content first," because this is how you build a business -- by building relationships and by simply doing what you said you were going to do. In today's day and age where "showing up" makes you look like a superstar, and where mediocrity is the new excellent, doing what you said you're going to do and more, is all you need to do, to build a loyal following.

'Nuff said.

Some important keys to upselling:

✓ **It is best done right there at the point of sale. Your buyers are MUCH more inclined to buy at the point of sale, than after the sale has been made.** This doesn't mean you should stop talking to them after they've purchased from you, it just means they are more likely to buy at that point in time than afterwards. I've tested this umpteen times and it's always proven to work this way.

I've already shown you how I do this online, let me share a little secret about how to do this offline. One way is to include an irresistible offer for something else, with a deadline on it, when you ship your product out to your customer. This takes literally NO extra money to do, outside of whatever it costs to print the sheets of paper. In fact, if you don't do this, you should be shot for wasting a great opportunity.

Another way to do this is by telephone. You have a sales person or staff person properly trained to do this, follow up with your customers, or else you drive them to order by phone in the first place, by telling them in your order form, "Order by phone at (phone number including area code) and get a FREE (whatever)!"

Then when they get on the call, you can do what Thomson Cigar does, or what

Bottom Line does (see the article at the end of this section). These companies will say something like this, right after you've place your initial order, "Craig, we have a VIP special today for all our customers. This (product name) normally sells for $57.95, but because you've ordered today and because we value and appreciate your business, you can have it on special for half-price at only $28.95. This is a one-time offer only for you to save 50% on (whatever)."

Now DON'T do this unless you have your offers scripted, and unless you have a good telephone sales staff and you continually test and improve the performance of your sales script. But this is a very effective way of upselling your customers, again... for virtually zero additional costs.

✓ **The way I do my upsells online is VERY basic.** There are loads of different kinds of pop-ups and exit pop-ups (pop-ups that come up after your page has closed), that allow you to make a follow up or lower-priced offer to someone who didn't buy, that I'm not using right now. This adds even more opportunities for you to connect with your customer, that make this process even more profitable. I'm NOT a techie -- my strength is selling and marketing. But if you can build a better or more efficient mousetrap using technology, don't be afraid of using it.

✓ **Timing can vary.** Online, some folks wait until the purchased item is actually in the shopping cart, before offering the upsell. I don't do this but that doesn't mean you can't do it and test the results.

✓ **Again, when you're offering continuity, especially forced continuity, make sure you're offering FULL disclosure.** We provide full disclosure about our continuity programs in our sales materials, on our ordering page, in our shopping cart, *and* on our offline ordering fax forms as well. I believe in being 100% transparent in my business dealings, and this is one reason our persistency rate (how long people stay on your continuity programs) is much higher than industry standards. I have no desire to bamboozle someone into any one of our continuity or membership programs.

I don't want to "trick" someone into ordering and then depend on their ignorance or disorganization to letting me whack them for a few months worth of charges. That is real lowlife behavior if you ask me, and yet it is unfortunately, very common. If you come across someone who's burying the fact that you're buying into a continuity program in small print, RUN! You can be certain they will under deliver on content, and not give you the service you need or the quality and responsiveness you deserve.

Remember, how someone does one thing is how they do everything.

✓ **When someone wants to cancel your continuity programs, do it right away.** Most people also don't do this. Instead, they offer a bogus or unresponsive e-mail addresses, or they bury their contact information or don't even show it at all.

✓ **You can definitely offer multiple upsells, but if you do this, make SURE you offer them in a decreasing price point order, from most expensive first, to least expensive.** Like we talked about in the last Chapter it's easier to convince someone to spend less money (relative to what you just asked them to spend) with you, than to spend increasing amounts of money with you. **Here's an article from the November 2007 issue of the Seductive Selling Newsletter, which explains exactly why:**

That's A Whole Lotta Upsellin', Ain't It?

Since it's the Thanksgiving Season, now's as good a time as any to say "Thank You." And so without any further ado… let's dig in to this month's feast:

I was recently preparing for a client project, and I thought getting on Bottom Line's customer mailing list might help me. I'd been a customer of some of their publications before, but it had been a few years. So timing was perfect one evening as I sat down to watch television, and sure enough, there was an infomercial running, on Bottom Line Secret Food Cures.

Since I was in research mode, I didn't just hop online and order their product, I called up to find out their selling PROCESS.

Now before I go ANY further, let me stop and point out two HUGE lessons. One, if you're not comparison shopping -- especially from great marketers (Bottom Line is a long-standing successful publisher of information, all marketed using superior direct-response marketing methods.) -- then you are missing out on opportunities, ideas and short-cuts, like the one I'm about to reveal.

And in business, since there aren't many short-cuts, I suggest you take advantage of them when you can.

And you'll notice I was concerned about their selling
PROCESS. All too often, people forget we're in the
"selling" business, and it's the uniqueness of whatever
selling process you can create for yourself, that generally
sets you head and shoulders apart from your competition.
NOT the uniqueness of your headline or the color of your
order form. Yes, these things are important, but your
PROCESS is what drives your revenue and controls who comes
into your funnel and who gets (hopefully and purposefully)
kicked out.

So here's Bottom Line's selling process: First they thank
you for calling and they restate the offer (A bunch of
books with VERY sexy titles like "Secret Food Cures." The
cost was $39.95.), and they remind you of all the bonuses
you're getting -- including (and this is important) the
value of the bonuses.

Two things here you need to pay close attention to: One,
I almost NEVER see people making their prospects aware of
the value of their bonuses or their teleseminars or
webinars, or even the value of their free in-person
seminars.

This is a BIG problem because if you don't give something
a value, then its value is presumed to be "zero," by
default. Values are a must, especially if you want your
prospects to get off their butts and buy something or take
some sort of action.

Even when something is free you need to give it a value.
What, do you think someone wants to listen to a FREE
Teleseminar that's worth nothing? Even my teenaged sons
wouldn't want that one.

Second, subscribers often ask me if the value of their
bonuses is realistic. Meaning, can you value something TOO
high to the point where it's not believable. The answer is
"Yes," but I don't think that's the real question you
should be asking. For the most part, the only people
valuing an e-book that literally every other "internet

175

marketer" is giving away as a free bonus, at $997, are the folks who are one-trick ponies. NOT entrepreneurs with real businesses, who are interested in making lifelong fans out of their customers.

The REAL question you should be asking is -- if something is intangible or unknown, and you want to give it a higher value -- what can you COMPARE it to, that has a KNOWN value, to justify the value you want to assign it?

So for example, I once valued a LIVE Four-Hour teleseminar (the one that's part of my Lead Generation Explosion System), at $3,250, because I compared it to the value of what it costs to come here and spend a full day of consulting with me ($7,500).

These are the kinds of comparisons you want to use, that justify your valuations.

If you've giving away a 756 page book, like Bottom Line is, would it be unreasonable to make the claim that, "This book is priceless. In fact, outside of these pages, it would be literally impossible to find all these remedies and cures neatly summarized and categorized in one place.

In order to gather up this much information, you'd need to spend three weeks in the Library Of Congress, and another two to three-THOUSAND hours interviewing the world's top clinical nutritionists practicing at the world's top universities (good luck finding them!)...

And besides, what's it worth to you, to *completely* eliminate the constant agony, and all the aches and pains you're having, *and* to eliminate all the needless suffering you're going through right now?"

See, when it comes to value, what you're comparing your product against, is FAR more important than the number you assign it. The more realistic your **value comparison** is, the more valid and logical, and the more readily acceptable to your buyers, that value will be.

This is because human nature naturally makes comparative judgments on a *relative* basis, when there is no other way

176

to determine or assess something.

In other words, your prospect simply can't value what "X" information is worth, unless they compare it to something. Make sure *you* offer that comparison -- don't leave it up to them. Do NOT forget this, it's very important.

Oh, and don't be concerned at this point if some people STILL think it's not a realistic number -- they won't be buying anything from you, anyway, right? You only care about your BUYERS.

Now before I get back to my phone call ordering products from Bottom Line, I'll tell you that Bottom Line MAY break even on these front-end orders, which is why every single dollar they are upselling you, is critical. Even though their infomercial is very well done, customer acquisition costs are quite high with infomercials.

Here's what they DO make money from:

✓ **Their monthly newsletter subscriptions (and Lord knows they have LOADS of different ones:** Personal, Health, Women's Health, Natural Healing, Tax Hotline, and Retirement

✓ **They make a TON of money from list rentals.** They have the perfect prospects: mail-order buyers interested in each of the above categories. And in case you didn't know, the health and wellness market is one of THE most reliable and evergreen (meaning, it never ends) marketplaces you can work in. My good friend Christian Godefroy has made much of his $300 Million dollars in sales, from this marketplace.

✓ **Their back-end.** Let's put it this way: If you think I try and sell you a lot of things on the back end... and if you think I e-mail you a lot... and if you think I'm always coming up with something new, or some creative and clever way to introduce something -- these guys make me look like a rank amateur. You will think they are your long lost childhood friend, they e-mail you so much.

✓ **And... they also make a TON of money from the inserts they include with their deliverables.** Not surprisingly, here's the inserts I received with my order -- and remember, they are sending inserts out every single month to those folks who subscribe to each of their newsletters as well:

☞ **Super Prostate Formula.** There were two of these -- looked like they were split-testing "Call for details" versus "Not Available In Stores." Each coupon had a different toll-free phone number to call, so they can track their results.

☞ **Omega 3 Fish Oil.** Same as above -- two different phone numbers to call, but for the life of me, the ONLY thing I can think they were split-testing was insert placement positioning. One ad was in an envelope with all the other inserts, one was loose with your invoice, and would clearly get more visibility.

☞ **A Discover Credit Card Application**

☞ **Woman Within** clothing brochure

☞ **"John Wayne" Bradford Exchange Knife**

☞ **One Spirit book-of-the-month club** (spiritual healing books)

☞ **AARP Life Insurance** (many of their customers are seniors)

☞ **An entry form for 6 free chances to win a Craftmatic Adjustable Bed.** This is lead generation for Craftmatic bed sales, and also for Craftmatic to build up names for their own list-rental business.

☞ **Prevention Magazine offer.** This is similar to the offer Bottom Line makes to get you in their funnel (free special reports, free three week trial).

☞ **Victoria Principal's Cosmetics**

☞ **Classical CD Membership Club**

☞ **Better Sex For A Lifetime videos** (clearly couples oriented, and also clearly NOT pornographic)

☞ **FREE Sample of Pain Vanish cream.** Again, this has a dual purpose. One, to generate sales, two, to generate leads and names for their mailing list rental business. And by-the-way, the leads these coupons are generating are good ones, since you have to fill out a very small post card and then drop it in the mail to get the stuff -- no "instant gratification", like "download your free report." Which is also another lesson, of course -- the more hoops you're making your leads jump through, the more qualified they'll be -- always.

Just one more thing I want to tell you before I finish my story. If it turns out that for whatever reason, you have a significant percentage of your buyers who are elderly and concerned about their health, you'd be well-served to now carve out a niche product JUST for this marketplace, and JUST to market to them by renting the Bottom Line mailing list of buyers.

Like let's say "Real Estate Investing Secrets For Seniors"... or "Health Secrets For Seniors Living In Warm Climates."

Think about how effective this might be.

So now let's get back to my phone call. The original product I bought was a book called Secret Food Cures, and the bonuses were 3 Free books, and 3 Free Special Reports (6 x 9 catalog sized, between 12 and 30 pages -- looks bigger because presentation is nice: glossy covers, smaller print, neatly printed).

After the operator finishes taking my order, they offer me the upsell, which goes something like this: "Now Mr. Garber, Bottom Line TRULY appreciates your business today, and because we value your time, we want to make you aware of a special offer we've got available for you today only. It's a 562-page manual called The Natural Physician's Healing Therapies."

She then goes on to tell me a few curiosity-provoking bullets about what's inside, plus the offer of "FREE Shipping Today," and how the bonus is only $19.95.

"Of course I'd love it," I say. "Let me ask you something, if you don't mind: How many people usually order this book?"

The operator tells me that over the course of every two-day period, she'll talk to 100 people, and that basically EVERYONE orders it. Now I'm not sure if she's been prepped to say this, but seeing as how she was SO specific, when I didn't *ask* her for specifics, I think she was being genuine. If she was prepped for this answer, Bottom Line's REALLY on it, but I think she was being spontaneous and sincere. I also don't suppose many people ask her this question.

She then offers me the next book, a 756-page guide called The Complete Encyclopedia of Natural Healing." (side note: "The Complete " is a great name to use for almost any niched product.) This one's only $14.95, and of course I say yes, and then ask her the same question again, about the percentage of callers who take this second upsell. And, I get the same answer.

Now assuming she's being genuine, what lessons can we extract out of this? One, the ORDER of your upsells is VERY important. Pricing should ALWAYS go DOWN for each successive offer, not up. This is why it's much easier to sell a $997 dollar information product, and tack on a free trial newsletter subscription to it, than to offer a $49 dollar product, and try and add a $397 upsell product.

Two, regardless of whether or not you like it, HEFT is important. I can tell you now, if those upsells were 150 pages long, they'd sell a LOT less of them. The truth is, no matter how valuable your item is, BIGGER is *perceived* to be BETTER.

Of course, this is also more of an issue with consumers over entrepreneurs, or with new or lower-level and lower price-point customers. As your customers ascend your funnel -- at least in the publishing business -- the better ones do value content over heft.

Three, the BEST time to sell someone something else, is when you're accepting their money in exchange for goods or services. (Remember the National Enquirer counter at the check-out line.)

This is why smarter, and larger mail order operations *WANT* you to call-in your order, instead of mailing it in, or going online. You can't upsell someone online anywhere NEARLY as effectively as a well-trained telephone sales person can.

Four, upselling often makes the difference between you paying for leads, or having your lead-generation system (in this case, an infomercial), being a self-liquidating lead generation system. Meaning, having an up-front lead generation process that pays for itself.

This reason alone makes it worth your while to create some sort of back-end upsells you can start offering, immediately.

Oh yeah, Bottom Line also offered me the free trial of their magazine for 3 months, which I declined. I'm very surprised they didn't make this a forced continuity product (meaning, you get a free trial automatically, whether you want it or not, and then you get billed for it), but I'd imagine they tested this and found the way they are doing it, to be most effective.

I also received a direct-mail piece offering me a shot at the newsletter subscription again. The piece was great -- it wasn't "selling" anything. Instead, it was a "Thank You For Your Order" letter with some very special gifts, including a FREE gift certificate for free special reports and a free trial of their newsletter.

I'd bet a sizeable portion of their initial "no's" -- folks who turned down the newsletter offer the first time, like me (I turned it down specifically to see how they'd try and upsell me.), sign up once they receive this. I will DEFINITELY be using this tactic for a few projects I'm in the middle of.

If you didn't think paying attention to your competition was either valuable or important before, I hope you're now convinced. And if you didn't pick up at least a half-dozen things from this experience, see if you can go and fog up a mirror, because you might be dead.

But don't worry, if you're dead or sick, I have a boatload of natural medical remedies sitting here in a 12-inch pile on the floor right next to me, that will probably be able to fix you up just right.

Remember, the toughest sale you're gonna make is the first one. Don't waste the opportunity to make a second sale.

In a couple of Chapters I'm going to tell you a story about how "Don't waste the opportunity to make a second sale," launched my coaching business out of nothing. This business took in $135,903.55 in its first year -- NOT including back-end sales or upsells, or copywriting and consulting days.

Money-Making Action Steps Checklist

☐ **Your action step for this Chapter is very easy.** Look through your products or services and figure out how to break them up, create something new, or do something to offer your buyers upsell products or services.

☐ **One thing you can think about doing is making your upsells unique to that particular offer.** Meaning, the only way your customers can get their hands on a particular upsell you offer, is by getting it as an upsell with the actual product itself. This is a sneaky way of creating scarcity.

Chapter References

- **To see how upselling works, check out the sales pages here and then click through to the ordering pages to see the upsells:**

    ☞ Magic Marketing Guide, kingofcopy.com/magicmarketing

    ☞ 22 Ways, kingofcopy.com/22ways

    ☞ ABC's of Real Estate Investor Marketing, kingofcopy.com/abcre

    ☞ How To Make Your Dreams Come True (Most Important Sales Letter I Ever Wrote!) kingofcopy.com/dreamscometrue

- If you want to see the structured coaching program I used to offer as a second forced continuity program with my Seductive Selling System, you'll find a .pdf of the calls listed at kingofcopy.com/seductivecalls. Not all of the calls are still available, but you'll get the gist of it.

- **To see how "forced" continuity works -- to see how the offers are structured and how to present items, check out the following sales letters:**

    ☞ Seductive Selling System, kingofcopy.com/seductive

    ☞ Lead Generation Explosion, kingofcopy.com/leads

- To see a "loss leader" offer, check out my Seductive Selling Newsletter offer at kingofcopy.com/ssnl

Strategy # 14

The Incredible Power Of Your Back End

Listen closely here, because this is important. With a small mailing list, reality is, you simply MUST be able to get as much money out of every one of your customers as possible.

In the last two Chapters, we talked about two different ways of doing this, along with a bunch of different examples:

1. Creating different levels of goods or services, and...

2. Upselling.

In this Chapter let's talk more about the basic concept of "back-end" selling, and how you can apply it to whatever business you're in. This is a fantastic way of making maximum money with minimum customers.

This Chapter's going to be short and sweet, and more conceptual than anything else, because I've actually gone over all the strategies involved in back-end selling over the last two Chapters. So here goes...

As I said earlier, the most difficult sale to make, is your first sale. After this, if you've done your job and provided the service or product you said you'd deliver, and you made good on all your promises, then you are no longer a stranger to your customers. The largest and most difficult hurdles of "trust" and "skepticism" have now been successfully overcome.

As a side note, here's the kind of reaction you get from your customers when you do this. It's a note my assistant received from one of our customers last week: "Craig, I ordered your Seductive Selling System, and there is certainly no shortage of content! You definitely under-promised and over-delivered on that.

The issue I'm having right now is, I've spent the last 3 days going through your complete system and I feel like I just took a sip of water from a fire-hydrant. I have all these ideas running through my head, and I somehow need to sort through all my notes so I can start taking ACTION NOW! I'm suffering from anxiety like a runner at the start of a race, and I want to run already!!!!

I wanted to see if you have a system you use from start-to-finish, in putting together a sales campaign? I'm sitting here trying to create this on my own, and it seems that if you have something you routinely use, that would be wonderful.

Much thanks and appreciation. I'm excited to get this going, and realize a ROI on my investment in your course. I love all the content, and I'll definitely let you know my success. If I can see a return on my investment in this course, it seems that it would only make sense to make an additional investment in your Mavericks Marketing program. Looking forward to it." Gabriel Anderson - Santa Ana, CA

Yes, getting paid is great, but comments like this are icing on the cake. And from here on in, any other goods and services you sell, nets you a much higher profit, since you no longer have any customer acquisition costs associated with these customers. Meaning, it costs you a certain amount of money to get a new customer through your marketing or lead generation efforts, or through your joint venture splits. Obviously, there's no cost to "get" the customer again, a second time.

That means your second and all subsequent transactions, are where you really get to make hay while the sun's still shining.

Can you also see now, why it's so incredibly important to stay in touch with your customers on a regular basis, and to keep them entertained and engaged with the regular correspondence you're sending them?

You want each customer to stick around and buy from you for as long as possible! Imagine how much less cash you'll have, if you have to pay an acquisition cost for every single transaction you make?

Yet, this is exactly what's going to happen if you sell someone something and you don't keep up your relationship with them.

They move on... and you never get to experience the really high-profit transactions with them.

Conversely, are you getting excited about how much more cash you're going to now have, simply by making repeat sales to your *existing* customers?

And this, in a nutshell, is your backend. It's the subsequent sales you make *after* you've made your first sale and after you've already paid your customer acquisition costs.

There are plenty of mainstream businesses, which actually subsist entirely on their back-end sales. Their back-end is so strong they are actually willing to lose money on the front-end, just to acquire a customer. Let me give you a few examples of this.

Hewlett-Packard supposedly loses money every time someone buys one of their printers. Between the cost to assemble, package and distribute their printers, and the advertising costs to acquire a customer, they sell their printers at a loss. However, they more than make up for it, once their customers start consuming all the HP ink cartridges you need, over the life of the printer itself.

Assuming this is true, HP is willing to "go negative" just to get their customer, because the amount of money they make in back-end sales of ink cartridges over the life of their customer, more than makes up for their front-end losses.

A life insurance company is another example of a conventional business that takes an up-front hit and makes it up on the back-end. Between their marketing costs spent to acquire a customer, not to mention the fact that many agents earn 100% or more commission on first year policy premiums, they lose big-time, up-front.

In many cases, they won't make any money on any one individual policyholder, until the policyholder is *well* into their second year's premium payment. And while you've got to have lots of extra capital to support a business model like this, most companies that go negative up-front, are doing so based on the law of large numbers.

They aren't concerned whether any "one" customer won't turn a profit, because they base their profits on the law of large numbers. Meaning, overall... *most* of their clients will turn a profit for them, even though a small percentage of them won't. They are basing their profitability on something many smaller, independent entrepreneurs, either can't afford or don't understand: their numbers.

My original direct-marketing mentor, Gary Halbert, had an expression he used quite often, "Always remember you're in the numbers business first, and the marketing business second."

You can't make up for bad margins by selling more, and this is something most entrepreneurs lose site of or have a hard time getting their arms around. You *must* know whether or not what you want to do, makes financial sense, *before* you go out and create

186

the marketing for it.

It's critical you monitor your business health measurements, like cash-flow and client acquisition costs, the same way you monitor personal health measurements like your blood pressure and your cholesterol. If you wait too long to deal with these issues, by the time these measurements have gotten out of hand, it's usually be too late for damage control.

Because I was originally a CPA, I'm lucky that I inherently know and understand numbers and usually think of them first and foremost. (And "No," I don't like doing it any more than you do, but I'm aware of how important it is!)

And understanding my numbers has helped me avoid taking on projects that could simply never be profitable, no matter "how much" I sold. (This is often what I advise clients on as well -- it is very important.)

Getting back to the life insurance company, what's truly amazing is that these financial service companies have such large customer databases, and yet they do such a poor job at cross-selling all their other back-end services to these customers. It's bad enough their front-end marketing is so weak, but to have such a complete breakdown on their back-end as well, is a financial sin that's offensive to every single one of their shareholders.

Frankly, this is one of the reasons you see so much consolidation in the financial services industry -- the more products and services any one company has to offer their customers, the quicker and more rapidly that individual customer is likely to turn a profit.

Another industry that exists solely based on their back-end business is the infomercial business. Television time is so expensive today, not to mention the cost to product the actual commercial itself. That's why, when you see a product being sold on an infomercial for $19.95 or something like that, you can bet the farm that there's a HUGE back-end to this business, typically including list rental fees (renting the names of all the buyers to other companies who want to prospect to this same marketplace).

The article I included in the last Chapter about Bottom Line's business, is a great illustration of this. I don't think I mentioned that Bottom Line is also in the list rental business, which for some companies, is enough of a back-end on it's own for them to be willing to go negative up-front.

The lion's share of my own publishing business is a back-end business. When someone accepts the offer to take a FREE test-drive of my Seductive Selling Newsletter, between our marketing costs to acquire each subscriber, and the cost to create, manufacture, and fulfill the initial order, which includes 18 free bonus gifts, we definitely go negative up-front.

However, since most of the people who accept this trial, stay on as subscribers (and most of them as long-term subscribers), we quickly recoup our money, usually by the third month, on average, of each subscriber's membership.

And as you can see from my product listing in the back of this manual, we have a very strong (and growing) back-end product and consulting program, so we can afford to go negative up-front. I wouldn't want to have to go negative for a year, though, like a life insurance or financial services company. That's just not the kind of business model I want to be involved with, nor frankly, could I afford it.

Call me old-fashioned, but I want to get paid as rapidly as possible. But the nice thing is, you can set up your business whichever way makes the most sense for you, to accomplish whatever goals you're looking to achieve.

Now let me tell you one thing, and if you remember nothing else in this entire book, but this one thing, you will make back your investment in this manual, hundreds and thousands of times over during the course of your lifetime in business. So listen, and listen good, and commit what I'm about to tell you, to memory

ALWAYS have some kind of a back-end in your business!

One-trick ponies don't go very far. Without a back end you will always be looking for fresh meat to kill in order to eat, and that isn't a business, it's a commissioned sales job that's far less rewarding.

If you follow this rule, -- if you always make it a point to have something else to sell your customers, after you make your first sale -- then you will always be walking down a path of growing riches, as more and more customers fill up your customer list and your prospecting pipeline.

I'm really serious about how important this is, and how critical it had been to my success, and how critical it will be to yours as well. So please say this strategy out loud.

Ready?

O.K., good. Let's go, say this slowly, and out loud:

ALWAYS have some kind of a back-end to your business!

Great! Now just do this ONE more time and I'll let you go.

One… two… three… now say it out loud with me:

ALWAYS have some kind of a back-end to your business!

Awesome. Good job, well done.

Next I'll tell you a story that shows you exactly how important this strategy is, and how I would have lost $135,903.55 had I not followed it.

Money-Making Action Steps Checklist

☐ **This one's easy.** Between this Chapter and the two Chapters before it, I hope you're starting to understand how and why every successful business has a back-end. It is very different to making money simply by selling one model of one thing, to each single customer, only. If this hasn't been your business model prior to meeting me, I hope your greed glands are now salivating over what you've been missing!

What I want you to do, is figure out what else you can sell to your existing customer base. I'm willing to bet, you already know, or have some "sense" of what else you can sell, and probably what else you already *should* be selling your customers. In the off chance you are still stuck on this, please go over the Chapters on Strategies 2, 12, and 13. And then re-read this Chapter over again, as well.

With all this new information you have, if you weren't able to figure this out before, I'm positive you can figure something out now.

Chapter References

• **To see my entire back-end, check out my complete product listing at kingofcopy.com/products**

Strategy # 15

How I Turned A Small Failure Into A Small Fortune!

This Chapter *isn't* about how to run a coaching program. That would be an entire manual unto itself. But it *is* about how to get additional income out of your list, beyond whatever goods and services you're selling them, *through* coaching.

Remember, this book is about making as much money as possible with whatever number of list members you have, and coaching can be a very important, and very lucrative part of this.

Coaching is a big part of my back end, and as long as your buyers are passionate about whatever it is you're selling them, chances are outstanding you can add some kind of a coaching program or consulting component to your business, as well. This brings you in loads of fresh new dollars you'll otherwise be missing.

The way I got into coaching is pretty interesting. Let me share this story with you because you'll find it both instructive and motivational at the same time.

How I Failed My Way Into Coaching

Somewhere near the end of 2005 I got the "idea" that I wanted to have a seminar, and I began promoting it to my list, both online and offline. Now appreciate this is NOT the way to promote a seminar, and here's why: at the time, I had NO physical products at all, (not even an e-book), and my offline Seductive Selling Newsletter hadn't even been started yet. (This started in April 2006.)

And getting someone to attend a seminar when they've never purchased anything from you at all, is NOT good strategy. See, most people won't pay to attend an event of yours unless they've typically bought products from you before. Shelling out money to get on a plane and fly clear across the country, isn't something someone does casually, unless they "know" what they're in for.

However, when someone has already consumed (purchased and used) something of yours, they've had an opportunity to evaluate you, and now they can determine whether it makes sense to attend a workshop you're putting on, or not. Or, to get involved with you on a consulting basis.

But there's a lesson here, which you'll see in just a minute: while proper planning is definitely important, execution is FAR more important. **That's where all your money is made and where all your wisdom comes from.** 'Nuff said.

So getting back to my seminar story, I did have a few hundred postal addresses I mailed seminar promotions to. I had been giving away a small special report in exchange for this information, but many of these addresses (20%) turned out to be bad addresses, and frankly, none of the mailings paid off. I spent $2,000 bucks on mailing a large envelope with a cover letter and grabber, a long-form sales letter, and testimonials, along with the guarantees restated on a pastel-colored 4" x 6" cardstock insert.

The pitch for this event was very straight-forward. If you come and spend a day with me, I will tell you how to get your business on track, how to market it properly, and how to maximize opportunities you're overlooking. And of course, I offered a 100% money-back guarantee.

My thoughts were, promoting and conducting this event would give me great experience, and I somehow felt it would lead to other opportunities. I also knew I'd learn something by going through this process, and I knew I could (as usual) over-deliver as far as content goes. I had no idea if anyone would come, nor did I know if I'd make any money, or even recoup the $2,000 in marketing costs I spent. Not to mention the time it took me to put all this together.

It turned out I had two people come to the event. At $997 each, I broke even on my financial investment, and since today, I now charge $7,500 for a day of consulting... this was a hell of a deal for the two guys who attended.

We met in my home-office here in Tampa, so there were no other costs to put the seminar on, outside of the Chinese food we had for lunch. We ate on my dock overlooking the lake -- it was a beautiful, relaxing sunny Florida spring day.

I was definitely nervous and if truth be told, I was embarrassed at having an event that only two people came to. However, looking back and knowing what I know now, that's probably two more people than I should have been able to attract.

But frankly, this has been the story of my business life. I have consistently always had to work harder than most people, but as a result, I've also been able to get more than most, simply because of my consistent application of the strategies and techniques I'm giving you in this book.

And by the way, as a side note, I always look at every single project I get involved with and think to myself, "I'm going to hit a big home run on this one."

I don't think you can continually have the same high level of energy and enthusiasm you need, to create and make so many good things happen, if you don't have this attitude.

Now back to my "workshop." Both of the attendees at this event got a lot out of it and had a great time. And one of them is still an offline newsletter subscriber of mine, and credits a lot of his progress and current success, to the information he learned at this meeting.

So if you're going to take away anything from my mistake, take away that if you're looking for opportunities, and doing "something" to create them, then you will find them and they will find you. Remember, "action" is king and only action returns dividends. "Thinking" alone has never made anyone a dime.

But here's **the real magic** that happened -- check this out: The night before the event, I couldn't sleep. I wasn't really nervous about delivering good content -- I knew I could do that, no problem. What was bothering me though, was that I didn't have a back-end to offer them.

Here I was, getting two people to fly several thousand miles (one from San Francisco, and the other from Canada) to meet with me, and I had nothing else to sell them!

So, at around midnight I went up to my office and began working on something. At around 3am I finished my project and I went to bed.

What I put together was an offer to join a Mastermind Group I'd be starting soon, and I'm pretty sure I also offered these guys some extra bonuses if they committed to joining this group early.

I got one of them to commit (the guy from San Francisco), and about 6 months later I started the group and got it going. In the interim, I started my offline Seductive Selling Newsletter and completed my Seductive Selling System, and by the end of 2006 I had 10 people in this Mastermind Group, each paying me $1,497 per month.

And what happened as a result of this initial meeting that "flopped?"

Simply this: that year I brought in $135,903.55 in coaching fees, NOT including hourly consulting and daily consulting.

This revenue came from two coaching groups, actually: My Mavericks Group, which is a monthly group coaching call members participate on, to get individual business and marketing advice. Members also get the audio CD's of these calls, as well. (At $299 a month, this is a *great* deal.)

And it also came from my Mastermind Group meetings, which are in-person 2-day meetings that takes place here in Tampa three times a year. Mastermind Group members are typically very serious about their marketing and their commitment to their business. We also meet once a month on the phone, as a group, and there are also monthly one-on-one calls on all non in-person meeting months. The members of this group are also the only people who get direct e-mail access to me, as well, and I look at and critique their sales copy and their marketing strategies, on an ongoing and regular basis.

Who'd have imagined this kind of success... would come out of my initial "failure?"

Now if you'll notice, I was never concerned with making money on that initial "seminar." **I was concerned with making something happen.** The two grand was immaterial to the learning experience I wanted to create for myself. In other words, it was a $2,000 investment, not a $2,000 cost.

And see, this is the problem with most people. Most uninformed business-owners and entrepreneurs, look at the money they're spending on their education and on their actual marketing and advertising, as a cost, instead of looking at it as an investment. This is because they foolishly believe the money they're spending is what creates their results, and not the actions they're taking and the quality of their marketing.

Money doesn't create results, it's only the conduit for your efforts to travel over. Action, and nothing more, creates results.

Like I said, the big lesson here is that if you're looking for opportunities, and you're doing something to create them, you will, in fact, create them. The biggest problem is most people are afraid of doing something unless the results are going to be "big."

I am sure you'll agree, the results of my "failure," ultimately... were big. Very big.

Another funny story. Years ago, back when I first invested in that life insurance marketing coaching program, I heard someone on a call mention that "You really can have too much business."

At the time, I didn't think that was possible. I was dead-broke, and having even "some" business was a dream for me. Today, I know what having too much business means, and as a result of this, I actually have limits on my consulting as follows:

Hourly telephone consulting. You may purchase ONE hour of hourly consulting from me. At $500 bucks an hour, one time this would have been the cat's meow, but today it's an interruption of my time. Most of the people who buy hourly consulting are people who have specific questions they want answers to, or they are sort of "testing the waters" to see if it's worth coming down here and investing in a full day of consulting at $7,500.

Full consulting days. Currently, I am only taking on one day of consulting per month. Again, I have so many of my own projects I'm working on, I simply can't afford to take that much time out of my own schedule. Consulting days are also mandatory for clients who want to hire me to write copy for them. The procedure is, you come down for a full day of consulting and if you want to hire me to create your marketing promotions and write copy, I apply your consulting fee towards your copywriting project.

The truth is, because I'm so busy in my publishing and consulting business, I take on very few, if any, copywriting clients.

Mastermind Group. I routinely turn down between 1 and 3 people every few months, for admission to this group, and as I mentioned earlier, back in April of 2007 I actually threw out three members of the group. These people were basically holding the rest of the group back with negative attitudes and whiny complaining -- they were frustrated they weren't making more money "just because they were in the group."

That's like saying you're frustrated you're not getting in shape, just because you've joined a gym. You actually have to get on the machines and *do* something, and watch your diet, in order to get in shape.

Or, as I said earlier, *thinking* about things doesn't make them happen. Only *action* makes things happen.

Today, you actually have to fill out a detailed application to get into my Mastermind Group, because I feel a responsibility to the members, to only let those people in who are genuinely interested in moving forward and who are action-oriented.

Since implementing this "application" process, the quality of the group, and the progress of the members, has gone up, dramatically.

I have people in this group who have been with me since Day 1, and in today's day and age, that says a lot.

Like I said, this Chapter isn't about how to run a coaching business. But let me tell you that the best way to figure out how to get *into* the coaching business, or what kind of coaching program you should set up, is to get involved in a coaching program yourself.

This way, you'll see what goes on... what the biggest benefits of this kind of a program are... and what you like and don't like about any particular program *and* how to adapt it to your own business.

Most importantly, a good coaching or Mastermind program (initially brought into the public's knowledge, by Napoleon Hill in *Think And Grow Rich*) should enhance your own life, dramatically. And if you're working with a sharp leader and you are implementing some of that leader's suggestions, your income (if it's a business or marketing coaching program) should also be going up significantly, as well.

The other BIG thing that happens when you get involved in a business or marketing coaching program, especially a Mastermind Group, is... you see how *anyone* can grow as a person, and make loads of money as an entrepreneur. "Success" becomes very tangible when you see people sitting right next to you, who are making *loads* of money... and you suddenly realize that frankly, not much separates them from you.

In fact, there is absolutely NO better inspiration to get off your ass and really create the kind of business you deserve, than sitting across the table from someone and listening to all the incredible things going on in their business and in their life, and hearing how much money they're making from it.

That's what inspired me to take action, initially. And if you look at the testimonials from my own Mastermind Group, you'll come to find this effect is universal.

Running groups like this, *isn't* for everybody, though. To be effective and to make a lot of money from it, you have to be able to think quickly on your feet, and you have to be able to consistently motivate, inspire and entertain your group members. You must be able to lead and command respect -- not through fear and intimidation, but by who you are and what you do. In other words, you must lead from the front.

You'd also better be someone who is always moving and taking action and doing new things in your own business. You can't lead others and encourage them to grow as entrepreneurs and as people, if you aren't doing those things yourself. That's what commands respect -- leading by example. Not "talking about leading by example."

In other words, walk the walk, don't just talk the talk.

Oh, and by the way, last weekend in the middle of the worst recession America has ever experienced, I held my first Emotional Copywriting and Ad Writing Workshop, over three days. This is almost three years from the time I held that first meeting where only two people showed up. This time I spent $1,600 promoting the event. 11 people attended, but the admission price was $5,000 each.

And that... is progress! (And it's also not a bad chunk of change to make over a long weekend, is it?)

Money-Making Action Steps Checklist

☐ **Like I said, the best way to figure out if coaching is for you, or if it makes sense for you to start a coaching program, and the best way to figure out the optimal coaching plan to run, is for you to get involved in a coaching program yourself.** I'm a big proponent of practicing what you preach and the best way to learn is by doing.

☐ **Appreciate that you can run coaching or Mastermind programs for topics other than "How To Make More Money."** Hobbyist or personal interest groups like traveling to Costa Rica or Disneyland, or skiing or photography, would definitely work. These folks have a ton of passion and interest in their hobbies.

Chapter References

Here is the big snowball that started after that "failed" conference I held, where only two people showed up:

- **Mastermind Group information and application is available at kingofcopy.com/mastermind**

- Mavericks Coaching Group information is available at kingofcopy.com/mavericks

- **Hourly consulting is available at kingofcopy.com/consulting**

- Information on booking a full day of consulting is at kingofcopy.com/consultingday

- **And lastly, you can find information about my Ad Writing Workshop at kingofcopy.com/adwriting**

On the following pages, you'll find some of the material I used to promote my last Ad Writing Workshop. You'll find:

- **The original sales letter that was posted online**

- A 2-sided advertorial I wrote to promote the event via mail to my existing Seductive Selling Newsletter members. One of the attendees at this event -- a man who's been involved in direct-mail and direct-marketing since the mid 1980's, told me this advertorial is the best piece of copy he's ever seen. So pay close attention to it, you're likely to learn a lot.

- **And... the Registration Form to sign up**

Make sure you take your time going through all this information. You'll find literally hundreds of lessons in marketing strategy and in copywriting, from this information, so please comb through it carefully.

An announcement of unusual importance for every entrepreneur who wants to write more emotionally compelling sales copy that easily eliminates selling resistance:

I GUARANTEE (With My Own Money!) You Will Walk Out Of My January 2009 Ad Writing Workshop, With A Completed WINNING Display Ad, Website, Sales Letter, Or Lead-Generation Ad, No Matter WHAT You Do For A Living!

(And don't worry, you'll even get to go over it with me after the workshop, in case it takes you a little longer!)

Four reasons why this ISN'T just "another copywriting seminar:"

1. **Plenty of people can write copy. But NO ONE can write copy that compels readers at an emotional "gut" level, the way I do.** And as you know, the fastest and surest way to get your prospects to buy, is by pushing their "emotional buy-buttons." This will be the fundamental focus of every strategy and subtle nuance we discuss at this workshop. **Magic bullets that make people buy?** We'll go over them. **Special "hot" words that stop people dead in their tracks?** I got 'em and I'll give 'em to you. **Making your prospects well up with optimism and hope for a better tomorrow because of what you have to sell them?** *That's* what selling is all about.

   I'll take you by the hand and show you, step-by-step, exactly how to do this, by giving you an easy and systematic process to go through, so you wind up spending your time ONLY on those things you need to do, to sell effectively.

"Join me here in Tampa and I'll give you everything you need to know, about how to create effective sales copy that makes you a small fortune. I will hold absolutely NOTHING back, and you have my personal word on this."

2. **This is a ONE-TIME ONLY event! It is NOT a workshop I plan on running this year, and then next year, and then the next year again!** With so many projects, new developments, and new businesses I'm working on, I thrive on change and on new challenges. **This is a one-shot deal only**, where I'm going to reveal all the behind the scenes secrets to writing **clean, emotionally compelling sales copy** that eliminates selling resistance.

3. **I am going to show you how to take the "headache" out of writing sales copy, and the pain out of writing sales letters!** When you have a step-by-step process of doing things, all you do is follow these steps in order, and then you're done. It's just like going to the grocery store. You look at your checklist: do you need butter this week? Yep. How about milk? Sure, just ran out. How about cookies? No, not this week. With your sales copy checklist, writing winning sales letters and powerful ads is just as easy.

4. **I will also, this one time only, reveal the 15 most important secrets Gary Halbert taught me, when I worked with him back in 2003, that I've never revealed before, and do NOT plan on discussing, ever again!**

Lutz, Florida
Thursday, 11:47 AM

Dear Friend,

Nobody *reads* ads.

People read what *interests* them and *sometimes* it's an ad. That's why emotionally compelling copywriting, is "the Swiss Army knife" of selling. It is the single most *important* and most *reliable* skill you can have, that directly generates the *most* money for you, in the *shortest* amount of time.

Take myself, for instance. Back in the late 1990's, prior to getting involved with writing copy, and with understanding how to apply emotional direct-response marketing strategies to business, I was just another average dead-broke financial planner. I had no idea how to get my next client, and I spent most of my time riddled with anxiety, hoping "something" would change in my business.

But as you and I both know, "hope" is *not* a very good business strategy, is it?

Today however, things are very different. Last week I just turned 45 and I am now on track to have the mortgage on my lake-house fully paid off before I "semi-retire" at age 50. Not that I'll stop working then, but I won't HAVE to work any more at that point. And that's something most people don't ever get to achieve, let alone achieve it in such a short time-frame.

Last year, I made a hair north of $574,000, with a small list of less than 5,000 names. And in case you want proof of that, here it is:

Results 1-12 of 12		Print These Results	Actions: Please select one ▼
Previous 1 Next			Results Per Page 100 ▼
☑ Date	NumPmts	Details	AmtPaid
☑ January 2007	367	Show Details	$52,646.23
☑ February 2007	306	Show Details	$41,678.50
☑ March 2007	350	Show Details	$46,978.08
☑ April 2007	302	Show Details	$34,361.53
☑ May 2007	286	Show Details	$26,682.63
☑ June 2007	267	Show Details	$35,592.80
☑ July 2007	265	Show Details	$40,014.26
☑ August 2007	275	Show Details	$49,676.58
☑ September 2007	260	Show Details	$33,578.65
☑ October 2007	275	Show Details	$37,514.30
☑ November 2007	238	Show Details	$35,112.44
☑ December 2007	218	Show Details	$28,199.76
	3,409		$462,035.76

(The balance of my earnings came from consulting and copywriting fees that were not processed through my shopping cart. I have copies of canceled checks for the balance, here in my office, if you want to see them)

And here's proof of the size of my list. This snapshot was taken on January 16th, 2008, and is actually the GROSS number of people on my list, including 700-800 people who have actually unsubscribed from my list, *and* including 816 new people my friend Christian Godefroy had just referred over to me. So in reality, my list was

Autoresponder Name	Msgs in Series	Unique Clients
0-KingOfCopy.com Daily Tip	3	5675

much closer to 4,000 names than 5,000.

Today I am one of the most prolific and highest-paid freelance copywriters and direct-marketing consultants here in America. I see clients only in my home office here in Tampa, at $7,500 a day, and I won't even *think* about sitting down and writing a marketing campaign for someone unless they're willing to pony up $60,000 plus ongoing royalties. I also run an active consulting practice working closely with entrepreneurs from all around the world, in a variety of coaching and Mastermind Groups. But don't believe me, listen to what I've done for a few of my clients:

- **A lead-generation piece I wrote for Chet Rowland, the owner of one of the largest independent service companies here in Florida, produced a 7.5% lead-generation response, when mailed out to a cold list in what was assumed to be "a completely unresponsive" marketplace!** In fact, we split-test no less than THREE different versions of letters I created, and all three came within .7% of each other!

"You CAN teach an old dog, new tricks!"

"Craig, using only two of the ideas you gave me last year, I pulled in $304,044.82 in the last 7 days alone. The two strategies were, incorporating continuity into my business, the way you showed me... and sharing personal information in my emails - personal stories, even weaknesses, the same way you do. I have never earned so much cash, so fast. At 90% profit, I am in debt to you, forever." **Christian Godefroy - Chesieres, Switzerland** (Christian has been in direct selling for over 35 years, and has sold in excess of $300 Million worth of goods and services.)

- I suggested to a private consulting client, Brian Deacon, from Asheville, North Carolina that he "dump" his non-performing business, which was draining the life out of him, and instead get into one that would leverage his talents and relationships more effectively. To Brian's credit, he accepted my comments and did as I advised. **He also hired me to write his first mailer for this new**

business. Result: AN UNHEARD of 42.7% response on his FIRST mailing, and $152,751 in sales! (And no, you are NOT misreading this.) Oh, and by-the-way, Brian (a former VP of Global Marketing at Microsoft - who worked side by side with Bill Gates) recently told me he expects this new business to bring him in over $3.5 Million dollars in revenue over the next 12 months. Not bad for a guy who at the time, was drowning in debt and just a few months away from having to abandon his dream of becoming a successful entrepreneur, is it?

"Millions More!"

"All I can say is, I wish I found Craig Garber ten years ago. That would've saved me a lot of frustration and headaches, not to mention I could have made even millions more dollars than what I already have. Not to mention the money I wouldn't have wasted looking for someone like him. And if anyone wants to speak to me in person about this, they can call me at 813-920-9049." **Chet Rowland - Tampa, Florida**

- And two months ago, I started a new, niche business with a former client of mine. **Before even lifting a finger to develop the marketing systems for the initial clients, I was able to collect $84,000 in fees, ahead of time!** (Oh, and by the way, this was the second time I did this. The first time, with the Pre-Foreclosure Success System, I collected $45,000 in advance.) What made this particularly rewarding, was that **3 weeks prior to signing up, these participants (who paid me an average of $6,000 each), had never even so much as heard my name before!**

See, THIS is what good marketing and great sales copy does for you -- it provides you with HUGE sums of money when you need it most.

And now, YOU can copy my formula for success!

Here's the deal: Last month, my Mastermind Group met here in Tampa, and it included entrepreneurs who came from as far away as Australia. At the end of the meeting on the second day, after everyone's had their turn, I opened the room up to questions from everyone.

One of the most popular questions I got asked at this meeting, was... "How do you write so much?" And, "How can I write better sales copy?"

Since I get asked this question so often, I am putting on a small, power-packed

Emotional Copywriting Seminar And Ad-Writing Workshop. This event is for those entrepreneurs who want to get a better handle on writing emotionally compelling sales copy, and who want to take the "headache" out of writing sales letters. **(Oh, and by the way, it is actually quite easy to be so prolific -- it has to do with HOW you write and the ORDER you write things in -- and it'll take about 5 minutes for me to show you both of these things at this event, as well.)**

And if you are an attendee, I have even more good news: **Since I will be working directly on your business and on your sales letter or ad, attendance is limited to 25 people only.**

"Craig said No!"

"Craig is awesome... I did a day of consulting with him a while back and it was worth every penny I paid him! After spending time with Craig it was obvious my current business was not getting me where I wanted to be... he really helped me reinvent a new business.

Additionally, I wanted to hire him to write copy for my old business and he told me that he wouldn't do it because he didn't see how it was going to improve my current business situation. When any other copywriter would agree, Craig said no because his reputation was on the line!

I have found Craig to be very straight-forward...he is not going to BS you or tell you what you want to hear." **Brian Deacon - Asheville, NC**

But wait, there's more! See, using the inside secrets you're getting, you're going to be walking out of this event on Sunday afternoon, with a WINNING ad or sales letter, put together using the *exact* same system I use to create one winning ad after another, for myself and for my clients.

I have **_never_** revealed this formula before, and I've certainly *never* gone into it in such detail, the way I'll be sharing it with you at this event. In fact, **there is literally NO other way on earth you will ever be able to get this information,** simply because this isn't something someone taught me. **It is a systematic, formulaic (and incredibly effective) process I developed myself,** the same way Jonas Salk developed the polio vaccine, or the same way Bill Gates developed Microsoft's Operating System. After thousands of hours of painstakingly hacking away at it, desperately seeking a better way of doing something -- I finally cracked the code and made it mine.

With that in mind, let me tell you what this workshop is all about, and then I'll also tell you what this workshop is absolutely NOT about:

The Secrets Of The Ages... Now Yours
When You Register To Attend:

1. **You'll get a simple checklist breaking down an effective sales letter into 17 easy-to-understand one and two-word parts.** Now the good news is, **you generally only need 8 or 9 of them in any one piece**, but I will lay them *all* out for you in plain and simple English, in a grocery store-like checklist format.

   Without this pre-launch checklist, you simply can *NOT* put a winning sales letter together, any more than you can fly an airplane without going through a pre-flight checklist. See, there really is a systematic and orderly way of doing things, that makes writing copy MUCH easier, and much more profitable for you. And having this checklist is one of the big reasons why I can write so much, and so quickly. **If you can fall off a log, you can use this checklist to start making money, right away.**

2. **Overcome "Weak Closing Syndrome!"** Listen, closing *isn't* easy -- and in fact, some people can't close at all. Some people list the benefits of what they're selling too late... and some don't offer *enough* benefits. **You'll find out exactly *when*, and *how* to close, so you'll never feel "awkward" about asking for money, ever again!**

3. **EXPLOSIVE Benefits!: The REAL truth about presenting the benefits of your goods and services, that make your prospects salivate!**

   This one's so easy, I'll explain the lion's share of it to you right now. See, first, you need to understand the *difference* between features and benefits. A feature is what something is, and a benefit is what something does for you. So let's take something as simple as a hammock, for example. Most people will tell you how strong and sturdy the wood is, and how it's a new model that just came in. But those are just features (what the thing is), not benefits (what it does for you). No one's going to give you money because the wood is sturdy. Think about it, it's a hammock, the wood is *supposed* to be sturdy. That's like saying "You can use this toothpaste on your teeth." Duh...

   The benefits to having that hammock are that it's guaranteed to be the most *comfortable* hammock you've ever laid down in... it's guaranteed to last at *least* 5 years, no matter what kind of weather conditions you subject it to... it's got a special balancing mechanism that won't let it tip over if someone comes along and sits down in it with you... and when you want to clean it, all you need to do is hose it down with water.

Now *those* are benefits.

See the difference?

And once you combine this understanding, with my hard-hitting way of presenting benefits to your prospects, **there won't be a single question in your prospect's mind about what you're really selling, about how it can change their life, or about why they need to buy, NOW!**

4. **How to make irresistible emotional offers that sell!** Next to your headline, your offer is the *most* important part of your marketing. **I'll show you, again, an easy and formulaic approach to making your offers as sweet as pie and mouth-wateringly irresistible!**

5. **Oh my gosh, I almost forgot -- what about headlines?** When it comes to headlines, you want to whack your prospect over the head, while being as subtle as a whisper about it. This is where using emotional copy that hits 'em in the "guts," *really* counts!

   See, above and beyond anything else, your headline is the most important part of your marketing piece. I've made two-word changes to headlines that resulted in a **five times increase in response!** So you do NOT want to dick around here -- you have to be as selective choosing your headline as you are in choosing your spouse! **I'll give you over 50 different "fill-in-the-blank" headline formula templates to choose from, and I'll explain the psychology behind headlines, and how to test them out.**

6. **What about increasing demand?** Did you know, there's an old adage, that if applied correctly to your promotion, creates a **burning desire** for what you're selling, that's unlike anything else? The problem is, most of the time people try to use this "strategy," they wind up looking *completely* unbelievable. This actually winds up *costing* you money instead of *making* you money. I'll show you the "Penthouse Centerfold " technique, that works as reliably as a Swiss watch, and creates the *surge* in demand you're after.

7. **Most marketers mistakenly believe empathy means telling your prospect "I'm not that much different from you." If you're a rank amateur, maybe so, but if you want to pony up to the bar with some real coin in your pockets, nothing could be further from the truth!** You'll learn the ONLY way to use "empathy," which is THE most important emotional buy-button to push. **(Screw this one up and your headed for the trash bin!)**

Look, being REAL is what makes you a small fortune. At this workshop, I'll show you how to be as real as a beautiful Hawaiian sunset, so your customers, your prospects, and your subscribers respect, and listen to you.

8. **How about introducing your product in your sales letter -- when's the best time to do this?** If you do it too *early*, you alienate your prospect... but if you do it too *late*, you blow the sale and they lose interest. Discover exactly when to introduce your product and what you'd better follow it up with! **(Free giveaway: if you don't follow it up with benefits, right away... then you're toast!)**

9. **What about making irresistible guarantees?** When should you give them and what kind of guarantees should you give? **I'll give you at least one-dozen different examples of "clean," ethical, and profit-boosting guarantees you can make, and I'll show you when and where to use them (there are three places, actually).** Lifting the buying risk off your prospect's shoulders is absolutely *critical* to your success, so pay *very* close attention here.

10. **The opening line of your sales letter is like the eye contact you're making with someone, just as you finish shaking their hand: if something feels even "slightly" off-kilter, you lose your prospect, <u>forever</u>.** See, this is a critical point in your selling process. Since you've gotten them past the headline, it means they're more likely to be a qualified buyer, so you *don't* want to mess this one up. Talk about walking the emotional tight-wire! **I'll give you at LEAST two-dozen ways to open your sales letter or ad, so you can sell *anything*!!**

11. **Destroy "The Competition Myth:"** Contrary to conventional wisdom, you almost never need to consider your competition, and yet... most people waste loads of time worrying about, and trying to *eliminate* their competition. **Discover the one sure-fire way to make sure your competition never even enters your prospect's *mind*!** (And wouldn't it be nice never to have to deal with *that* again?

12. **You've probably heard something that says you always have to give your prospects a "reason why" you're doing something.** Right? **Well, unfortunately, this has been misunderstood and misused to the point where it makes absolutely NO sense at all.** In fact, I'll reveal why, with one exception, giving the "reason why" you're making your offer, or why you've created your product, is an absolute waste of your time and won't even put one thin dime into your pockets! (Again, this completely flies in the face of conventional wisdom.) However... you will save *countless* hours of writing wasted copy, once you understand this.

13. **I'll also reveal the one single reason why most space ads never even have the slightest chance of selling *anything*.** (Hint: if you had any questions about

two-step lead generation before... you won't have them after this!)

14. Critical to your success, is the concept of 2-step lead generation: **you MUST understand the four selling situations when using two-step lead generation is mandatory --** I'll reveal this in great detail! **This ties the entire "emotional buy-button" concept together -- without this, there is virtually NO marketing... and NO money to be made!** (This takes approximately 15 minutes, yet it will change your life, forever.)

15. **You will take home a prolific swipe file, *filled* with a stable of proven, emotionally compelling ads!** You'll find enough fodder in here, to give you ideas to work on any campaign you will *EVER* want to create.

16. **We'll dig deep into the psychological underpinnings of what makes people "tick" and how to identify these emotional buying triggers in YOUR marketplace.** Unless you understand why your prospects buy and what their REAL motivation is, you simply will *never* be able to sell things to them with *any* kind of consistency or predictability. **I will also give you the ONE brain-dead question you need to ask, to figure out your prospects REAL motivation, no matter *what* you're selling.**

17. **Why you often must *understate* things to make yourself more credible.** I'll show you live examples of this almost always overlooked glaring mistake that *completely* blows your credibility.

18. **You'll uncover at least 21 of the most important emotional buy-buttons as possible, and find out *how* to push them and when!** Discover how to tap into the inner emotional recesses of your buyer's mind, using compelling sales copy that attracts *only* those prospects you *want* to deal with and sell to. **After this, you'll be able to save *thousands* of hours of *endless* frustration, by eliminating all the looky-loos and tire-kickers who insist on doing *nothing* but wasting your precious time without parting with a penny!**

19. **You'll get the 4-step method I use to come up with my "big bang boom" strategy that instantly shows you the right "differential" to use!** This secret formula is how I came up with the spin in my Loan Officer consulting business, that allowed me to collect $84,000 before I even wrote a headline! **(And I _swear_ under oath, this took me a whopping 10 minutes to come up with.)**

20. One of the most frequent comments I hear once people meet me in person, is "Wow, you're so much nicer than I thought!" This is by design, and it's called... "Positioning." And you *must* position yourself effectively if **YOU** want to control how your clients interact with you, as opposed to your clients calling the shots. **I'll give you the FIVE key secrets of positioning, and explain how to use them so you will never have to cow-tow to anyone, ever again.** (And by-the-way, this is one of those necessary evils of business, but I'll reveal a few secrets

no one's ever told you, which makes this *much easier* than you thought.)

21. **I will also, this one time only, reveal the 15 most important secrets Gary Halbert taught me, when I worked with him back in 2003, that I've never revealed before, and do NOT plan on discussing again!!** I learned more valuable cash-producing information from Gary in the 6 months I worked with him, then I learned from everyone else I ever worked with, combined. **You'll get the top 15 takeaways, before the weekend's up!**

22. **You'll get a slew of bonus marketing gifts you'll be able to use forever, personally hand-picked and hand-created by me!** I want this to be an experience you remember, so you'll walk out of here with loads of Audio CDs, DVDs, and Special Reports with even *more* winning secrets, strategies and emotional copywriting short-cuts!

23. **Every attendee will even get a post-workshop one-on-one phone consultation with me, to review any ad you've created.** This way you can roll it out with confidence, in case you don't get to finish it during the weekend!

24. **I will also be accessible in the evenings, after hours, as well.** Maybe not until the wee hours like everyone else -- but long enough for you and I to hang out and have a quality conversation. And "Yes!," I will be available... for drinks!

25. **If we have time, we'll also spend a few minutes talking about what I've observed (and what proper scientific tests have verified) to be the ONE personality trait most responsible for the degree of your success or failure!** And "No," it's not persistence... optimism... or believing in yourself. It is far more basic than this and it's identifiable in young children as well as adults. This'll be engaging and provocative -- 'nuff said.

26. And lastly, **I'll tell you the real reason why the Internet is so popular and how to leverage this in your business, and in your dealings with your prospects and customers.** And "No," it has nothing to do with making money... with communication... or with any other silly thing academics, gurus, and whiz-bangs tell you. **It has to do with something much simpler than that, and it's actually the reason why most cheating spouses become unfaithful in the first place.**

Plus, since there's a Don Shula's Steakhouse on the first floor of the hotel where we're having the event, I'm taking the first five people who register, out to dinner with me at Shula's.

Holy smokes! That's a *TON* of good stuff, isn't it?

As you can see, you're going to be walking out of here armed for bear, with enough information not only to make yourself tens of thousands of dollars in extra revenue, but... you'll also have so many *NEW* ways of making extra money, your head will be spinning trying to find the time to spend it all! So now that you know what this event is all about...

Let Me Briefly Tell You What This Event Is NOT

☞ **This is NOT a big giant free-for-all.** Because I'm going to be so hands on with you, I am limiting this to a small group of 25 people. Frankly, outside of coming to me for a day of consulting, no one else has *ever* worked this closely with me for this much time, *including* my private copywriting clients.

☞ **This also isn't some grandiose pitch-a-thon where I bring a procession of people across the stage**, each telling you about their latest successes and then offering you their own version of the Sacred Scrolls of Egypt, for only $997.

This is just going to be you and me working on your marketing, your business, and your sales copy, and a small handful of other entrepreneurs who'll be able to give you input and advice, based on their own experiences as well. In fact, Dustin Mathews, one of the members of my Mastermind Group, is constantly saying how I'm "all about the content." And if you are one of the first 25 people to register for this workshop, you'll get to profit and benefit from this, for yourself.

I can *assure* you, **it is impossible for you to *ever* learn what I'm going to reveal at this event, on your own**. And here's why: There are three reasons, actually.

1. **One, over the last year alone, I've probably spent an average of no less than 8 to 10 hours a day, 6 days a week, writing sales copy and coming up with killer marketing ideas. And I'm actually at the stage of my career where I'm starting to slow down!**

    For the first six or seven years of my career in marketing, I worked closer (again, very conservatively) to 11 or 12 hours a day, at writing. **That means, over the last 9 years, I've spent well over 29,640 hours doing this one thing alone. And "Yes," I really *do* work that much.** In fact, if you ask anyone who knows me personally, they'll probably vouch for my work ethic first, above anything else. But don't believe me, you can ask my wife, since she'll be at the workshop as well.

    So unless you have an extra thirty-thousand hours to spare (the average person actually "works" less than 2,000 hours per year), **you simply have no**

way of gaining this kind of experience.

How else are you going to get a short-cut to this kind of wisdom, laid out in such an easy and "common sense" format?

2. **Two, I had a pretty crazy childhood that forced me to hone my "radar" and sharpen my ability to understand and anticipate people, pretty early in life.** See, my father was a violent man, so I tended to walk around on eggshells quite a lot. And as Malcolm Gladwell said in his best-selling book, "Blink," "People who have had highly abusive childhoods... **have *had* to practice the difficult art of reading minds**. In their case, the minds of violent parents." So I *had* to know what made people tick.

   I excelled at this when I was a kid, in order to survive... **however I excel at this now, *not* to survive, but to prosper**. Add to this, a 167 I.Q., and the fact that I grew up in The Bronx, squandering tales of a misspent youth, and you've got a very unusual combination of street-smarts and intuition, you simply cannot replicate at this point, any more than you can replicate Tiger Woods' golf swing.

3. **And lastly, add to the mix, the exposure to Halbert and the unique insight he added...** and you can see, there's a reason why I *intuitively* and *easily* do things marketing-wise, few other people can do.

"O.K., Craig... <u>I'm in.</u> When, where... and how much?"

<u>WHEN:</u> This Emotional Copywriting Seminar And Ad Writing Workshop is taking place on Friday, Saturday and half-day Sunday, here in Tampa, on January 16th, 17th and 18th.

<u>WHERE:</u> At the Intercontinental Hotel, which is a twelve-minute shuttle ride from the Tampa Airport. I personally checked out the meeting facilities last week, and it's such a nice place, I'm actually moving my Mastermind Group meetings to this facility, as well.

Plus, the hotel rooms were recently upgraded and they look great -- flat-screen TV's and sleek smooth lines throughout -- the whole shebang. Anne and I actually stayed at this hotel last year, and the place is first class!

<u>HOW MUCH:</u> At my daily consulting rate of $7,500 alone, this event is worth close to $20,000, *not including* all the physical takeaways you'll be getting. But since this is a "shared" event, where you're actually not getting me "all" to yourself, you won't have to pay this much to attend.

In fact, you won't even have to pay *half* this much. The registration fee to attend this workshop is only $5,997, which is actually less than even *one* full day of consulting, and rest assured, *no one* walks out of a day of consulting with anything even *remotely* resembling a completed ad.

Early-Bird Registration Discount: **When you register before December 1st, you will also receive a $1,000 Early-Bird discount, and you can even make 2 or 3 EZ payments on your registration fee as well.**

Plus, Mastermind Members receive an additional $1,000 discount on top of this, and Mavericks Coaching Group members receive a $500 discount. (Again, call me old-fashioned but I believe in taking care of those folks who support me.) So it winds up looking like this:

Admission To Ad Writing Workshop (25 people only):	$5,997	
Early-Bird Registration Discount Savings (before 12/1/08 or once the first 25 people sign up)	**$1,000**	**six EZ-pay**
Current Workshop Registration (payable in 2 or 3 EZ installments, if you'd like)	**$4,997**	**$897 x 6**
Workshop Registration - Maverick Coaching Members	**$4,497**	**$797 x 6**
Workshop Registration - Mastermind Group Members	**$3,997**	**$697 x 6**

Also, if you have a **bona-fide business partner** you'd like to bring with you to the event, they may attend for only $997.

My Guarantees for this event are very simple and straight-forward: You have my personal promise, if you are unhappy with the content of the seminar, or with your experience, I will reimburse your registration fee. Plus, if this isn't one of the most content-rich and meaningful workshops you've ever attended, I will also reimburse your registration fee. This way, the workshop should MORE than pay for itself, before you've even finished making your payments.

I can't be fairer than that, now can I?

As to the registration fee, if you think this is "expensive," then you're missing something: See, if you can't use these strategies, which have literally been responsible for millions of dollars in sales, to get 1 stingy $5,000 sale... or 5 measly sales of a $1,000 product... then this event isn't expensive, it just isn't for you. Not to mention all the new ideas you're going to pick up, that show you **key positioning strategies that let you charge *much* more money, and that will have you selling *more* products to your *existing* customers. How much do you think all *this* is worth?** Lord only knows what this workshop is *really* worth.

The truth is, if you think it costs a lot to *get* this information from me, then you have no idea what it's ultimately costing you right **now**, every single day in your business, because you *don't* have it. The skills and strategies you'll walk out of this workshop with on Sunday afternoon, after the event is over, profit you **<u>forever</u>**.

It's like I said earlier, **"Nobody *reads* ads. People read what *interests* them, and *sometimes* it's an ad. That's why emotionally compelling copywriting, is "the Swiss Army knife" of selling. It's the single most *important* and most *reliable* skill you can count on, that generates the *most* amount of money for you, in the *shortest* amount of time."**

Besides, reality is, based on early registration interest, **less than one out of every ten people who said they *want* to come to this event, will actually even *get* to come to this event**. So if you want to be here, side by side with me, then I encourage you to act NOW and register immediately. **If you are registration number 26, you will be put on a waiting list and your registration will not be processed.**

"Yes, Craig! I want an emotionally compelling sales letter that eliminates selling resistance and brings in cash, fast!"

How To Find The Hidden Money In Your Business, *FAST!*

Look, in reality this is all about finding the "hidden money" in your business. This is all you really want, and frankly, this is why people hire me and are so willing to pay a small fortune for my services. Because once you find the hidden money in your business, what you spend to find it, isn't a *cost*... it's an *investment* that quickly returns itself and pays off for you, over and over again, forever.

And what you need to know about me, if you don't *already* know me, is that basically, when you strip aside all the business veneer, when it comes down to it... I am a simple family guy. You can take every significant accomplishment I've made... every obstacle I've overcome... and all the money I've made... and none of this means anything to me, compared to my family. My wife and children are THE most important thing in the world to me.

The good thing about this, is when family is most important, you tend to treat everything and everyone you come in contact with, as if they were *all* family. Remember, how you do one thing in life, is how you do everything.

The simple secret to my business success has been nothing more than taking that same commitment I have to my wife and children, and just extending that natural nurturing and attention to detail, to my business and to my clients.

Along those lines, what's going to happen is, the people who attend this workshop won't just leave here as "happy customers." We will have a much deeper and far more meaningful relationship than this. You will now be part of my extended business family, which is significantly more important.

It's for this reason, I ask you NOT to register for this event, unless you meet the following three criteria:

- **One, you already have a business, or you're in the process of launching one.** This isn't a business opportunity seminar for dreamers or for people who won't take action.

213

- **Two, you genuinely believe people buy based on emotions, and you understand how critical it is to be able to push your prospects emotional buy-buttons.**

- **And three, you must also genuinely believe, the words you say make a HUGE difference in the results you get.** I don't imagine you'd be reading this if you felt otherwise, but I just want to make sure we're both on the same page here. So...

Has the time finally come for you to strike it rich?

If so, then you already know that in business, there is no greater skill you can have, or improve, than knowing how to create and write effective, emotionally compelling direct-response sales copy. And there is actually no greater gift you can give yourself, no longer-lasting benefit to you or your business, than attending this workshop.

Reality is, **this workshop can make you financially independent for the rest of your life.** Heck, who are we kidding? One solid sales letter *alone* can make you financially independent for the rest of your life!

Remember, just the same way you never get hit by the bus you saw coming, your income will always be limited by the amount of wisdom and knowledge you're missing. What I'm offering you is a chance to make dramatic changes in your business, and therefore in your life, by giving you the fastest and surest way to rapidly ascend any marketing and income limitations you previously may have been hampered by.

And let's face it, if you're going to work hard, then you might as well get rich at it, right? And the quicker, the better. Getting these strategies under your belt means you will never, *ever* be beholden to anyone, for anything, ever again.

So obey that impulse and register for this rare opportunity, right <u>now</u>.

"Yes, Craig! I want an emotionally compelling sales letter that eliminates selling resistance and brings in cash, fast!"

Whether you attend or not, I wish you nothing but the very best. Thank you for reading this message, and I'm looking forward to working with you and helping you here in Tampa at my Ad Writing Workshop. I know this workshop will make 2009 your best year ever, and I know we'll have fun working together. Please contact my office at 813-909-2214, with any questions you might have. But **do not wait**, there are less than 25 seats remaining as of this very moment.

Now go sell something,

Craig Garber

Craig Garber

P.S. Look, I don't pretend to know you at all. But if you're anything like me, you're probably thinking, "Craig, this sounds great. I know how important this stuff is, but how do I know I can do it?" This is an excellent question and it's one you deserve an answer to, and I'm going to answer it in a story:

A tired businessman traveling by horse, pulled in front of his hotel for the night. As he went to tie his horse up to the post in front of the hotel, he realized the rope was missing. So the elderly owner of the hotel, observing the predicament his guest was in, stepped outside to see if he could help.

"What seems to be the problem?" said the hotel owner.

"There's no rope to tie up my horse, sir. If I leave him here, surely he will run away and I won't be able to leave in the morning."

"That's not a problem," said the hotel owner. "I'll just use this invisible rope to tie him up, and then tomorrow morning he'll be waiting right here for you."

Thinking this was some sort of a cute joke the old man was trying to play, the traveler figured he'd play along, so he simply said, "O.K., why don't you do that. I'm sure that'll work."

And with that, the old man removed an invisible rope from around his shoulder and proceeded to loop it around the horses neck several times, making sure it wasn't too tight. Then he gently slipped it around the fence-post, and tied off a secure "knot" at that end.

Continuing to play along, the traveler shouted to his horse, "Here boy... come on!" And while the horse began to move forward, as soon as he reached the end

215

of his invisible "rope," he stopped in his tracks and jerked back, tethered to this invisible rope.

The traveler's jaw nearly hit the floor! Bewildered, all he could say to the old hotel owner, was... "I guess... I'll check in and go up to my room for the night."

The traveler had a wonderful sleep, and in the morning, when it came time to saddle up, he felt refreshed and filled with life. Then, after wolfing down a delicious breakfast of toast, raspberry jam, and fresh coffee, he headed out front to saddle up his horse and get moving onto the rest of his journey. Sure enough, just like the old hotel owner promised, his horse was right there beside the gate-post where he'd left him the night before.

The traveler saddled the horse up, hoisted himself up onto the horse, and slid his feet into the stirrups, prepared to leave. But sure enough, the horse would only go as far as the invisible "rope" let him go, and then he stopped short, right in his tracks. Just like the night before.

Once again, the old man saw the commotion going on outside, and he came out front to see what the problem was. When the traveler explained the situation, the old man simply sad, "Of course he isn't going anywhere -- you haven't untied him yet." And then the old hotel owner looped the rope back around the horse's neck in the opposite direction... and untied him from the fence post.

And with that... the traveler went off, in a cloud of dust...

What I want you to get out of this story, is whether you realize it or not, you too, have an invisible "marketing rope" tied around your neck, that's preventing you from getting what your really want -- and from making the kind of money you deserve. You have old habits and doubts, and perceived marketing handicaps in your business, that hold you back and prevent you from moving forward.

 For example, so many times I hear things like, "It's a difficult economy. People just aren't buying." Or, "My customers only want the lowest price." Or, "In order to do this, it's going to take me a year or two, right?"

Wrong. Dead wrong.

Here's an example of what I'm talking about. Bob Maunsell, a member of my Mavericks Coaching group, came to me with what he felt was a 2 to 3-year marketing plan. He was SURE he could do what he wanted to do, but he was also sure this couldn't happen overnight. Well, Bob was right on both accounts.

See, using my advice, Bob created an extra $43,000 of revenue, straight to his bottom line, that he didn't have before. But it also didn't happen overnight -- it took him a full 30 days to do this, not 2 or 3 years.

And you heard before what happened with Brian Deacon -- someone who was literally just a few months away from having to abandon his dream of becoming a successful business-owner, and was faced with the cold, harsh reality of having to go back to corporate America. Then, as he says, I "reinvented" his business and he went off and made $152,751 on his first mailing.

Bob, Brian, and even Christian Godefroy (remember, he's sold in excess of $300 Million over the last 35 years), let me lift the invisible ropes off their necks. And while I can't promise you'll get the same results they did -- if you will let me lift these invisible ropes off you, I promise dramatic changes in your business, and therefore in your life. And I can also promise your investment in this workshop will be repaid many many times over, for sure.

"Yes, Craig! I want an emotionally compelling sales letter that eliminates selling resistance and brings in cash, fast!"

P.P.S. The truth is, **knowing how to write a solid emotional direct-response ad or sales letter, may be the only way the little guy can still make big money today**. It's truly the "secret of the ages," and it's all yours when you attend this workshop.

Look, my goal is to make you the highest paid "whatever it is you do," that's humanly possible. If you have the same goal, and you're passionate about your marketing and about what you do, than I urge you to attend this workshop.

Remember, greatness is NEVER a matter of circumstance. It is purely a matter of design. By design, I've become the person who many people consider to be one of the greatest copywriters to ever set ink to paper. If you saw where I live today (The picture of me at the top of this page was taken in front of one of the many Cypress trees in my back-yard, directly in front of my lake and just next to my boat-house.), and compared it to where I came from (An apartment housing project in The Bronx.), you'd see for yourself the kind of transformation emotionally compelling copywriting creates, first-hand. **And at my workshop, I will download everything I know about writing emotionally persuasive, cash-producing sales copy... along with all the proven marketing strategy short-cuts I've seen and used, directly to you.**

Don't forget, since there are only 25 slots available, in a case like this... it is far better to be a few weeks too early, than even one minute... too late! See you in Tampa!

"Yes, Craig! I want an emotionally compelling sales letter that eliminates selling resistance and brings in cash, fast!"

"Half science... and half dark art!"

Recently, Cameron and Tanya Outridge flew in from Kawana Island, Australia, to see me for a day of consulting. **They did not come to the States for a vacation, they came solely to see me.** Here's what Cameron had to say about their experience:

"Craig's awesome. I would thoroughly recommend Craig to anyone. **This guy really is THE King of Copy.**

But really - apart from copywriting - **his other great strength which is just as important, lies in his ability to conceptualize, design and build an automated business system**. He's putting that in place for us for our Herbalife business.

So he's not only the best, most natural and intuitive copywriter I've ever seen, but he knows how to make a business run like an automated money-making machine. He's given us a step-by-step blueprint to build our business. It is based on two-step lead generation providing leads and taking them through an automatic process that will qualify them and even sell them. Only after they have bought, will we have to have contact with these people. We're going to engage him to do all the copywriting etcetera for that. He's not cheap but we wanted the best and I don't want to go through any more years of trial and error and guessing games.

The thing I found put my mind at rest was that he asked us to send him a heap of material so he could research our business before our one-day consult. He said he likes to mull things over a couple of weeks before the meeting. **I was relieved that he is the kind of guy who genuinely cares about giving value for money.** I would have been worried if we'd got there and he had to start from scratch with us. But by the time we got there he was thoroughly versed with our business. He'd even read a book on the subject! He basically had our business machine concept laid out and ready to action.

I think what Craig does is half science and half dark art. It requires street smarts, empathy, a strong work ethic, an intimate understanding of human nature and an ounce of genius.

Craig has all of the above in spades. Plus he's a very genuine, lovely guy who will have your best interests at heart."

218

Obama Will NOT Save You Or Your Business... And Neither Will Unbridled Optimism!

Q: What's the best way to make a small fortune in this economy?
A: Listen to this story about the Old Mule And The Arabian Bazaar:

TAMPA - Has the economy got you down?

Are you sick and tired of "waiting" for things to get better?

Has the beating you're taking financially, become the "pink elephant" in the room no one wants to talk about, because you're so stressed out all the time?

You know what? The truth is, in spite of what people would love you to believe, almost *everyone's* feeling the pinch from the economic downturn we're having. And let's face it, tightening your belt, especially when you've been living the good life for the last few years, *isn't* easy!

After all, who wants to work like a dog, and stay up all night long in front of their computer, just to "get by?"

You deserve better than that, and in a

There's nothing like the thrill of victory (And the windfall of cash!) that comes after you've created a sales letter that works like *gangbusters*. Join me here in Tampa, and I'll show you every little subtle secret and powerhouse strategy you *must* know, and about how to create emotionally compelling sales letters that work, in good times...*and* in bad.

minute, I will *shower* you with the good fortune you deserve.

But first, check off which one of these boxes you've recently experienced:

❐ **Have any of your clients recently left over pricing or continued affordability?**

❐ Have some of your formerly excellent clients, suddenly become "slow payers" because they're suffering a cash-flow crunch themselves?

❐ **Do prospects tell you they're "waiting for the economy to improve"** *before* **making any kind of a commitment?**

❐ Are even practical clients suddenly allowing their fears to outweigh their common sense? **Even when they, of all people, should know better?**

❐ Have you heard some people mention they're waiting to see what happens once Obama takes office -- that perhaps he'll turn things around?

❐ **Have some people flat-out just stopped spending** *any* **money at all?**

❐ And how about you? **Are you typically very positive and optimistic, yet lately you find yourself having a hard time staying that way, when all you see on television and in the newspaper, is how everything's going to hell in a hand basket?**

If you marked off *any* of these questions, then you **must** listen to this story. It's called...

The Old Mule And The Arabian Bazaar

Lost and somewhat foggy from his long trip, a weary traveler found himself smack dab in the middle of an Arabian Bazaar.

Having ran out of gas in his car, and not familiar with the terrain, the oppressive heat was beginning to overwhelm him. And the burden of his heavy luggage, which he now had to schlep around himself, was staggering.

So when he spotted a sign that said, **"OLD MULE FOR SALE,"** he immediately inquired about it.

After negotiating a fair price for the mule, he next asked the street vendor who sold it to him, how to communicate

with it.

"You just talk to it, sir. And it will do whatever you ask."

"That sounds easy enough," said the weary traveler, and he began hoisting his luggage up onto the mule.

When he finished, the traveler turned to the mule and said, "OK mule, let's go." However, the mule just stood there motionless, without batting an eyelash.

So the tired traveler gently stroked the mule's head, and once again said "C'mon boy, let's get moving." Yet still, the mule did nothing.

Becoming impatient, and truly exasperated by now, the traveler tried *pushing* the mule... and then *pulling* the mule, all the while encouraging the mule to get moving. But alas... nothing happened.

"Damn Mule."

Finally, shrugging his arms in defeat, the traveler returned to the vendor who sold him the mule and said, "Hey, this damn mule just won't budge. I thought you said all I needed to do was talk to it, and it would do whatever I ask."

"*Hovno*," the street vendor muttered to himself, in some foreign language. Then, he suddenly reached up under his table and grabbed a long wooden stick hidden underneath it, and leapt out of his seat.

He stopped short in front of the mule, and then, without any warning at all, he raised the wooden stick up over his shoulders, and he *whacked* the mule straight in the center of his head, bringing it to his knees.

"Why'd you do that?" said the traveler, startled by what just went on. "I thought all you had to do was talk to him?"

"Yes, this is true," said the vendor. **"But first... you have to get his attention."**

And see, this too is the secret to selling. The first thing you have to do is get your customer's attention. And although you must be as *powerful* as a whack on the head, you must also be as subtle as a whisper, all at the same time.

Your goal is to get your prospect to react. To take action. To respond. And the difference between just a few words placed in the right place, at just the right time, is almost *always* the major difference between incredible *success*... and yet another crushing failure.

You must *entice* without being needy, *persuade* without being pushy... all while making your customers feel great about what they're doing, and enthusiastic about what you're offering them.

Street Vendor Or Wealthy Prince?

If you're comfortable whacking prospects over the head to get their attention, then throw this article away -- there is nothing here that can help you.

If, however, you prefer to seduce and persuade, to lull your prospects into a trance and have them pay you *huge* sums of money, over and over again... then listen, and listen good.

On January 16th, 17th, and 18th, I am hosting an Ad Writing workshop for 25 people who realize **your ability to control your destiny and make a bushel of cash, is solely based on your ability to communicate and persuade in print**. It's for those people who realize the **most important skill** *any* **entrepreneur can have**, especially in today's unpredictable economy (which isn't about to turn around *any* time soon), is your ability to write an effective sales letter.

See, times like this separate the true sales people, from the mere order takers. If you have been an order-taker all along, counting solely on being in the right place at the right time, then without the ability to write effective sales copy, you are now, in *this* economy, dead in the water.

And this isn't a question of "if," it's only a matter of "when."

If on the other hand, you refuse to let anyone else determine your destiny and your financial future, then knuckle down, and make what is probably the most profitable and highest return investment you will *ever* make in yourself and in your business, and join me at my January 2009 Ad Writing Workshop.

But... is this workshop really for you?

Because this workshop is limited to 25 people, it's important you know who this event is for, because it is *not* for everybody. It is only for you if you can answer "Yes" to any of these questions:

- **Are you an entrepreneur or salesperson who needs more qualified leads?**
- Do you have a "million-dollar idea," but you're stumped about how to make it pay off?
- **Are you stuck in a low profit-margin business, sick-and-tired of trying to figure out how to make *more* money?** Are you ready to get out of the "I'll make up for it in volume" rat race?
- **Are you a marketer who needs to stay on the cutting edge, and you need fresh ideas and proven strategies to help your clients -- and to make a small fortune for yourself?**
- Are you an entrepreneur who's simply looking for that one "missing link" that'll *finally* get your business to take off like a *rocket ship*?
- **Are you a real estate investor, loan officer, realtor, financial planner, insurance agent or other financial services professional, who'd love to have a predictable and reliable way of attracting a steady stream of *qualified* clients?** Do you want to get rid of all those tire-kickers and looky-loos who insist on wasting your precious time?
- **Do you own a jewelry store, an upscale restaurant, a spa or gym, a feed and grain shop, or some other kind of retail establishment, and you'd love to see it BURSTING with customers?**
- **Have you had it "up to here" with clients who *demand* first-class service, even though they're on a Walmart budget?** Would you instead like to deal exclusively with *ultra-rich* clients who are *thrilled* to be working with someone of your caliber?
- **Is there anything you want to sell?** A car? A boat? How about ten boats? **Consulting services?** Self-improvement products? **Pre-foreclosures?** Vitamins? **Information products?** Upscale dog grooming? **Yourself?**

If you answered "Yes" to any one of these questions: then you MUST attend this workshop. I will reveal every single strategy I use, to create winning sales promotions and effective copy that sells and persuades your prospects at the gut level -- **which is the *only* way this works**.

You'll discover how to subtly whack your prospects over the head, create instant rapport, and give them more value then they ever imagined, in exchange for more cash than *you* ever imagined.

It's Completely Risk-Free

If you *are* one of the first 25 people to register, I don't want you to feel even the slightest bit uncomfortable about coming to this workshop. So you can sleep easy knowing you have not one, but **TWO GUARANTEES**:

First, you have my personal promise that if you are unhappy with the content of this workshop, or with your experience, I'll reimburse your registration fee.

And second, if this isn't also one of the most content-rich and meaningful workshops you've ever attended, I will reimburse your registration fee.

See, I don't want you here unless you feel great about it. The last thing you want to do is have buyer's remorse about an experience as important as this one.

$1,000: Now Yours, FREE!

Oh, one more thing and this is important: You'll also get $1,000 bucks off your registration fee, as long as you register before December 1st.

How To Register: "I Ain't No Mule!"

There are three ways you can grab one of the remaining seats, and get to walk out of there with a completed display ad, website, sales letter, or lead-generation ad, no matter *what* you do for a living:

1. **Complete the enclosed "$1,000 Early-Bird Savings Ad Writing Workshop Form," and fax it into my office at** 954-337-2369.
2. Register online at kingofcopy.com/adwriting/registration.html
3. Or simply **call my office at 813-909-2214, and leave your name and telephone number, along with the message, "I ain't no mule!,"** and Anne will get back to you within 2 business days, to get you registered.

And don't worry, all faxes, online orders, and telephone messages will be logged in, on a first-come, first-served basis, so everyone has the same fair shot at getting into this workshop.

Look, the old way of doing business is gone. The only sure thing in business today, the only reliable thing you can count on to get you out of *any* jam in *any* kind of economy, is your ability to write an effective sales letter.

And if you keep your mind open, and you're willing to take a chance and **come to this workshop, you will be able to laugh at money worries for years to come. So obey that impulse and register for this workshop, right *now*** while this is fresh in your mind, and before anything else comes up.

P.S. There are only 25 slots here, and if you sign up and you're number 26, you miss out, period. So don't sit there thinking this workshop costs too much for you to attend. This isn't a cost, it's an investment with a darn-near infinite return, that starts paying you, as soon as you get back to your office first thing Monday morning, when you begin applying these techniques.

Look, this recession is going to be here for a *l-o-o-n-g* time. So don't regret this, because "regret"... unlike opportunity... will never make you... even one thin dime.

Here's to all the money you'll be making, after attending this workshop here in Tampa!

Ad Writing Workshop Registration Form

☐ **Yes, Craig! I want to attend your Ad Writing Workshop on January 16ᵗʰ, 17ᵗʰ and 18ᵗʰ, in Tampa Florida!** I understand your no-nonsense personal Guarantee: <u>If I am unhappy with the content of the seminar, or with my experience, you will reimburse my registration fee.</u>

"He's not only the best, most natural and intuitive copywriter I've ever seen, but he knows how to make a business run like an automated money-making machine... He's given us a step-by-step blueprint to build our business. It is based on two-step lead generation providing leads and taking them through an automatic process that will qualify them and even sell them. **Only after they have bought will we have to have contact with these people.** *We're going to engage him to do all the copywriting etcetera for that. He's not cheap but we wanted the best and I don't want to go through any more years of trial and error and guessing games."* **Cameron Outridge - Queensland, Australia**

"After spending time with Craig it was obvious that my current business was not getting me where I wanted to be... **he really helped me reinvent a new business**. *I have found Craig to be very straight forward...***he is not going to BS you or tell you what you want to hear**. *When I left my day of consulting I had 14 pages of notes* plus I recorded our conversation. I have referred back to my notes numerous times."* **Brian Deacon - Ashville, NC**

☐ **Craig, I also want to bring my business partner with me for $997 (paid in full). Their name is** _____

Select Which Registration Group You Are In!

←

☐ **I am not in either of your coaching programs:**
   _____ $5,497 (one-pay, $485 Savings)
   _____ I want to use your EZ-6 plan. **Please charge me $997 now and 5 more installments of $997, every 30 days.**

☐ **I am in your Mavericks Group:** **Slash $500 off the regular registration fee of $5,497**
   _____ $4,997 (one-pay, $385 Savings)
   _____ I want to use your EZ-6 plan. **Please charge me $897 now and 5 more installments of $897, every 30 days.**

☐ **I am in your Mastermind Group:** **Slash $1,000 off the regular registration fee of $5,497**
   _____ $4,497 (one-pay, $512 Savings)
   _____ I want to use your EZ-6 plan. **Please charge me $797 now and 5 more installments of $797, every 30 days.**

☐ **Craig, count this registration form to reserve my seat... but please have someone from your office contact me <u>immediately</u> about membership in either your Mavericks or Mastermind Group. My daytime phone number is** _____

For Fastest Service, Complete This Information, Then Fax This Form To 954-337-2369

☐ Charge my   ☐ Visa   ☐ MasterCard   ☐ American Express   ☐ Discover Card

In order to split your installments over two cards, please fill in your secondary credit card information and % of split. Your primary credit card will always be used first. **We are NOT a collection agency! Any delinquent payment voids your participation in this workshop and your seat will be given to the next person on the waiting list. Voided seat registration fees will be refunded.**

Credit Card #1 _____   Exp Date _____   Security Code _____

Credit Card #2 _____   Exp Date _____   Security Code _____

Name_____   Signature_____

Ship to address: _____   Fax #:_____

City, State, Zip Code _____   Day Phone_____

Credit Card Billing Address (if different)_____

City, State, Zip Code _____   e-mail _____

✓ **To pay by check or money order, complete the above information and then mail it to: kingofcopy.com 3959 Van Dyke Road # 253, Lutz, Florida 33558. If you have any questions, contact my office at 813-909-2214.**

If after reading these sales letters and ads, you are starting to realize the importance of good copywriting, and of being able to push your prospects emotional buy-buttons in print, then you're in for a treat!

Later on in this book, I'll be going over the basics of writing sales copy, and you'll get a lot out of this.

And in the meantime, if you want to speak with me about writing your next promotion, contact Anne in my office at 813-909-2214, or to find out more about working together, go to kingofcopy.com/workingtogether

Part Two: How To Think

Strategy # 16

The Most Profitable Investment You Will Ever Make

"Drop out of school before your mind rots from exposure to our mediocre educational system. Forget about the Senior Prom and go to the library and educate yourself if you've got any guts. Some of you like Pep rallies and plastic robots who tell you what to read." **Frank Zappa**

"I have never let my schooling interfere with my education." **Mark Twain**

The smartest and most profitable investment you can ever make isn't in real estate and it's certainly not in the stock market. I've made all kinds of investments in both of these vehicles and I've watched others do the same thing. Some of these investments have paid off big time, and some have gone bust.

But without a doubt, the most profitable investment you can ever make is in your own ongoing self-education and self-development. After all, it is literally impossible to know any more than what's inside your head right now, so unless you are constantly filling that mind of yours up -- where you are today is as far as you're going to go.

Right?

If this isn't a scary thought for you, then the likelihood of you being a long-term student and practitioner of success, isn't *very* high. And this isn't some kind of artsy-fartsy new age nonsense I'm talking about, it's cold harsh reality.

The truth is, investing in your own ongoing self-education is the surest way you can make a lot of money, very fast. It's also the fastest way to surpass any pre-conceived notions of what you *thought* you could accomplish, or what you thought your role in this world was.

This is an experience literally every single successful person knows. There isn't a wealthy entrepreneur I've met who isn't constantly immersing themselves in self-education.

Like I tell my kids, **"If you can read, you can literally do anything."**

Actors study great acting methods, artists are constantly studying great artists, musicians are always trying to learn new techniques and riffs used by other musicians, and successful entrepreneurs are always trying to learn more about marketing, and about new ways of making money and improving the quality of their lives.

**For the successful entrepreneur and sales person,
pushing the envelope of personal growth is the rule, not the exception.**

Here's an interesting story about this. One time I was at a seminar and the speaker was selling some information on copywriting at the back of the room, and at some point I went back and made my purchase. Later on that evening, another attendee who knew me, approached me about how revealing it was that even though I'm one of the best copywriters around, I was still back there buying more information on copywriting.

Frankly, that's one of the reasons why I'm so good at what I do -- my relentless pursuit of knowledge, and my insatiable desire to always be better tomorrow than I am today. I have, on many occasions, paid several hundred dollars for individual books that were hard to find, simply because I believed the information inside them would open my eyes to something new and inspiring I couldn't find anywhere else.

This is no different from a collector of music paying hundreds of dollars for a rare or out-of-print record, or for a bootleg CD. After all, the value of anything is directly related to the passion and enthusiasm you have for it, and to the benefits you get out of it, right?

But please remember, if you never implement what you're learning, a book is nothing more than paper and ink, an Audio CD nothing more than molded plastic.

Now there's a marketing lesson in here as well. You see, even though I'll be the first person waiting in line to get new marketing ideas, unfortunately, the people who *really* need this kind of information in the most *critical* way, are usually the last ones to have any interest in it.

Think about it, if they were interested, they wouldn't be in such dire straits in the first place, wouldn't they? And this is true whether you're talking about marketing information and business growth, fitness or weight loss, raising a family and being a better spouse, or buying real estate.

The marketing lesson is, people who *want* your information are the only ones you want as prospects, not people who *need* your information. **Want drives consumption, not need.**

Getting back to self-development though, no matter what category you look at, those people who are the top performers in their fields, inevitably have the largest libraries on this topic.

See, while school may give you an opportunity (I'm a college educated CPA.), only practical knowledge -- the wisdom of experience carefully laid down in books, and the words and impressions recorded onto Audio CDs and DVDs -- is what you profit from. Experience gives you the secrets you need, to transform yourself from a burn-out into a billionaire, changing your life dramatically along the way.

Napoleon Hill referred to this as the principle of "specialized knowledge." This was one of the 17 principles he discovered all successful people have in common, which he discussed in his 1937 landmark book, *Think And Grow Rich*.

And let's face it, there isn't any college or trade school here on God's green earth, that's going to give you even one-tenth of the secrets and specialized knowledge, successful entrepreneurs have already laid down for you to absorb, in the books and media that's already out there.

People often ask me, "What's the best way to get specialized knowledge?" After all, there are so many people out there offering so many different things, it's hard to tell what to invest your money in, and who to buy it from.

How do you decide whose advice to take and who to listen to?

If you've ever asked yourself these questions, then here are a few guidelines:

- **Good knowledge is like good music -- there is no right or wrong.** Invest in those people who have proven track records and that you resonate with. Meaning, what they have to say should move you, in some way. However, keep in mind, many times, the best source of wisdom may actually be that person who at first blush, rubs you the wrong way.

    This is simply because he or she may be asking you to confront a few issues you don't particularly like, or want to deal with. But that's how growing works. If you want to have big breakthroughs in life, you actually have to "break" something. And what you break most often, is a preconceived notion, a limiting belief or way of thinking, or a way of marketing yourself or doing business "you've always done" in the past.

You'll find the most successful people are in tune with this, and usually look for discomfort as a signal which means there's something big lying behind this discomfort. Discomfort often leads to big breakthroughs, and the *most* successful people are *always* looking for big huge breakthroughs!

- **"How someone does one thing, is how they do everything."** One of my long-time newsletter members, Cris Chico, a successful real estate investor and information marketer from Hollywood, Florida, told me he heard someone say this one time, and it's absolutely true.

  For me, I look for little behaviors to get insight into someone's real character. For example, how someone treats their server at a restaurant is much more revealing than how they treat someone they're trying to impress or get money from.

  Whether they hold the door open for they wife or do they make her get into the car by herself, is a good indication of how they will treat you. On the internet, however, you rarely get this kind of a glimpse into someone's life, so you need to look for other clues.

  Things like consistency and work ethic are very important here, as are testimonials. You'll find some people have the same old testimonials from the same old industry gurus and marketing friends in their circle. However, testimonials from "average Joe's" often give you a much better glimpse into what's really going on, since they're truly third party testimonials.

  Keep "How someone does one thing, is how they do everything" in mind, when you are trying to evaluate who to work with and who to avoid.

- **Don't limit yourself to only one source of information.** You probably have several different favorite actors you like, and you probably listen to more than one band on your iPod as well. Likewise, you shouldn't only have one business or marketing mentor, either. NOBODY has a monopoly on ideas, including me. Everybody has their own unique take on things.

  Listening to any bright person about a situation you're "stuck" on, usually leads to at *least* **one** new idea. And many times, that's all you need. Just yesterday, my younger son Casey and I were in the car coming home from the gym, and I casually mentioned to him about something I was struggling with in my workouts. Sure enough, he came up with a great idea that solved my problem, right away. Which leads me to my next point...

- **Always be open-minded!** I grew up in a close-minded household, where new ideas and different ways of doing things were shunned. Early on, however, I had a financial planning client of mine who really opened my eyes about how important it is to be open-minded. He was the owner of a very successful, very busy distribution company, and yet, he always took and returned all his calls. Yes, there were loads of people on the phones trying to sell him something, but as he used to say, "What if one of them had a new idea, or wanted to sell him something he needed?"

  He explained to me, if you aren't open-minded, then how can you ever get new ideas and find out new ways to prosper? Since then, my perspective changed completely. And lo and behold, it turns out, the most intelligent and successful people out there, are also the most open-minded as well.

  Reality is, smart people realize how little they know, and how big the world around them is, while stupid people think they know everything.

  Here's a story you'll find interesting about being open-minded. I recently found out how Walt Disney got his inspiration for the animated figures that are prolific throughout the Disney theme parks. Apparently, one day, Disney stumbled across a century-old miniature animated mechanical bird, in a New Orleans antique shop. Walt purchased the mechanical bird and then showed it to Roger Broggie, the head of his machine shop. Then he asked Broggie if he could use modern technology to develop life-sized birds that would be capable of moving and talking like the mechanical bird in the small antique shop.

  And the rest, as they say... is history.

  So keep an open mind. You never know where ideas will come from, but you'll never be able to find them, unless you're open to them in the first place.

- **Don't just sit on your ass learning -- DO something!** Ultimately, even the most specialized and advanced knowledge only becomes wisdom when you take action and apply it to something by implementing. Remember, you learn *from* your mistakes, so don't fear them. Instead, embrace them as the learning tools they are.

- **Take advice from the RIGHT people.** If you want to learn how to be a better marketer, or a better copywriter, learn from someone who's made a small fortune from marketing and writing sales copy. If you want to learn how to be a better anything, listen to someone who's done it, and who's paid their dues! You shouldn't ask your uncle, the thrifty school teacher, what he thinks about your sales letter, any more than you should ask your cardiologist about fixing your roof. **Seek out advice from experts, not expert wannabees.**

- **Beware of frauds!** You have to be careful -- especially in today's day-and-age, where anyone can put up any kind of a web page and call themselves an expert. **Look for consistency in the tone of someone's messages, and consistency in the quality of their content.** If someone changes their philosophy of business or their thoughts on their craft, as often as they change their underwear... then head for the hills!

  And don't deceive yourself -- free stuff is only usually worth what you pay for it! Even my own information -- the free daily e-mail tips you get on my website and on my blog, absolutely *pale* in comparison to the paid content in my offline Seductive Selling Newsletter or in the other information products I publish.

  In life, and especially in business, the old adage "you get what you pay for" is amazingly true! The problem is, most people are far too afraid to pay for things, not because they don't have the money, but because they don't feel they deserve the rewards of their investment, or frankly because they're just too cheap! If you're like this, sadly, you're losing out.

  So stop doing that. **Please -- don't have regrets about things.** You only get one shot at life, so make it a life worth living, and fill it with robust memories and time well spent.

  I've already explained my philosophy on investing money in learning new ideas and skills. Frankly, everything I've learned and all I have today, comes directly from money I've invested in my own ongoing education. You couldn't convince me to stop, for anything.

- **Don't be afraid of success, or afraid of change.** Make the most of your life -- that's the *only* true "debt" you owe yourself. When it comes down to it, we have no control over how much time we get to spend here on this big ball of mud, and time goes by *very* quickly. There are no do-over's in life, no dress rehearsals. **TODAY you are up on stage. Stop "preparing" for life, and instead start living it!**

  On my facebook profile it says, "I'm a family man first and foremost, but I also love my business. My goal is to suck as much as possible out of life while I'm here." Make it a life worth living, and start right now!

- **Keep in mind, what you think about most, you do... and what you do over and over again, becomes your habits. And your habits become who you are.** Stop doing things like watching television and playing video games. I watch almost NO television -- haven't for years. Almost nothing on television gets me closer to my goal of becoming a better businessman, a better marketer, or a better husband and father, so why should I focus my attention on it?

The bottom-line message I want you to get out of this Chapter, is that ultimately, your success, and your final destiny, is entirely up to you. And nothing gets you there faster, than self-education.

I graduated with a degree in accounting and became a CPA. However, the biggest differential in my life is when I spent roughly 2,000 intense hours over a 12-month period delving into everything I could learn about marketing and copywriting. Then, I turned that knowledge -- through trial and tribulation, and through a lot more hiccups and failures than I'd have liked -- into a small fortune for myself and my family. Most important, though… the result of this is that I'm now doing what I love, and living the lifestyle I want!

I come and go as I please, and account to no one. I work only with who I WANT to work with, under MY terms and conditions. I've said "no thank you" to large sums of money more than once, because I've either had better things to do with my time, or because the pain of dealing with a particular individual wouldn't be worth the pot of gold at the end of the rainbow.

I wake up and go to sleep when I want to, take my wife to lunch, and pick my daughter up from school when I want to. Some mornings I'll sit out back on my dock overlooking the lake, with a good book, a cup of coffee, and a cigar. Other mornings I'll be up at the crack of dawn and I'll already have banged out 3 to 5 hours of work before most people are even getting started.

Last year, I started a brand new coaching and consulting business in a new niche, and I wound up bringing in $92,000 just on the initial launch. This year I am working on diversifying and getting into several new niches in another publishing business. These niches are virtually empty and devoid of any competition, so with relative ease I expect a modest income of $2,000 - $4,000 per month, within the next 6 months or so.

The point is, I've got lots of options, and I use them. And I invite you to live your life to the fullest and do the same thing. My greatest accomplishments so far (and I truly believe I'm just starting to scratch the tip of the iceberg here) have been done not through formal education, but through self-education, an open mind, and enthusiasm for what I do. And for the common man, which is you and me -- this, by *far*... is also the fastest way of getting what you want out of life, as well.

The library in my office is filled with books, binders, cassette tapes, CDs, VHS tapes, DVDs, and remnants and memories of the many consulting groups, workshops, and seminars I've attended. These are the "friends" who've have helped me elevate my life.

In a recent interview, I was asked what my 3-step plan for tackling big goals was, and here is the answer I gave:

1. **Research what you are trying to do.** Regardless of what you're looking to accomplish, from training your dog to writing a book, someone out there's already done it, so why not make your life easier and get a head start?

   No sense re-inventing the wheel when someone's already given you the blueprints for how to do it, right?

2. **Lay out your plans.** If you know where you are now, and where you want to go -- once you've finished your research, you should be able to fill in the preliminary steps it's going to take, to get you from here to there. I find laying out each of my action steps individually, makes getting there much easier, as opposed to solely just writing down the big picture about what I want to accomplish. Often there are so many steps in-between, the big picture is just too overwhelming or intangible.

   For example, "Write a book" may seem overwhelming. But "Write Chapters 1, 2, and 3," is much easier to digest, accomplish, and manage. Plus, it's also more tangible and you can see progress being made in small increments.

3. **Execute -- start taking action!** Fall down, scrape your knees, get back up and put a band-aid on, but don't stop moving. As Gary Halbert once told me, "Things happen when you're in motion, not meditation." I know I've said this before, but you really can't "think" your way to success, it happens *only* through action!

The truth is, unless you go out of your way to change things, we're all limited and confined only to the world that exists inside our head. And as I said, since it is literally impossible to ever know more than what's already inside your head, your *only* hope of making progress and moving forward, is to expand that world by expanding your knowledge base. And the fastest and surest way of doing this, is by listening to what others -- who have already gone through what you are looking to do -- have to say.

I wish you much luck and success on your journey.

Money-Making Action Steps Checklist

☐ **Is there a book, course, marketing system or coaching program you've avoided getting involved with, simply because you've either been afraid of success, or afraid to confront some other inner demons you have?** If so, get real with yourself about it, make the investment NOW, and start digging in!

☐ **Don't be afraid of growth!** You were put here on this earth to be the absolute best you can be. If you are afraid of growth or have some issues with feeling undeserving because you're not _____ (fill in the blank) "enough," then read *The Science Of Getting Rich* by Wallice Wattles. This old book, written in 1911, helped me get rid of all the undeserving garbage I had in my head, and if you're sincere about getting rid of this same negative programming in your mind, it will help you, too.

Chapter References

- **Earlier, I mentioned a quote from my facebook profile, and you can find that profile at kingofcopy.com/facebook.**

- **I've re-published The Science Of Getting Rich, and it is now available, along with a couple of very personal stories of my own "down and out" experiences, at kingofcopy.com/science.** This is the book you want to delve into if you're uncomfortable or afraid of competition, or if you can't look at the world through abundant eyes, but instead… you tend to view things through eyes of scarcity.

Strategy # 17

How To Make BIG Money... Really Fast!

Money loves speed. Nothing transforms desire into money, *faster*... than fast action itself.

In fact, once you make a decision to do something, your greatest rewards will next be received when you *rapidly* implement whatever it is you're looking to do.

Do you remember the story I told you, a couple of Chapters ago, about how I got my coaching program started and what the ultimate outcome was? This is the net impact of what happens when you take fast action. Remember, what I did wasn't "right" but it was deliberate and focused, and implemented very rapidly.

Sitting around waiting until something is perfect -- or even "just right" -- is the kiss of death. You see, it's impossible for *anything* be perfect, because in business, you never know what's going to happen or how your customers and clients are going to react to something until after it's done, anyway. So in reality, the very reason why you are delaying launching something, may turn out to be the actual flaw in your ointment.

This doesn't mean you need to jump into something without thinking about it, or without evaluating whether or not it makes sense. It simply means, once you decide to go for it, then **GO FOR IT!** Stop dicking around and being so anal-retentive that nothing gets done.

Do it, and get busy NOW!

Let me share a couple of stories with you about how fast success can come to you and what happens if you just get on something instead of thinking about it. There's a fellow in my Mavericks Coaching Group, Bob Maunsell. Bob's from Worcester, Massachusetts and he runs a very successful residential and commercial security system company, and he's a successful real estate investor as well. I mentioned him earlier, in one of the sales letters for my Ad Writing Workshop.

One of Bob's goals in joining my coaching group was to become a guru to other security system company owners, and counsel them on how to become successful in their local territory, using the marketing materials he's developed, that have made his own business very successful. Anyway, Bob joins my Mavericks Coaching group and on our first or second call, he says something like, "Craig, I figure over the next two or three years, I can really build up a following and become a major player in this industry."

And my response was something like, "Bob, why are you going to wait so long to do this?"

See, the truth is, your success in any marketplace is limited only to the time it takes you to mail out a letter -- or if you already have an e-mail list -- it's limited to the time it takes you to set up an e-mail campaign and make the right offer.

So within 3 weeks after Bob mailed out his first direct-mail campaign, he had 11 people paying him $347 a month for a coaching program. That's not bad -- it's an extra $3,817 a month, or $45,804 per year, assuming they all stick as members. Now they definitely won't *all* stick around -- but he's got lots of letters to mail between now and then anyway, that will more than replenish the ones who drop out.

The point I want you to takeaway from this is that money only appears as fast as you ask for it. Or, as slow as you ask for it, as well.

Here's another interesting story about this: I recently launched a new business with a business partner, Mike Miget, who I've known for almost 3 years now. Mike was originally a Mavericks Coaching Group member and then he became a private client of mine.

Mike's been a successful residential loan officer for the last 16 years, and he also runs a territorial exclusive consulting business for loan officers in a certain niche marketplace. I enjoyed working with Mike during this time, and we decided to do something together. (To me, nothing shows you who a person really is, better than how they act once you put money between the two of you. It doesn't matter who's paying and who's receiving -- either way, over time you'll see their true colors -- good, bad or otherwise.)

Within 2 weeks of initially speaking, I developed a formula for our business launch. We launched the business over a 4 week period, and as I mentioned, the net result of this was that we were able to collect $92,000 from 14 complete strangers who'd never even heard of me before this... and another $16,000 from 2 subsequent participants in this same program, who heard about us subsequent to our product launch.

Mind you, we didn't even have a product when we sold those first 14 programs! We actually got paid ahead of time, to create the product, which is a turn-key lead generation system for residential loan officers looking to pick up clients who are interested in refinancing their adjustable rate mortgages.

Basically, I got all these people to "chip in" and hire me out on a group basis, at a much lower rate than it would cost them to hire me individually.

Now don't get me wrong -- during this business launch I worked my butt off, and of course, I made loads of mistakes. But look at the end result!

Who else do you know who's been paid this much money AHEAD of time, to **make** a product. Most people have a difficult enough time getting paid *after* they've made a product, but getting paid to make a product *before* you've even created it, is simply unheard of.

(And by the way, this was the second time I did this. The first time was in the Pre-Foreclosure Industry, when I created the Pre-Foreclosure Success System.)

This all happened though, because once we made our decision, we took FAST action, and I strongly suggest, the biggest successes you will have, will come about the same way. It's not just enough to "do something," you must implement *rapidly* for the best results.

Now you may be concerned about failing when you do this, but I've got news for you -- you're going to make a bunch of mistakes along the way, anyway -- so you might as well make them sooner than later.

This way you can make the adjustments and improvements you need, quickly.

The other thing you need to realize, is that in reality, procrastination is what prevents most people from becoming successful. Not just in business, but in life in general. **Not taking action, not doing anything at all... is a far greater success-killer, than actually doing something and then failing at it.**

This is true whether it comes to making money, losing weight, getting in shape for a certain sport, or preparing for the local county bake-off.

Along these lines, here are a few articles I've written, you will benefit from.

Is youth wasted on the young?

My father used to say "youth is wasted on the young." I'm not so sure he was right, but I do know that experience and wisdom teaches you a lot, and you can't gain wisdom until you get the experience, that's for sure.

When I was a kid, I had no patience at all. I still don't have much patience, but one thing I do have now, is more realistic expectations, and these expectations have a way of sort of "regulating" your patience a little more effectively.

So for example, when I first picked up a guitar, years ago, I was expecting to play Stairway To Heaven like Jimmy Page did, within a month or so, of "pretty heavy" practicing. Turns out it really doesn't work that way -- even Jimmy Page didn't get to be Jimmy Page after a month. But not knowing any better, I got discouraged.

The truth was, I was a damn good guitar player. I have the kind of musical ear that can hear something one time, and then play it. But expecting to play like Jimmy Page -- let's face it, that's a pretty unrealistic standard of comparison to use, especially straight out of the starting gate, no?

But I did continue playing for a little while, and I had fun with my instrument during that time.

There's a similar problem I see in business, and frankly I see it often, especially with people trying to get something off the ground. They are too preoccupied with making sure they'll have a "million dollar" business!

These folks don't stop and consider that the first time you do anything, whether it's picking up a guitar, riding a bicycle, or starting a business -- the end result down the line is always going to be dramatically different than it is today.

For instance, this year we'll do close to 7 figures -- but three and a half years ago when I started my business online, all I had was a webpage and a few people who knew me from writing copy. If I'd have "waited", guess what would have happened?

Nothing!

So if you're having trouble getting started, here's something that will help you: Don't sit there pressuring yourself to roll out something that's going to make you the next Bill Gates. At least, don't think that until your doors are open, anyway.

Just try and make ONE dollar doing whatever it is you do.

Then, as soon as you've made that ONE dollar, guess what?

Go for two dollars.

Then go for $100 dollars... then maybe $100 a month, or $100 a week.

If you do this, chances are your business will be profitable. And the other thing that soon happens is your experience and your learning curve grows exponentially -- along with your increase in profits.

New ideas will come to you, new strategies will appear in front of you, and you'll suddenly find yourself in the same position Napoleon Hill mentions in *Think And Grow Rich*: the money will be coming in so fast and so furiously, you'll wonder where it was hiding all this time!

Of course, many people don't want to hear this because they're so afraid of taking that fist step. It's much easier to justify their delay by saying they're just "not ready" yet.

But the truth is, *everybody's* ready to make ONE dollar, right?

***

This next story addresses many of the undeserving feelings people often come up with as excuses for procrastination.

Who are YOU to be brilliant, gorgeous, talented and fabulous?

He was a quiet man, outwardly very successful, but inside being eaten alive by something horrible.

Not something tangible (But there again, fear never is, is it?), but a fear brewing inside him for many years now, nonetheless.

It was his fear of succeeding. His, fear of being brilliant, talented, and fabulous.

Children never have these fears, do they?

Little Sammy runs around like a diva dressed in her Sunday best, microphone in hand, standing on the living room table singing made-up songs at the top of her lungs.

Fear? What's that?

What happens between the time she's on top of the living room table, and the time she's scared to death and sick with fear years later -- the crying kind of fear -- afraid of succeeding. Makes no sense, does it?

Want to know what happens? I'll tell you.

Someone steps in and squashes her microphone. Tosses it aside and says "Shut up, you're annoying." Or you watch the person you look up to most in the entire world, toiling away for pennies, nothing but a sore back and a bum leg, after 25 years of this.

Or else you get let down and disappointed, and instead of erasing the experience from your memory like an episode of Gilligan's Island, you replay it, over and over again -- "if only..."

But you see, as Marianne Williamson said in *What We Have To Fear*, "Our deepest fear is not that we are inadequate. Our deepest fear is that we are powerful beyond measure. It is our light, not our darkness that most frightens us. We ask ourselves, 'Who am I to be brilliant, gorgeous, talented, fabulous?' But actually, who are you not to be?"

So I ask you, "Who are you to be brilliant, gorgeous, talented, fabulous?"

In reality, the question ought to be, who are you not to be?

***

Finally, this story is one I've thought of so many times since I first heard the original message. It will, no doubt, leave a lasting impact on you, as well.

"3 Clever Ways To Dramatically Change Your Future!"

Do you know who Roger Waters is?

Yes? No?

I'll tell you a little story about Roger in just a minute, but first, let's talk about the very best way to kick-start your new year into high gear, straight away.

One early January, many years ago when I owned a financial planning practice, I was listening to a motivational tape.

237

It was more "institutional" or corporate-oriented, and less entrepreneurially oriented, but hey, you've got to start somewhere, right?

The guy on the tape was telling me how I needed to have a business plan for the year, detailing all of my upcoming strategic moves. Otherwise, I wasn't going to be successful.

I really had no clue what this guy was talking about. I mean, I took a look around my office -- which consisted of me and an assistant -- and I said to myself, "This isn't Microsoft or Bank of America here, what's he talking about?"

The only kind of "business plan" I had, was to make money. After all, I wasn't planning any mergers and acquisitions this coming year... no initial public offerings... and I certainly wasn't adding any new board members either.

So what on God's green earth could this guy be referring to, that I was totally missing the boat on?

Well, fast-forward the clock a few years... after listening to several hundred more hours of information about success, and after reading over one hundred or more books about success... I now understand what this fellow really meant was, to be successful...

You've Got To Set Goals!

Not setting goals for yourself is like getting into your car and going on vacation without having a map. Or like going fishing without knowing where the fish are biting or what kind of bait to use. You'll wind up sitting there casting your line out over the water all day long, but it's really going to be hit or miss whether or not you catch something, unless you know what you're doing, right?

Now, far be it for me to give you advice on what *kind* of goals you should be setting -- Lord knows I'm not qualified to do that.

But I do want to tell you 3 things you must consider, if you want any chance at making your goals become a reality.

First of all, you've got to write your goals down, and set yourself some kind of reminder to go over them on a regular basis -- at least weekly.

You see, doing this makes you accountable to them and it lets you modify them along the way. It also keeps you on track for how you're progressing... how far you're moving forward... and even more important...

How Far You Aren't!

And sometimes, the discomfort of seeing "How Far You Aren't" moving forward, is just what you need to force you to get off your ass and start taking some action!

Remember, you don't usually do something until the pain of inaction is greater than the pain of *taking* action. I call this, the "Law Of Action."

And I don't care whether you're talking about losing weight... going to the dentist... or tying up all the loose ends of an existing project that's been nagging you, the "Law of Action" is always going to rule your time constraints.

So you *must* write your goals down, regardless of what they are, and then you *must* re-commit yourself to achieving them, by going over them on a regular basis.

The second thing you should do when you're setting your goals, is to...

Shoot for the moon!

Or, as the big blue wooden fence-post sign hanging on the wall in my office says, "Dream Big." After all, if you can't dream big on paper, than how the hell are you going to do it in reality? Also, is there really any reason why you shouldn't be living out your dreams?

After all, why are you waiting?

Do you really think you'll be more "prepared" or more "deserving" for that big house by the lake 10 years down the road, than you are right now?

What Can You Possibly Be Waiting For?

Besides, I can tell you from experience, it's going to take you as much work to launch a project that'll make you $100,000 dollars, as it will to launch a project that's going to make you $25,000 dollars, so why not go for the big numbers?

Why not dream BIG?

Or perhaps this makes it even *more* tangible: You have to work as hard at selling a $500 dollar item as you do at selling a $1,000 item, so go for the big dollars since you're going to have to hustle, regardless.

239

O.K., now let me tell you that story about Roger Waters, the guy I mentioned at the very beginning of this article. See, Roger Waters was the bass player, lead singer, and co-author of many of the powerhouse band Pink Floyd's songs.

Back in March of 1973, the band released a ground-breaking album you've no doubt heard of, called "The Dark Side Of The Moon."

The process of creating and releasing the album was extremely difficult, because the band's leader, Syd Barrett, had just been institutionalized as a result of a nervous breakdown and a serious drug problem. That left the band rudderless and somewhat uncertain about "what was next."

Nevertheless, with David Glimour (the band's new lead guitarist) and Roger Waters splitting the writing and vocals, the album was a major coup, staying on the Billboard Top 200 charts for 724 weeks, a record at the time.

They cracked the code, because to date, this album has sold well over 41 million copies.

Anyway, I recently saw Roger Waters being interviewed and he had some very revealing and insightful things to say, that sort of sum up what I'm talking about.

The Waters interview took place in 2003, while he was discussing the 30th anniversary of "The Dark Side Of The Moon".

What you may not know, is when Waters made the album, he was just about to turn 30, and this is what he had to say about what was going through his mind at that time:

"I suddenly realized then, that year... that life was already happening.

I think it was because my mother was so obsessed with education... and the idea that childhood and adolescence, and well... everything, was about "preparing" for a life that was going to start... "later."

And I suddenly realized that life wasn't going to start later, that it starts at "dot"... and it happens all the time.

And at any point, you can just grasp the reins and start guiding your own destiny.

And that was a big revelation to me.

I mean, it came as quite a shock."

I don't believe Waters is alone in his thinking -- every successful person reaches a point in time when you grab your balls (sorry again, ladies) and you suddenly realize, "the future really is now," or some sort of similar epiphany.

And once you realize this, and once you fully embrace the freedom that comes along with it, you begin a very prolific and long-lasting period of creativity and success.

I mean, think about it: if you're no longer "preparing" for the future, you're no longer "auditioning" for it either. And there's a tremendous sense of "letting go" once you realize you're already past the audition. You *won* the part... and you're the lead role.

And your job as the leader, is to lead. In this case, to lead yourself. And that's lesson number three.

Make sense?

Good.

Now here's another thing I've noticed, time and again:

Everybody wants to "get in" on the action... but nobody wants to TAKE any action!

But if you want to have an amazing life, you must...

Take Action!

Because you can have the most ambitious goals, written down and reviewed weekly... and the highest level of motivation to succeed, but if you don't ever get out there and actually put the key into the ignition and put the car in drive, and you never step on the gas pedal... then you're never going to get moving.

Listen, I talk to new people almost every week. And for whatever reason, people feel pretty safe and comfortable speaking with me, so they usually feel compelled to share many of their innermost feelings and secrets.

And one thing that's fairly consistent amongst almost everyone I talk to is that they're all scared of something. Some are scared of failure, and some are scared of success. And some may be scared of being "less than perfect," so they wait... and wait... and wait... and things ultimately never get moving, because... they're never "ready."

But see, you've got 2 choices: You either live in fear and let that fear hold you back from living your dreams, or you overcome your fears... do what you need to do... get busy, and start enjoying all the wonderful experiences life has to offer you.

Remember, your future is out there waiting for you, and your future... is...

Happening Right Now!

So get moving.

P.S. Now you know the evolution of Roger Waters' lyrics, "Every year is getting shorter, never seem to find the time. Plans that either come to naught, or half a page of scribbled lines."

***

On the upper left hand corner of the corkboard hanging on the wall of my office, just next to my desk, I have a card with a quote scribbled down on it from Maxwell Maltz, the author of *Psycho Cybernetics*. It says, "Only today can be spent wisely or unwisely."

Spend your day wisely by taking fast action -- NOW, not later.

What are you waiting for?

Money-Making Action Steps Checklist

☐ **Your action step here is... to take action!** Don't sit around trying to figure out why you're waiting, just do it and the answer will come to you afterwards. Nothing gets you over your fears, as effectively as making that first dollar. So get off your ass, NOW!

Chapter References

- For information on my **Mavericks Coaching** program, go to kingofcopy.com/mavericks

- For information about becoming **a private client** of mine, go to kingofcopy.com/workingtogether or kingofcopy.com/consultingday

- You can find information about my **ARMs Lead Generation Program for loan officers** at loturnaround.com/arms

Strategy # 18

When To Fail

Back in 2003, when I was working with Gary Halbert, we worked on a few promotions that never really took off.

One day we were talking about this, and I noticed it didn't really seem to bother him. I asked him why and he explained that it bothered him quite a bit, actually. But, he'd been in business long enough to understand not everything you do is going to work.

And what you *must* understand is that just because something doesn't work, it's *not* a failure. Everything you do in direct-response marketing is testing, plain-and-simple.

There are SOOOOO many moving parts involved with every promotion you're working on, you'd have to be some sort of a mind reader to get it right all the time, or even half the time, for that matter.

So whatever the results are, it's ALL just part of your testing, remember that. And never take it personal -- it's just business. Regardless how your projects wind up working out, at least you're out there in the arena, not stuck in some cubicle sucking high ninny from an overbearing boss who goes home at night and gets his balls handed to him by his wife.

Be proud you're an entrepreneur. You're the lion that roars, out there on the firing line. NO ONE I know, gets it right all the time. Even professional athletes don't get it right all the time. If you look at baseball, for instance, someone with a *great* batting average only gets a hit between 3 and 4 times out of every ten times he's up at bat, right?

This is why you must avoid anyone who pretends to be perfect or infallible, or anything less than human. They are simply lying, flat-out. I have a damn good track record, but I've had my share of flops, believe me.

This is another HUGE myth perpetuated by some people. For some reason they want

243

you to believe that everything they touch turns to gold. That they've never had hard times. I will tell you now, that's just not true. Most of the projects I work on, don't hit big. My success is the result of making hundreds of moves, and each one adding a little here, a little there. Then, you work on some of them so that you can expand your reach, you firm up a little bit of this, you tweak a little bit of that, and soon, you've got yourself a viable ongoing system that works.

As I said earlier, I'm a steady singles and doubles hitter, NOT a home run hitter. But I get up to bat so much and I take so many swings at it, I wind up getting enough singles and doubles that in the end, I win the game.

The good news is, all you need to do is get 2 or 3 projects right out of every 10 you take on, and you'll be making a small fortune and living life on your own terms.

Here are just a few of the many projects I tried to get going, that didn't work:

- **Trying to sell consulting services straight from my website with NO other physical products sold prior to the sale.**

- Trying to sell presidential tax returns.

- **Trying to sell free tourist books for money on eBay.**

- Trying to get free research for a product I was thinking about making, by using an "ask campaign" on a topic WAY too vague -- "Jeep Wranglers."

- **Giving away free books I should have been charging for, and giving them away incorrectly.** (Not making people give me their contact information first.)

- Giving away free consultations thinking I'd get business from them.

- **Getting in bed with the wrong partners.**

- Paying huge sums of money to have someone promote me to their list, without doing enough research on the list itself. In other words, being lulled into a trance simply because I saw large numbers (which, to be 100% honest, I never even verified). Remember, the size of a list is mutually exclusive to your compatibility with, or the quality of the list. And a massive list of non-buyers is always worthless.

- **Trying to focus on product creation first, without knowing what my list wanted to buy, and sometimes without even bothering to create a list, first.**

- Thinking becoming well-known on free discussion forums makes you any money. **Appreciate that nearly 100% of the people who spend their time in free online forums are dead-broke.** They have nothing else to do with their time, and since any shepherd can easily step up and command respect from a bunch of other sheep wandering around the online forum desert, forum members are always ready to join someone's flock.

This is truly the "blind leading the blind" space of the internet. If you are one of these folks, admit this to yourself and do something about it. Stop being so cheap! Find yourself a good mentor, pay them money and start doing something worthwhile with your time. Being a "professional gossip" isn't a very high-paying job and it doesn't give you any kind of self-respect, either. When you wake up in the morning and look at yourself in the mirror, ultimately... there's no sense of pride in this. You are far better off **doing** something and failing, then doing nothing and being safe and hidden.

Lessons like this are the most valuable tuition you can get.

- **Trying to work in industries where there simply wasn't a marketplace.**

And these are just the ones I can think about! Lord knows there's probably dozens in there I can't recall. And many of the ideas I just mentioned, I got from other "gurus" who said they did these things and they worked like gangbusters.

This also goes to show you, what works for one person may not work for you, and... it also may imply that there may be more going on than meets the eye. And this is why the lessons you learn from the mistakes you make are so important. Mistakes teach you what books and CD's and DVD's simply can not.

See, no matter what happened on any of these projects, I learned loads of new lessons and skills on each of them! Things like how to use a new piece of software... or a new way of thinking... or a new approach to generating leads. Something positive always comes out of whatever you do. (Remember my "failed" 2-attendee meeting I held!)

Again, to paraphrase Halbert... one time we worked on a project that simply never came alive. I put in lots of time on it, and was a little bummed out that this thing never even saw daylight. Gary just said, "Nothing is ever wasted."

And I can tell you today -- hindsight being 20/20 -- he was right. This is a marathon, not a sprint. And everything you do, and all the lessons you learn, are all part of your "training," so you *can* eventually cross the finish line.

Money-Making Action Steps Checklist

☐ **Next time you're thinking about throwing in the towel, think about Theodore Roosevelt's speech he gave at the Sorbonne in Paris, France, on April 23, 1910, when he said:** "It is not the critic who counts; not the man who points out how the strong man stumbles, or where the doer of deeds could have done them better. The credit belongs to the man who is actually in the arena, whose face is marred by dust and sweat and blood; who strives valiantly; who errs, who comes short again and again, because there is no effort without error and shortcoming; but who does actually strive to do the deeds; who knows great enthusiasms, the great devotions; who spends himself in a worthy cause; who at the best knows in the end the triumph of high achievement, and who at the worst, if he fails, at least fails while daring greatly, so that his place shall never be with those cold and timid souls who neither know victory nor defeat."

Chapter References

- If you're still struggling, then check out this semi-autobiographical program that shows you exactly how I got my start in marketing, along with many of my own personal struggles and failures. It also comes with an Audio CD called "Excuse Busters," that basically smashes ANY excuse you may have, for not taking action. It's called "How To Make Your Dreams Come True!" and I think you'll enjoy it. You can find it at kingofcopy.com/dreamscometrue

Strategy # 19

Be A First-Class Act, Always

What I'm about to tell you may sound like common sense. But if there's one thing I've learned it's that common sense isn't so common any more. All of these little intangible things are very critical to making loads of money, especially when you have a small list and when you don't have thousands of customers. These are the little things that count big-time, when it comes to getting as much money out of your buyers as possible.

A Seductive Selling newsletter member of mine, sent this e-mail to me just the other day, and I think it summarizes what I'm going to talk about in this Chapter, in a nutshell:

"I doubt it will take very much for you to bribe me. The free material that you have on your site is better then some of the $1,000/$2,000 courses that I have seen sold and pitched as the greatest thing since sliced bread...

Some of this stuff, though, when I look at it... I'd be ashamed to be giving away, but I guess if you have 73 emails nailing you all at the same time that this is the greatest thing since God created the vagina, it's a lot of social proof and pressure to buy.

It obviously works well but I'm not sure I'd be comfortable selling like that. Especially since it seems like to be "in the club" they just pretty much all agree to promote whatever each other puts out.

I've always had a rule that if you're on my list I treat you like a guest in my house: i.e. I wont feed you shitty food and I won't let you drive home drunk, same kinda thing should apply to the people who trust you enough to give you the information I think. One thing I have liked about you is that you obviously have a similar feeling...

Anyway I've got to get running here. It's been a pleasure getting to know you a bit and I look forward to learning from you for a long time to come."

This is very true. I do feel a strong sense of obligation to my customers and clients to always "do the right thing" for them. This runs deep through my core and I have a great deal of pride of ownership in my work. Meaning, if my name's on something, it had better be damn good. And while trying to be "the best," is simply too intangible and unrealistic, "the best I can do," certainly is not. And this is what I strive for.

I've talked about my work ethic before, and this is just a by-product, or an extension of that work ethic.

I mean, let's face it, if you're a consumer of anything, then you've no doubt been disappointed by a product you've purchased that didn't live up to its expectations.

As a dad, I can tell you this has happened to me dozens of times when Anne and I have bought or ordered things for the kids. Items that looked great on television or on the pictures on the box, but were literally plastic pieces of junk that looked and performed dramatically different once you ripped open the packaging and tried to use the thing.

This always leaves you with a bad taste in your mouth and an experience you're not going to repeat again with that same company.

And no doubt, I've experienced this in business, many times. But listen closely here, because in business, you usually only get one shot at it. In business, **nothing** is worse than disappointment, so you should **only** be offering first-class products. Always go the extra yard for your customers. Always.

And since, in today's day and age, mediocrity has become the new excellent, when it comes down to it, it really doesn't take very much for you to impress people, other than actually "doing what you said you were going to do."

This commitment to over-delivering, to having integrity, and to simply "doing what I promised" is also responsible for the lion's share of my income. People have come to rely on me and count on me as the "go to" guy who simply fulfills his promises.

Simple, right?

But apparently not easy.

Want to know one of the key ingredients here?

Integrity. If you don't have a good work ethic, or if you're lazy... then ultimately, your ability to make money is limited by the number of people you can find, who you're able to bamboozle -- once. You won't *consistently* make the kind of money I earn, without any integrity, or with a weak work ethic.

Write this down: "Your ability to differentiate yourself is critical to your success." And having integrity in what you do is a HUGE differential.

See, once you've overcome your prospect's skepticism, the world is your oyster. When you over-deliver and exceed expectations, you will easily be able to run a highly profitable business that makes you tons of money. You'll have a loyal following of devoted customers who'll buy from you, again and again. This is because you've shown them you are who you say you are, without question, and they can trust you.

This fits right in with a concept I emphasized earlier on, which is to be in the continuity business. See, you can fool someone once... but you the only way you're going to survive, and thrive, long-term -- especially if continuity business is a significant portion of your overall income -- is by giving people *more* than they're expecting, month-in and month-out.

And frankly, this isn't easy. To do this, you must be disciplined and you must have an inherent sense of pride in what you do. And you must genuinely believe it's your *obligation* to give your customers two dollars in value for every dollar they've invested in you, and then some. **Not your *right*, but your *obligation*.** These two mindsets are very different, but so are the results of having them.

Let me tell you a story about how much work ethic counts. I mentioned earlier on in the book, that my younger son Casey was born with a mild case of cerebral palsy. He walks with a slight limp and when he was younger, he lagged behind with some of his fine motor skills.

Now the harsh reality of life for Casey is that many people see his physical disability and automatically deem him mentally disabled as well. So he has to work harder than most people to show them he's not only mentally sound, but mentally *stronger* than the average non-disabled person.

Only then can he hope to level the playing field for himself and be on an even starting ground with other people.

Casey has been working as a cashier at our local supermarket, since he was 16. Casey truly hustles at work, and as a result, he's well-liked. (Lord knows we wish he'd hustle around the house, but that's teenagers for you, right?)

He was saving up to buy his first car because he didn't want to have to get in debt to buy it. So his first Summer working, regardless of how many hours he was scheduled for, every single day he'd call in, asking if he could either come in early, or stay later. All he wanted to do was pick up some extra money for his car.

And even though he was the new man on the totem pole, about 90% of the time he was told "Yes, come in. We need you." He works more hours than most of the kids there, even though nearly all of them have been working there much longer than he has. He also makes more money than most of them, as well. His quarterly and semi-annual raises are always maxed out.

He has loads of pride in what he does.

Last week, I happened to be doing some grocery store shopping (Which, to be honest, is extremely rare for me. The truth is, I am trying to lose a few pounds so I was shopping for some spices to add to my grilled chicken.), and I saw one of the managers walking down an aisle.

I introduced myself to him as Casey's dad, and the guy stopped what he was in the middle of what he was doing, and shook my hand firmly, and said, "Sir, I want you to know how much we appreciate Casey and how glad we are to have him here. His work ethic is second to none, and we wish all our employees were like that. Thank you so much."

Needless to say, I am very proud of my son. Not because of the accolades I heard, but because I know he's taking personal pride in what he's doing, which ultimately makes him feel better about himself, and helps him succeed in life.

He has the same work ethic in sports and in school. Last year he won the "Commitment Medal" on his wrestling team, for the amount of effort he puts in. I'm not sure if you're familiar with wrestling, but it is one of the most difficult sports to train for. Most people who come out for the team, leave not because they don't have the talent. They leave because they can't complete the training.

No one ever talks about this, but effort counts -- a lot. I outwork nearly every one I know.

Let me tell you a story about the value of effort and intensity. When I lost custody of my sons, back in 1995, I was absolutely devastated. I was trying to remove them from an abusive situation they were in with their biological mother, and I felt helpless over this. Because of my own abusive childhood, and because I knew how much this environment harms them, losing this court case was a devastating blow for me.

But let me tell you something -- fighting for custody, putting out the effort to try and do the right thing, bought me "sleep insurance."

I was able to sleep at night because I knew in our loss, I went to the wall and did absolutely everything I possibly could have done, to win. I also happened to learn one of the most important lessons of my life, and that is to never worry about the things you can't control. And this lesson has given me invaluable peace of mind since then, in dealing with other hardships.

The whole point I am trying to make here, is to just do what you say you're going to do, and always put 110% into the creation and delivery of all your goods and services.

Be a first-class act, *always*.

Hopefully, in sharing some of these stories, you've come to understand just how important this is, not only in business, but in ALL areas of your life. And how much your customers and clients appreciate you, when you're consistently doing this.

Remember the Golden Rule: **Do unto others as you would have them do unto you.**

Follow this rule in your business, and you won't just be happy, you'll be happy and wealthy.

Money-Making Action Steps Checklist

☐ **Sometimes doing the right thing is hard to do, because you have no frame of reference.** This is yet another reason why it's important to be a consumer of whatever it is you're selling. See what it feels like to be on the other side of the coin and then do a better job.

Chapter References

- Another tremendous benefit of giving 110%, is that when you're doing a better job than everyone else, you can get paid more than everyone else! See, people generally don't have a problem paying, they have a problem paying in the absence of value. I did an interview a while ago where I revealed my specific formula for charging higher prices than anyone else, as well as my mindset. I think you'll get a lot out of it, and you can listen to it online, for free, right here: http://www.kingofcopy.com/media/interview/christian

Strategy # 20

How To Start A 1,000 Mile Journey

Confucius once said, "A journey of 1,000 miles begins with a single step."

And the truth is, too many people never achieve success because they start off by looking at where someone else is, and they say to themselves "Holy shit... it'll take me a hundred years to get where that guy is!"

But there are three things wrong with this, and please pay very close attention to what I'm about to tell you.

First, looking at where a successful business person is today, and trying to "be" that person, is like thinking about swimming across the Atlantic ocean on your first day of swimming lessons. It makes no sense.

We talked about this a little bit earlier in Strategy #17, but I want to expand on this.

Here, come closer and listen to this story. Anne was in the hospital one time (she's fine now, don't worry), and I was sitting around the waiting room, getting bored and antsy. I'd already read through the giant pile of magazines, old-emails and e-books I brought with me, and I was looking around to see if there was someone close by to chat with, to pass the time.

And by the way, this is one of the things I miss most about New York City. It's funny -- New Yorkers have such a bad reputation as being rough and rude, but the truth is, you will find no one group of people easier and more willing to stop and chat about anything, than New Yorkers.

Anyway, I saw a man sitting nearby, reading a book about retirement planning. He was there with his wife. Her mom was having surgery, and he was waiting for her to come back from her mother-in-law's recovery room.

Since I used to be a CPA and a financial planner, I know quite a bit about retirement planning, so this was an easy conversation to slide into.

"How's that book you're reading?"

The fellow was a very affable guy. Late 50's, average shape, hair thinning, pleasant smile, easy-going disposition. Dressed very blue-collar, civil-service like. The way my dad used to dress. He was wearing the same kind of clothing people who used to shop at Caldor's in the Bronx used to wear.

(Not that I'm going to be on the cover of GQ any time soon... I'm just making an observation.)

Anyway, turns out the guy works for the post office. Originally from Boston, he was as sweet a guy as you could talk with. Told me his whole life story.

Never had any kids, his wife was a teacher and he was nearing retirement, so that's why he was reading the book.

Couple of things I remember, besides his story, which I'll tell you about.

One, I was very impressed by the fact that he was willing to invest time and money into getting accurate information from people qualified to give it to him.

When he started thinking about how to prepare for retirement, he was fully aware that he didn't know a thing about it. He advised me that if I ever needed any kind of information, it always pays to pay an expert for it, rather than trying to screw around and learn it yourself.

And by the way, I didn't tell him what I do for a living, how much I make, the extent of my experience, "how smart I am," or anything else like that. When I meet someone, I'm inherently curious about them, and about learning something from them. And since you can't learn if you're mouth's running, I like to listen, first.

He said the few hundred dollars he paid his accountant and a financial planner, to sit down and educate him about retirement, was worth thousands of dollars in mistakes he could now avoid.

This is such basic, practical advice, and yet it amazes me how many people simply won't follow it. They instead try and do everything themselves, thinking they're "saving money." These folks can NEVER make any real money because they simply don't value their time or appreciate how much "specialized knowledge" is really worth.

These folks spend time doing all the mundane tasks when they instead should be working on the highest-paying jobs only. They foolishly assume that by doing it all themselves, they'll save money.

They are all dead wrong.

See, by doing it all yourself, it's actually *costing* you money.

In my business, I literally spend all of my time: thinking, marketing, selling, creating products, consulting, and writing. And that's it, period. I don't install crap on my website, and I don't make copies or pay bills or do my own taxes, either. (And remember, I'm a CPA!) Paying other people to do these things frees me up to spend time working on tasks that are going to make me a lot more money.

And if there's something I need to learn, I'll either pay someone to get me up to speed on it, really quick, or I'll invest money into information that shows me how to do it, *or*... I'll hire someone to do it for me.

For example, when I switched over from PC to Mac, I had to change the software I use to create and publish my Seductive Selling Newsletter. I went from Microsoft Publisher to Adobe InDesign. Now I could have spent a week or more likely two weeks, learning InDesign, but instead I paid an expert to set up the template of my newsletter in InDesign, and then she spent a few hours on the phone with me and showed me how to use it.

Total investment, somewhere around $700. Total savings to me in terms of time I didn't have to spend learning this on my own, that I could instead devote to making money doing what I'm good at: at least $8,000 - 10,000.

This is a *great* example of what I mean about using your time wisely and looking at checks you write as investments instead of costs.

Doing things like this makes my life easier, and allows me to focus on those things that make me money, and avoid making the mistakes that are going to *cost* me money.

Make sense?

Good. Now back to this guy in the hospital waiting room. The second thing I remember is his sense of regret. This fellow was clearly an intelligent man who had potential to be more than he was, career-wise. He explained his circumstances that led him to take this job. Basically, when he got married, the economy wasn't doing very well, and he was concerned about safety and providing for his wife. He knew working at the post office would give him both of these things.

But yet... I could "sense" he regretted his decision. He had an overriding sense of "I wish I would have at least tried something else along the way."

For me, there are a few principles I've always been firm on when it comes to the way I live my life. "No regrets" is one of them. More specifically, **I'd rather regret the mistakes I made, than the mistakes I didn't make.**

And I try really hard to apply this to *all* areas of my life, not just business.

If you want to achieve your maximum potential, you can't get there with a load of regrets piled high up on your back. They weigh you down.

See, time is the one thing you simply can't get back. You can make more money, but you can never *ever* make more time.

Right?

O.K., so now let's get back to this guy's story, because it's a really good one.

His wife grew up in Lake Placid, New York. Lake Placid is a small town about 60 miles south of the Canadian border. The town is famous for being one of only 2 cities (L.A. being the other one) to host two Olympics, the 1980 and the 1932 Winter Olympic games.

One time, before he got married, he went up to visit his wife's family in Lake Placid. It was smack dab in the middle of a bitter cold winter snowstorm. (Boy am I glad I live in Tampa!)

There was this big giant ski slope in town, he wanted to see. So in the middle of this snowstorm, while his wife is at her parent's house, he goes up to visit this ski slope. He took the elevator from the bottom of the slope, all the way up to the top, where a big strapping ski instructor was waiting around.

When he got off the elevator, he went over to the edge of the slope and he looked down the hill, straight through the raging blizzard. He'd never skied before and was completely overwhelmed by this entire scenario.

So he turns to the ski instructor and points down towards the bottom of the slope and says, "How does anyone get down there? It looks so scary."

And the instructor simply said, "**You don't... start... *here*.** When you first start skiing, you start down there at a point closer to the bottom."

Do you see where I'm going with this?

And see, this is the main reason why people don't succeed. It's also why looking at someone who's already done all the legwork they need to become successful, and then using this as your basis of comparison for where you are now, is completely unfair.

Where someone else is right now, *isn't* where you start.

You don't start there, you start at the beginning, and *that's* where you want to look. And see, the beginning of *any* journey, usually has the widest openings and the easiest ski trails. Anyone's welcome to start at the beginning.

Right?

I'll never forget when I closed my financial planning practice and I decided to make a go out of writing copy and being a publisher and a marketing consultant. It was VERY difficult. I was spending all my time building my website and trying to get traffic to it.

I was almost ready to throw in the towel. In fact, I even applied for a low-paying job at a local company, just to get "some" money in. Then, suddenly, things started happening for me. I started getting some decent traffic to my site -- people began calling me -- and I began getting copywriting jobs.

Over the next 18 months, my life changed dramatically and so did my finances.

Now don't misconstrue what I've said here to mean "don't give up." Because there are times when you *should* give up. For example, if you've tried selling something and there's just no marketplace for it and you're sitting there "waiting" for something to come to you. Or you're "hoping" to get noticed.

"Waiting" and "hoping" aren't good business strategies, and they're absolutely *horrible* marketing strategies.

My point is, hang in there as long as you're making some kind of trackable or measurable progress, moving forward and accomplishing things that get your name and your business out there in front of the *right* prospects, using the *right* marketing techniques.

Persistence is wonderful. But blind, dumb persistence just for persistence sake, won't get you anything other than ulcers and blown dreams.

The other thing you're going to find is that as you do more, and as you accomplish more, your dreams automatically get bigger. As an example, Matthew Jones, who spends 30 hours on a plane each way, just to attend my three Mastermind Group meetings a year, now dreams bigger than ever.

In one **recent three-week stretch, Matthew did over $70,000 in his software business, acting on a "whim" based on an idea he got at our last meeting**. And yesterday, I received this e-mail from him:

"Ended up doing $28,430 for the launch which finished today... and $1,200 onto monthly support plans (38 took the support)... so this launch, plus the internal launch 2 weeks ago brought in just over $50,000 - not too bad!

Now we need to keep this moving. Need to work on the current purchases and get them onto the support plan and start working on growing the list to bring in the next lot for another release in a few weeks time, we might even be able to tie in the trip to Tampa as part of the story line.

I have budgeted to make $110,000 gross for May and June – I'm currently right on budget.

I also secured a deal today with one of the biggest accounting firms in Australia – they give me an annual fee and I have developed a hybrid of my software for all their clients, which prepares financial reports in their required format to upload into their software. They have 15,000 MYOB users they are going to distribute this to!"

The most incredible thing about this is when Matthew first got started in business, he used to think he was the cat's meow making $14.50 an hour and being booked all week -- today, if he's not making a minimum of $25,000 a month or more, he knows something's REALLY wrong.

So dream big, but dream smart as well. Because dreams really do come true.

And remember, we all started at the beginning, not at the end.

Money-Making Action Steps Checklist

☐ **Be brutally honest and ask yourself if you're being realistic in your expectations.**

Are you expecting too much too happen, too soon? This doesn't mean "settle for less," because Lord knows I don't settle for less, *ever*. But are you really doing the mundane things you need to be doing, to move forward, or are you stuck thinking about the fact that you're not a multi-millionaire right NOW?

☐ **Are you practicing your craft?** By far, the most common question I get is, "How can I become a good copywriter?" No one wants the answer because it's not very sexy: **write LOADS of copy!** I recently added up all the time I've spent working at my craft over the last 9-plus years, and the total was well in excess of 30,000 hours. That's a lot of time and effort, isn't it?

And you know, when you do something for that long, chances are... you're going to be pretty good at it! If you're touting yourself as an expert on something -- then make sure you're an expert at it. While nothing can take the place of good marketing, if you want to make a small fortune from a small but loyal herd of people, then you'd better be able to deliver what you're promising.

You know the old joke about "How do you get to Carnegie Hall?"

Practice, practice, practice.

☐ **Always be in motion.** Although I do plan things out, I'd sooner take action and *then* plan, than delay action for a long period of time, TO plan. Like Robert Ringer said, "Nothing happens until something moves." In my world, I'm not "just" moving -- I simply don't sit still. And I was the same way when we were broke, but it's paid off. Are you pumped up and excited and always moving, or are you lethargic and unmotivated?

I have an incredibly high energy level, and if I can attribute my high energy levels to a few things, they'd be:

✓ **Exercise** - I've been lifting weights for over 20 years, and for the last 10 years I've been doing cardio work as well. I usually lift 3 or 4 times a week, and I do cardio the same amount, usually for 35 minutes a shot. I can't recall more than a handful times during this period of time, where I've missed exercising for longer than 2 or 3 weeks at a time.

✓ **Diet** - I eat 5 smaller meals a day. All natural foods, never anything from a can, or that isn't grown from the earth. I do eat beef once or twice a week, the rest of the time fish, chicken and turkey, as well as whey protein shakes (chocolate). I almost never eat refined sugar or processed foods (like cookies or white bread), I don't snack at night, and although I drink liquor, I don't drink often or regularly, and when I do have a drink, I don't go out and get blind, stinking drunk.

✓ **No diet soda.** After drinking 2 or 3 cans a day for over 30 years, I recently stopped drinking diet soda. I cannot tell you how much clearer I can think, and how much more energy I have now. And I'm someone who NEVER wanted for energy.

✓ **Supplements** - I've been taking a good daily multi-vitamin supplement for as long as I can remember. I also take fish oil and Kyolic (Garlic), based on a recommendation from my friend Christian Godefroy. He told me Garlic is great for your heart, and considering he's made a ton of money in the health and wellness field, I listen very closely to what he has to say on these matters.

✓ **Love** - I'm very happily married to a great woman who I've been with for over 16 years now. Don't get me wrong -- we have our ups and downs like any other couple. But she has ALWAYS supported me and encouraged me to grow and develop. She saw and believed in my potential long before I saw and believed in it myself, and she's been a great friend and source of support, ever since we met.

We have three children, and I'm not going to sit here and tell you raising them has been easy. Raising children is incredibly difficult, but they too, have always been here to support me, and I love having them around. They are definitely a source of my energy, as I always try and lead by example. My dad was a "do as I say, not as I do" kind of parent, and he was also a bully, which is one of the reasons why he and I don't speak and were never close. I feel a tremendous sense of obligation to my children and I work hard to deliver on this.

✓ **Passion** - I truly enjoy what I do. In some ways this is a blessing and a curse, because as a result, I tend to work more than I probably need to. I'm constantly working on "weaning" myself from work and onto other hobbies I'd like to spend more time on, like drawing, photography, and fishing... and maybe even playing guitar again some day. Passion is raw energy.

✓ **Maverick Spirit** - I've always rooted for the underdog and I've always gone against the grain. To the point where it's now almost a knee-jerk reaction for me, that when I'm making a decision, one of the things I look at is what everyone else is doing and then I just go the other way. See, I know the odds of making the right decision are in my favor when I do this.

My daughter is exactly the same way, and my older son is somewhat like this as well. "Doing what you want, and on your own terms," for me at least... is a tremendous source of energy and freedom.

Because of my upbringing (having an abusive father), I'm actually emotionally allergic to being told what to do. So while I have no desire at all to boss around or control anyone else, I thrive on living life on my own terms. In fact, that's mandatory for me.

Chapter References

- Since I've been around the block with respect to this, many times, a good portion of the consulting work I do, focuses on helping people overcome some of the mental obstacles that are in their way. I don't pretend to be some kind of a therapist, but I do believe in confronting and then conquering your demons head on, and the first thing you need to do, is to identify them. To work with me in this capacity, you can either book an hour of consulting time at kingofcopy.com/consulting, or you can book a day of consulting (must get approval from my office prior to booking) at kingofcopy.com/consultingday.

  In any case, getting the "mindset" aspect of business nailed down is like getting your diet nailed down when it comes to weight loss. All the exercise in the world won't burn even an ounce of fat off you, until you start eating right. Similarly, all the hard work in the world won't pay off for you financially, until you really believe you deserve to make big money.

- The other tool that helped me overcome many of my self-sabotaging issues as a result of my abusive childhood, is an old book I've re-published, called "The Science Of Getting Rich," by Wallice Wattles. This will be the best $10 bucks you ever spend, and I've even included some personal stories of the things I experienced in my own life, that held me back (in my own mind, anyway). You can find this book at kingofcopy.com/science.

Strategy # 21

Why You MUST Have Brass Balls

Success *isn't* for the weak and timid. You need a strong stomach and incredible tenacity to become successful.

You're going to have to jump over many hurdles and be very focused, but if you stick it out, the rewards are well worth it.

I'm going to tell you three stories that illustrate the point I'm trying to make here. Then we'll talk about some Money-Making Action Steps you need to take.

Wrestlemania

Success is FAR more difficult than anyone -- except someone who's done it -- can imagine.

It's like when you see a band suddenly appearing all over the radio and on television shows, and their videos are in regular rotation on MTV. You think they're an overnight sensation, but no one knows about how they spent the last 10 years of their lives traveling around the country in an old van. Then, sleeping in that van in Pontiac, Michigan in the dead of winter, while they were playing in one dingy club after another, night after night.

This is the unglamorous part of success no one discusses. It's not exciting and no one's going to get pumped up about becoming successful, dwelling over this part of the story.

In reality, there are few iPods and Walkmans. And although the press loves to dote over the "1 in a million" business that takes off like a rocket ship, these businesses are such an incredibly small minority, you can't even measure them in terms of hundredths of percentage points.

261

These stories *do* keep the dream alive, but they also paint a very false picture of what success is really like.

I'm currently trying to explain this to my older son, Nick. He's finding it difficult to achieve the success he wants, on the wrestling team. The truth is, anyone who achieves success, in any endeavor, must have an incredible burning desire to succeed, and they must be prepared to sacrifice a lot. Usually a lot more than they thought, in fact.

Over the years, Nick used to tell me every night, "go to bed Dad, it's not good for you to work so much." I loved hearing this from him, because I knew he cared about me, and I never took even *one* of his comments for granted.

But in reality, I was doing what I had to do, to become successful. To give the airplane that is my business, enough energy, to finally get that big machine off the ground and soaring through the sky.

Today, my late nights are *much* fewer, but Nick understands that the lake-house he lives in is one of the many things we've been able to attain, from the sacrifices I made by putting in all those late nights and all-nighters.

Success is NOT for the weak and timid, and it's not for the wishy-washy either.

You need a game plan, you need to be flexible enough to adjust it as you move along, and you'd *better* be prepared to go balls to the wall, to get things done.

You're going to have loads of ups and downs along the way. Many successful people, myself included, have either experienced a bankruptcy (mine was in 1997), or some other financial crisis on their journey.

Not to mention, your life outside of business doesn't stop. Family, children, health, and other issues will crop up from time-to-time as well. That's just life and there's nothing anyone can do to change it.

Like everything else in life that's worthwhile, there really is no free lunch when it comes to making money and doing things on your own terms. And it takes guts to put yourself through something like this.

It has to be this way though. That's the filter success has, to see who gets through.

Do as best you can to squeeze in through that filter -- it's a steep price to pay, but nowhere near the price you're going to wind up paying by not squeezing in.

'Nuff said.

When Do You Get Results?

Last week I received an e-mail from longtime Seductive Selling Newsletter member and a member of my Mavericks Group, Dwight Miller from Marlton, New Jersey.

Dwight's a successful Corporate Online Marketing Strategist and the marketing brains behind some very well-known SEO gurus. I've personally known him for over 4 years -- he's a kind and gentle man, and a friend.

Amongst other things that were very heartfelt, Dwight had this to say:

"Hey Craig, Hope you and your family are well, just finished reading the "back-end" and I gotta tell you it's great to read about your life and your family.

Forced some reflection on my part about my own life and how I've lived it so far and thanks for that. A few experiences have recently been interesting in that they are helping me clarify how I want to live the rest of my life. All that said, the "back-end" was great and I must say the days you lose with your family cannot be regained.

Enjoy each one and squeeze all of the juice out of them. Thanks again. Be well, Dwight Miller"

There are lots of reasons I enjoy getting mail like this. Writing a newsletter is very much like doing a teleseminar or speaking at the podium -- you really have NO idea how you're doing, until someone tells you. Yes, of course how long people stick around, and how many referrals you get is one measure, but you don't know the level of impact you have on your members, until you hear things like this, from them.

Feedback like this lets me know I *am* reaching people and making a difference. That I'm compelling people to think and stretch beyond where they were before sitting down to read my newsletter.

Getting my members results, is what makes things real for me. This validates my effort, beyond the dollars and cents.

And that's what I want to talk about right now: results. So let's get right into it.

Both of my sons work out in the gym after school, daily. My younger boy, Casey, who's got a typical solid but wiry build, came to me one day last week after a particularly hard-fought biceps workout and asked me when he would "see the results" of the days workout. He wanted to know when he'd visibly see the progress from that day, measured by increased muscle mass in his arms.

Unfortunately, that's just not how it works, as we all know. It doesn't work that way in bodybuilding, and it damn sure doesn't work that way in success and in building a business.

The truth is, he won't see the impact of that particular workout at all, unless he follows it up with another 3 to 6 months of workouts just as hard, and then he'll see the aggregate effect of each of these workouts, across that time line.

You can't see the results of one workout, any more than you can step on the scale after a bike ride or run, and measure how many pounds you've lost from the weigh-in you did a few hours ago.

And unfortunately, you can't measure your success because of the one all-nighter you've pulled, either.

It's extremely rare that one big thing alone is going to "finally" make things happen for you.

Generally, it's a consistent, dogged series of sequential steps moving you forward. Each one of them, repeated over-and over again, tweaked and modified as you're going along. Oh, and add a ton of hard work and painful mistakes on top of that, and having serendipity cross your path every once in a while, as well. You also need hours of preparation, execution, chaos and damage control, and evaluation and feedback from your results.

Yeah, I know that's not real popular now, and "fast, easy, and simple" is what all the gurus out there are telling you, but that's nonsense. Anyone who's making money "fast, easy and simple," is only making that money in their dreams.

As for me, well... It's 2:40 am right now, and even though I'm taking off tomorrow morning, believe me, the guy making $75,000 a year working as a store manager at Publix, isn't working at 2:40 am, that's for sure.

THIS is what it generally takes. There really is no "fast, easy, and simple."

But... here's the flip side of this:

✓ **We're taking FOUR vacations this year, staying in two rooms (one for Anne and I, and one for our 3 kids), doing whatever we please.** However, keep in mind I had no vacations at all for many years, along the way. (Note, I no longer fly first class on domestic flights. The service is only incrementally better, for the significant extra costs involved, except when flying overseas. One thing I learned, is that making money is easy -- keeping it *isn't* so easy. I try and be good at both.)

✓ **I haven't looked at the prices on a menu in a L-O-O-N-G time.** This is particularly rewarding since at one time we were so broke I couldn't even afford to pay attention. Pizza was a delicacy!

✓ **I take off 2 or 3 times a week to spend time with my wife, have lunch, go the mall, whatever.**

✓ I hit the gym most mornings or afternoons, and often I'm working out with my sons.

✓ **I've never missed a sporting event, recital, activity or game any of my kids were in, unless I was out of town, which is rare.**

✓ **And most important, I don't have to work with anyone I don't want to.** Which, for me, is worth all the money in the world.

This is how you're going to see the results of today's workout... or of tomorrow's sales letter.

Success is not for the weak and timid, but the freedom you have is well worth it, if you have what it takes to complete the journey.

The good news is, there's no qualifications necessary. The only requirement is discipline and faith in yourself.

Oh, and as far as my son goes, he's packed on close to 10 pounds of quality muscle in the last year and he looks great.

Now if I could only get him to clean up his room... ☺

How Much Money Do You Want To Make?
This Depends Solely On How Much You Want To Charge.

About five years ago, I was at a seminar in Dallas, where I met a man I'd later wind up becoming friends with. Today, he's not only a friend, he also happens to be a long-time Seductive Selling Newsletter member, and a member of my Mavericks Coaching Group. At the time, he wanted to get better at writing sales copy, and he also wanted to know how he could charge his clients more money for it.

He asked me, *"Craig, can you get me up to the point where I can charge $10,000 dollars for my services?"*

I said, "I'll do one better. I'm going to tell you exactly how to charge $10,000 for a sales letter, right now."

"Really?"

"Yes, really."

"Now are you ready? Because I'm only going to tell you how to do this, one time. And, it's going to be the only free advice you ever get from me, because frankly, I don't think you're going to take it. And as you know, people value the advice you give them only to the extent they've paid for it, so I'm leery about doing this in the first place, as I'm sure you can understand."

"No, really Craig, I'm ready for it."

"O.K., here goes. The way you charge $10,000 dollars for your services, is... you just charge $10,000 dollars for your services."

"That's it?"

"Yep, that's it."

See, most people are looking for permission to make their next breakthrough. But as an entrepreneur, you don't usually get this permission. You simply have to give *yourself* the permission you're looking for, or perhaps maybe you can find a mentor to give it to you.

In reality, the only person whose permission matters, is yours, anyway. You must be your own boss and you must give yourself permission to *earn* more money, *charge* more money, and take each one of the steps required to get to that next level.

In business, the only moorings and limits that exist on your income and on your progress, are the ones you make for yourself. And running a business and doing all these things on your own, *isn't* always easy.

Bluntly, you need brass balls to consistently charge big money for your services... you need brass balls to consistently believe you deserve to be paid well for your goods and services... and you need brass balls to succeed.

Today, I charge of $60,000 dollars plus 3% royalties to develop a full-blown marketing campaign and create the sales copy for it. I'll tell you right now -- you need balls to charge this much money.

For those people who hire me, however, they get to benefit from a tremendous return on their investment, over and over again, throughout the course of their entire lifetime.

And for those folks who believe this is too much money to "write a sales letter," they are simply not qualified to become a client of mine, or they are not in my marketplace.

Frankly, one of the reasons I charge so much is that writing copy for other people, interrupts my publishing and consulting business. After all, if you're a great copywriter and a solid marketing strategist, why would you limit your income solely to what others will pay you?

That's just trading dollars for hours, when it comes down to it. And I'd rather use this knowledge and the skill-set I have, to set up a variety of businesses of my own. This frees me from clients and gives me the *most* independence.

Anyone I meet who tells me they've been a copywriter for more than a few years, and who's still working with clients -- this tells me they have a problem. It's either a business problem, or it's a mental quirk about running a business they need help with, *or*... they really aren't very good at what they do.

Or, they're just "writers" and they don't know a thing about strategy, which to me is like being a surgeon but now knowing anything about medicine. But, whatever...

For me, this just has to do with my inherent fundamental need to have integrity throughout my life. How can someone possibly give out business advice for a living, but be too ignorant to listen to it, themselves?

True?

Like I said, success is not for the weak and timid.

I encourage you to be strong and I hope you have the courage you need. And I am also, right here and now, giving you all the permission you need, to be as successful as you deserve to be. You will see, the results are well worth it. And when you think about it, there's plenty of room at the top -- it's the bottom that's crowded, right?

So start climbing, today... now. The sky's the limit, and how high up you climb is only up to you. As for me, I believe I'm only at the beginning of my journey -- I've still got lots of climbing to go!

Money-Making Action Steps Checklist

☐ **If you've been holding back on something, grab a legal pad and a pen, and write these questions down at the top of the page:** "What am I holding back on and why?" Then, spend a couple of hours thinking about this and writing down your candid answers.

☐ **If you are smart enough to answer those questions, then you're also smart enough to figure out a step-by-step action plan that lists all the things you need to do, to get you from where you are now, to where you need to be.** Base these steps on your answers to the last action step, and on what you've learned in this book. The work you do on these sheets of paper, may very well be the most important work you will do on yourself and for your own progress, *ever*. It is very likely to set you on a course with destiny that changes your entire life. So set down a time to do this on your day-planner, and make sure you get it done.

Block out this time, right now.

When you're finished, don't hesitate to let me know what happened the end result of this action step was, and the kind of changes or growth you experienced. For information on how to contact me, see the "Contact" page at the back of this book.

Chapter References

• The fastest way to take action and get things moving, rapidly, is to get involved in a coaching or Mastermind program with other entrepreneurs who are like-minded in their thinking. I have two programs I run that are very effective and get my members results. My Mastermind Group is an application-based program only, and you can find information about it at kingofcopy.com/mastermind.

My Mavericks Coaching program is open enrollment and you can find information about it at kingofcopy.com/mavericks.

Bonus Strategy # 22

The Mother Of ALL Your Success

I know I promised you 21 strategies but I have a few more important ones I wanted to share. And since I'm more comfortable giving you *more* than I promised, here goes.

Remember the old television program "Kung Fu," from the early 1970's? In it, the late David Carradine played Caine, a Shaolin monk who roamed across the early American west on foot, looking for his brother, Danny Caine.

In flashbacks from his youth, you'd see a young Caine in training with his mentor, the blind Master Po. Po would often test Caine's reflexes by asking him to snatch a small pebble from his outstretched hand. In spite of the fact that Po was blind, Caine would never come up with the pebble.

The lesson Po was trying to teach Caine was that he had to work harder, and the only way to work hard (which if you remember, was the opening salvo of this book) is to be disciplined.

I want to talk about discipline in this Chapter, because it's a necessary ingredient to good habits, which of course, are a necessary ingredient to becoming successful in any endeavor.

In fact, **discipline is the mother of success, and consistency is the backbone of discipline**.

My good friend Christian Godefroy says that I am the most disciplined person he knows. He references my consistency in cranking out Seductive Selling, my 12-page newsletter with examples, every single month… my Audio Success CD monthly interview that goes out along with Seductive Selling… the weekly faxes I write for my coaching group members... the daily free e-mails and blog postings for my online e-zine subscribers… monthly coaching calls for my various coaching group members… and two or three product releases per year, on top of my client and consulting work.

And I do all this on top of marketing and running all 3 of my businesses and being a father and a husband.

You too, can be as disciplined as want, if you're willing to do just a few things. I will tell you what they are, but first let's take a look at what discipline means. After all, you can't be disciplined, unless you truly know what discipline is, so pay attention because this is important.

Discipline is when you sacrifice something today, in order to accomplish something bigger, tomorrow.

Got that?

Let me say it again: **Discipline is when you sacrifice something today, in order to accomplish something bigger, tomorrow.**

Again, simple… but not easy.

But the good news is, if you have ever been disciplined in one area of your life, it only takes this same sense of commitment to be disciplined in other areas of your life. And if you've never managed to discipline yourself, I'm going to give you a simple thought-process to follow, that allows you to be disciplined without becoming overwhelmed.

First, you need to know how the mind works.

For most people, what you think about most, is what you do. The more you think about something, the more likely you are to turn these thoughts into actions.

Make sense?

Good, because if you're going to get hung up somewhere, this next part is the most likely spot. That's because there's a big leap from "thoughts" to actions, but remember… the first time you do something is the most difficult.

From there on in, every other successive time you do something, it gets easier and easier, no matter what it is you're doing.

And so here's the big secret of being disciplined: All you need to do is focus on the one action you want to get done, at that particular moment. And that's it.

Don't focus on the outcome you want, and don't become overwhelmed by what might happen in the future, along with all the other things you need to get done. Just focus on that one particular action you're taking, at any given moment.

So for example, if you're trying to lose a lot of weight, and you're working out in the gym, just focus on getting through each workout, every single day.

Don't focus on how many pounds you still have left to lose -- just focus on doing each day's workout as best as you can.

When you're eating breakfast, don't become overwhelmed thinking about all the caloric restrictions you're going to have to deal with at every meal... just think about... enjoying breakfast. And then you do the same thing with every other component of your weight loss.

For instance, when I write Seductive Selling, my offline newsletter -- I don't sit and think to myself, "Oh my God. I've got to do this every single month for the next 10 years!"

That would completely ruin any sense of enjoyment and pleasure I get out of writing the newsletter, and it would take my focus away from the discipline I'm exercising every month.

In fact, I don't even concentrate on getting through the entire month's newsletter. I just focus on getting through each section of each month's newsletter at any given point in time. And then I move on to the next section, and so on.

And see, all you need to do is get through each of these steps on a regular basis, and before you know it, you've got a new habit. Then, once you're performing that action long enough (I've heard anywhere from 21 days to 6 weeks, depending on the source of your information), it's no longer something new for you. It becomes your new habit.

And once you get into the *habit* of doing something, it becomes normal for you -- it's just part of your daily routine.

At that point, the actual "discipline" part of doing whatever it is, is pretty much over. You should simply have this particular activity scheduled into your daily planner. At this stage, this activity just becomes a regular and ordinary part of your life, just like brushing your teeth is a regular and ordinary part of your life.

I know I've made this sound incredibly easy, but that's because it is. The difficult part is planning out what needs to be done, and simply taking that first step. And then making sure you repeat this process, over and over again. (Anybody can do anything, once.)

In some cases, like when you're trying to lose weight, you may have to repeat this process every day. In other cases, like writing my newsletter, you'll need to repeat it monthly.

Now you do need to be aware of the "sacrifice" part of discipline. Because you do have to sacrifice or invest something to bring that discipline to life. It's either going to be time, money, effort, food, whatever. But something has to actually be invested, in order for you to get a return on that investment.

Because like I always say, you can't divide by zero. If you don't put something into a project, there's just no way you're ever going to get something out of it. You've always got to have skin in the game or else there's no value in it for you.

No exceptions or short-cuts here, that's just the way it is.

But you are no different from me, and I <u>know</u> you can do this.

Money-Making Action Steps Checklist

☐ **In all likelihood there is ONE important thing you can't discipline yourself to do, that is preventing you from moving forward in a number of other areas**.

Focus on this one thing, and then create your daily action plan. List all the **specific steps** you need to do on a regular basis, to make this goal happen for you. Then, create an action plan.

Make sure you write down <u>each</u> <u>specific</u> <u>step</u> of your plan. Don't just put down something like, "write a book," because that's not specific enough.

Since there are perhaps 20 steps involved in putting a book together, what ultimately happens is that you lose interest in this project, since you can't visualize or measure the progress you're making against such a huge benchmark.

That's like saying "build a house." Building a house may involve hundreds of tasks before it's completed. It makes a lot more sense, and you're a lot more likely to start (and finish) something when you've broken it down into smaller, more tangible steps in your process.

So for example, if you're writing a book, you're much better off making a list like this:

1. Come up with a specific list of topics to write a book about.

2. **Do marketplace research to see what topics my marketplace is interested in, to narrow down my list.**

3. Look at the practicality of being able to sell each of these topics.

4. **Which of these topics will give me the positioning and leverage I need, to be a recognized expert and leader in my industry?** Which topic will be congruent with my overall current business philosophy and desired positioning?

5. **Which of these topics will make me the most money?**

6. Create headlines and titles for my book.

7. **Accumulate material and do research necessary to create book content.**

8. Hire out any experts needed to help me with research.

... and so on...

See, you've already got 8 items already listed and you haven't even got to the part about sitting down and doing the actual writing yet. And since we're all very driven by goal-setting and goal-seeking, as you knock off each one of these items, your feeling of accomplishment and progress is *dramatically* higher, than if you simply wrote down "write a book."

Organizing and planning like this, goes a very long way to giving you the motivation and persistence you need, to be disciplined.

So set realistic and specific step-by-step goals, that you will be able to discipline yourself to accomplish. Not "lose 40 pounds" but "eat healthy today"... or "do 35 minutes of cardio work in the gym on Wednesday..." or... "lose 1 pound by next Friday."

These are tangible and practical steps anyone can achieve, and taking action to complete them is easy. Breaking things down into smaller chunks makes discipline a lot less painful, and it makes your progress much more rewarding.

Part Three: What To Say

Bonus Strategy # 23

How To Write A Sales Letter That Sells: All The Copywriting Secrets You Ever Wanted To Know, But Were Afraid To Ask!

It is rumored that John Lennon, after buying a house, decided he needed a swimming pool to go along with the house. When asked how he was going to be able to afford the swimming pool, he simply told the rest of the Beatles, "I'll write myself a swimming pool."

Copywriting is no different. This is a skill, that when mastered, you can use to create money almost at will. Now please understand what I'm saying here, because I want to be clear on something.

I'm not saying you should *ever* make money by making something look good even when it's not true. You should never do anything even *remotely* like this.

What I'm saying is, once you know how to write, all you need to do is find something to sell, and then find the marketplace to buy it. Your writing is the bridge that connects these two components, to make the sale.

For most people, this is usually the most difficult part of this entire equation.

Finding stuff to sell and finding markets to sell it to, is generally easy. It's the selling that's usually the hard part for most people. If you can write, you therefore hold the keys to the kingdom.

Here are a few comments from a couple of very successful entrepreneurs who are part of my Mastermind Group.

DC Fawcett negotiated short-sales for six long-hard years for others, before deciding to become an entrepreneur and go into business for himself. Only 31 years old, DC just finished a massive launch that made him more in two months than most "successful" business-owners make in 20 years.

DC developed an entire new niche for real estate investors, Virtual Short Sale Investing, and created a marketing system that allows investors across the country to bring his team of experienced negotiators, luxury home short sale deals.

DC has spent the last year working very hard on his copywriting and marketing skills, and after his launch, sent this note around to all of his launch partners:

"The task of copywriting and video script writing is key to your success for maximizing conversions. I am fortunate to have Craig Garber on my team to critique my copy.

Copywriting is the most important skill you should hone as a marketer. I'm in Craig's mastermind group and I get to send him critiques of my copy. The amount of money that those critiques made for me during this launch have paid for his mastermind group for the rest of my LIFE. btw, I write most of my copy myself. You should too."

Another member of my Mastermind Group, Bill Parlaman, was up until recently, a salaried employee working for the man.

It's been a thrill to coach Bill and watch him grow, both personally and professionally. Bill started with me when he was an employee in a dead-end job. All he had was a dream of doing better and he also felt he deserved to do better.

Here's a note Bill recently sent me:

"Dead.

This was the opening Craig used in an e-mail he sent out announcing his ad writing workshop held in Tampa, FL in January of 2009.

With one word, Craig summarized exactly what your business is -- if you don't know how to sell in print.

And let's face it, if you update your website, if you advertise in the yellow pages, or if you simply send out an email -- you are a copywriter whether you realize it or not.

The cold hard truth is if you don't know how to write effective and emotionally gut wrenching sales copy that makes your prospects pick up the phone and call your office, or enter their name and email into an opt in box, then you're in a world of hurt my friend!

Now the great thing about studying copywriting with Craig is his uncanny "sixth sense" in combining sound business strategies with effective copywriting. As Craig will tell you, its doesn't matter how good your copy is, if your strategy is bad you're dead in the water!

You see, about a year ago I was stuck working a dead-end job. I knew I wanted to start a business but I didn't have a clue as to what to do or where to start.

I subscribed to Craig's Seductive Selling Newsletter and then his Mavericks and Seductive Selling Coaching groups shortly thereafter. I started learning how to write compelling copy and how to see opportunities in places I never saw them before. Today I am a member of Craig's Mastermind Group as well.

In short, Craig trained my mind to think like an entrepreneur!

So why am I telling you this? Well in the last month I have taken everything I've learned from Craig and applied it to my first real business venture and made $12,961.00 in just two hours! From the copy, to the strategy and to turning my ideas into a business! I learned it all from Craig Garber!

Because of Craig my knowledge of direct response marketing and copywriting is far superior to many other direct marketers who have been in the business for years. And none of this would have been possible if it were not for Craig's products and coaching and mentoring!"

While this may have sounded like an endorsement for me, what I want you to focus on is the resounding endorsement of the power of compelling sales copy and great marketing strategy.

This is what makes the cash register ring.

O.K.?

So let's talk about how you can make your life a lot easier and make a lot more money, by uncovering the mystery of copywriting.

You know, people call me the King Of Copy, but I sure didn't start off my career like that. I graduated from college as a CPA, (hated English and writing, by the way), then got into sales after I realized I didn't like working in accounting, where things are always black and white.

It's a gray world, and I like it that way. I love change, I'm fiercely independent, and I absolutely hate being told what to do. I'm also 100% prepared to live and die by the outcome of my own effort, which is the hallmark of a good salesperson.

It's also one of the reasons why I love what I do and why I'm basically unemployable. For me, working for someone is like having a noose around my neck. I just want to be left alone -- I know what to do and I'm all motivated to get things done by myself, thank you.

Not that I don't take criticism and learn from others -- I thrive on it, in fact. But I need to choose who those people will be, the same way you need to choose what kind of car you drive, instead of being forced into driving a car by someone else. Which is what happens in a conventional job: you can't pick your boss, they're assigned to you.

And that doesn't work very well with me.

See, in case you didn't realize it yet, there are a lot of really dumb people out there, and my biggest flaw is that I have little patience for any of them, so that's why I'm so stubborn in this area.

Now appreciate that for me to sit and tell you how to become an expert at writing long-form sales copy in one Chapter, would be like trying to learn how to become a doctor in one biology class.

I didn't become me in a week, or in a year even, and you're not going to do it, either. But mastering the art of writing compelling sales copy is probably one of *the* most important skills you can learn, when it comes to marketing. It's second only to understanding what makes people "tick" and how to push their emotional buy-buttons.

Before I take you through some copywriting basics, let me give you a tip on how to use a free resource with more information on it about this topic, that's growing daily: my kingofcopy.com website and blog

You can find any information you want about writing copy on my blog at http://blog.kingofcopy.com. All you need to do is scroll down a little bit and look for the box on the right-hand side that says, "Looking for something Here In The Kingdom?" Then, enter the words you're looking for, like "writing copy"... "headlines"... "direct mail"... "marketing"... whatever.

Then just click on the "Search" button or hit the return key, and you'll be given all the entries I've made to my blog and to my website (before the blog existed). There are literally hundreds of articles filled with useful information on many important topics, and over 1,000 pages of information online, so enjoy them.

As a side note, I don't use the word "copywriting" very much in my blog, so you're better off searching the term "sales copy" or "writing copy" or just words like "copy"... "opening lines"... "headlines"... "guarantees"... and other specific items you're looking for.

When you're speaking to someone and explaining how to write copy, you really don't use the word "copywriting" very much. I know my search engine experts would have preferred I used the word "copywriting" in every single post I make, but I've always felt that doing things naturally, or organically, is the best way, so I've just stuck to my guns. And judging from the results, it doesn't seem like I've suffered any, so I'll continue doing it my way.

Now before I get into all the details, let me just give you a summary of a few basic copywriting rules you want to follow, which anyone should be able to do:

✓ **Always write like you speak, no matter what you're selling and no matter how "elitist" or sophisticated you think your marketplace is.** Your sales pitch in print, should be almost identical to your sales pitch in person.

Now there *are* a few things you're going to have to add, simply because you don't have the benefit of interactive dialog, and because you can't respond to your prospects' follow-up questions and objections. So you have to anticipate some of these things and address them in your sales letter. I'll show you what I'm talking about in just a minute.

✓ **Be specific.** Just like in "real life," being vague and evasive smells bad and makes your prospects question what's going on.

✓ **Be simple.** No one ever lost a sale for being too clear in what they're trying to say.

✓ **Tell stories.** Everyone loves a good story and when you're telling a story, you're not selling something -- you're building rapport. You need to do things that put your prospects into a position where they're naturally lowering their guard. No one's going to trust you if they feel defensive or pushed up against the wall -- in person or in print.

On the other hand, stories get people involved and make them open to

278

suggestions.

✓ **Build your relationship through what you have to give, not through what you want to take.** Or, as my good friend Christian Godefroy said, "Always think of what you want to bring into this world, not what you want to get out of it." **Remember, people don't care how much you know, until they know how much you care.**

✓ **Always make an offer. <u>Remember, nothing gets bought unless it gets sold first.</u>** This is true even when you're "giving" away free things as lead generation pieces. Even the benefits of the free stuff you're giving away, have to be "sold."

✓ **Be liberal with your guarantees.** While you can't guarantee someone else's performance, you can guarantee your own. Figure out what you can guarantee and then let your prospects know about it.

Above and beyond these rules, we'll also briefly cover the 12 of the 17 components of a sales letter or advertisement. The other 5 items are beyond the scope of this book -- they are things I go through in my Ad Writing Workshop and in person. However, knowing even these 12 items, puts you way beyond 99.9% of all the marketers and copywriters out there. And they are:

1. **Headline**

2. Opening

3. **Discussion/Transition/Empathy**

4. Credibility

5. **Introduction to your product or service**

6. Bullets / Benefits

7. **Guarantees**

8. Who it's for / Who it's NOT for

9. **What it is / What it's NOT**

10. Eliminate competition (maybe)

11. Closing

12. P.S.

I'll cover each of these components in this Chapter. So without any further ado, let's dig into some of the many components of writing great sales copy.

✓ **Always write like you speak, no matter what you're selling and no matter how "elitist" or sophisticated you think your marketplace is.** Your sales pitch in print, should be almost identical to your sales pitch in person.

Here's some background on this: in 1905, a former Canadian policeman man named John E. Kennedy -- by then, a well-known successful copywriter and ad-man -- defined advertising as "salesmanship in print."

And since that's about as accurate a definition as I've ever come across, who am I to change it? So let's talk about how to speak with your prospects, no matter who you're talking to.

For example, many people think there's a difference between writing sales copy when you're pitching to a business (B2B), and writing sales copy when you're selling directly to an individual (B2C - business to consumer).

Frankly, nothing could be further from the truth.

I know this isn't what most people tell you but most people have no clue what they're talking about here.

Remember, when you do the things most people do, you're going to get the same results most people get. And most people are lucky to get even mediocre results, especially when it comes to marketing and running ads, so don't listen to them.

Few (if any) people have written ads that have pulled in a 42.7% response on a first mailing to a cold list, so listen to me when it comes to copywriting. I don't mean that in a boastful way, I just want you to succeed, that's all. So clear your mind of any preconceived notions you may have about this -- I'm giving you the real deal about what works and what doesn't work.

O.K.?

Good, so let's get back to writing to business owners versus consumers.

Think about it -- who are you talking to when you're pitching to a business -- a legal entity, or a person?

And who are you sending it from -- a legal entity or a person?

You don't need to be a genius to figure this one out, now do you?

The bottom line is, *people* have relationships with *people*, not with "businesses."

Keep this in mind, because one of the biggest problems people have in relationships, is communication. **You *must* know who you're dealing with and what's important to them, in order to communicate with them effectively.** (Which is why the research you do, to create your sales material, is so important.)

This is true whether you're talking about a business relationship... a marriage... or even a relationship between two friends.

And the last thing you can EVER afford, is to have a communication problem in your sales copy.

If you do, you're dead in the water and you will sell nothing.

O.K.?

That's why most ads are useless. They're saying the wrong things, and they're usually saying them to the wrong people. They talk about what the product is (features) instead of what the product or service does for you (benefits).

Look, you only get one shot at connecting with your prospect, so you'd better make it a good one. You know the old adage -- you never get a second chance to make a first impression. In print, this is even harder, so listen up.

To make sure your first impression is a lasting one, I'm going to share some examples of common communication errors I consistently see when I'm doing sales copy critiques.

It's important you get your arms around this issue because these problems make your prospects experience a "disconnect" from you. And this forces them into being *guarded* about what you're saying, instead of open-minded and receptive to what you're saying.

And when someone's guarded about what you have to say, your ability to sell them something drops to nearly zero. (Think how you feel every time you walk into an Auto Dealership, for example.)

So for example, one of the most common flaws I see, is writing sales copy like you're either sending it off to your 11th grade English teacher to be graded, or writing as if you're trying to get your letter included in the newest IRS tax code modification. Meaning...

It's Too Freakin' Complicated!

See, the thing is, sales copy doesn't have any grammatical "rules" -- at least not in the conventional sense you've been taught. So to be effective at it, you've got to re-program yourself by clearing your mind of any kind of "writing rules" you had drummed into your head when you were a kid.

Here, let me show you just a small handful of the "dis-connecting" words and phrases I've seen recently, along with what you should be saying instead:

Ineffective Sales Copy Used	What It Should've Said
... which one is appropriate	... which one's best for you? ... which one of these makes sense to you?
employment	**work**
order form	application form, 180-day free trial form
Contracts	**documents**
a cabal of	a secret group of
A strange anomaly	**A fluke**
Until the behavior you desire	Until the behavior you want
These pure essential oils were selected for their known benefits	**These 100% pure essential oils have a unique ability to make you feel more relaxed...**
We provide reliable health information from medical doctors.	Inside "X", you'll find medical secrets uncovered by medical specialists recognized as top experts in their field, world-wide.

You will find descriptions and recommendations for control over the more common...	**Here are some of the most common situations you might run across. Check off which ones apply to you:**
To date, you've achieved much.	Listen, obviously you wouldn't be in this situation if it wasn't for all the success you've already experienced.
It's difficult to comprehend.	**It's hard to understand.**

See, in most of these cases, what was originally written was either too complicated... used too many five-dollar words... or simply wasn't benefit-oriented enough. Like I said a few minutes ago, the copy was focused on what the product or service can do, instead of what it can do for you.

So please keep in mind, you will never ever get in trouble communicating too clearly in *any* relationship, but *especially* in business.

And how can you make sure you're not turning on your prospects "Someone's trying to sell me something" alarm, and alienating them from you?

Simple.

There are actually 3 ways of doing this:

1. **First, after you write your copy, you must read it out loud, and actively listen to what you're reading.** And I don't mean read it "out loud" in your head, I mean, actually read it <u>out</u> <u>loud</u> as in "words and sound coming out of your mouth."

    Another alternative is to use a text-to-speech software, or have one of your children read it back to you, out loud. Kids are good because you really shouldn't be writing at anything more than an 8th or 9th grade reading level, anyway. So if your 14 or 15-year old can't understand your sales copy, then chances are, it's too advanced.

    When I first started writing copy, my older son, Nick was around 10 years old, and he'd read all my sales letters out loud. That was really great. But after a while, the novelty wears off, and it's not much fun any more.

    So if you want to opt for the software, which is the next best option, one I've used in the past is called "Read Please" (readplease.com). I like this software because you can vary the speed of the reader, and you can choose voices with accents in them. Reading your copy out loud either slowly, or with an accent, exaggerates the flaws, so you can quickly identify where they are, and smooth them out immediately.

Also, don't write something you'd never actually say in person, if you were sitting across the table from your prospect and trying to pitch them your goods or services. It'll come across as either inappropriate, disrespectful, or disingenuous. And in today's day and age when everyone's so full of themselves, when you come across as a real person, it's like a breath of fresh air.

This alone is a big differential that helps set you apart from everyone else. In fact, I attribute much of my personality's appeal to this one item alone.

For example, if you were talking to your prospect, you'd never say, "To date, you've achieved much." But you would say "Listen, obviously you wouldn't be in this situation if it wasn't for all the success you've already experienced."

Right?

Do you get the gist of what I'm saying here?

O.K., good.

2. **Second, unless there's a specific reason you're using a word, use the shortest and most direct version of it.** Be economical with your usage of, and quality of words.

See, the biggest mistake people make when they're writing copy is, they take their "reading" intelligence level, and apply this same standard to the intellectual quality of their written sales copy.

Meaning, this: Just because you've got a genius I.Q. or whatever, or just because you or your marketplace can read and understand a certain level of words, you're probably not necessarily using these words in your everyday ordinary conversations, now are you?

You probably speak in plain old conversational English, just like the rest of us, right?

And see, that's exactly how you want your sales copy to sound.

Like I said, you want your sales copy to say the same exact things you'd say if you were sitting across the other side of the desk from your prospect, pitching your goods or services in person.

Or even better yet, you want it to sound the way you'd probably talk to an old friend of yours, telling them about your product over a cup of coffee or a Coke.

In other words, use your "ordinary"... and easy... "no-pressure" conversational speaking voice.

Believe me, I have a 167 I.Q., and one of the things I do when I'm editing my copy is I make sure it's not too smart. Yes, I dumb it down. Again, this isn't because people are stupid, it's because **conversational sales copy should sound like... a conversation!** (Imagine that.) Not like the Encyclopedia Britannica or like a scientific research paper.

The truth is, people speak at very different levels than they read at. We probably only use a few hundred words in our daily vernacular. So be consistent with that when you're writing.

3. And lastly, follow this rule: Make simple things complicated, and complicated things, simple.

A Blackberry isn't some complicated technological gadget, it's a simple hand-held global communication device that lets you run your business from any corner of the earth.

Similarly, a picture frame isn't just a picture frame. It's beautiful pressed wood, over 100 years old, imported from Brazil and carefully hand-crafted to store your most precious memories in.

See where I'm going with this?

Your ability to make complicated things simple, minimizes the effort your buyers are going to feel it takes to use your goods and services. And when you make simple things come to life by describing them in detail, they become vivid and tangible.

The more your prospect gets your product or service inside their head, and the more they can visualize themselves using it, the closer you are to a sale.

Now lets cover some more basic ground rules about writing compelling sales copy.

✓ **Be specific. Just like in "real life," being vague and evasive smells bad and makes your prospects question what's going on.**

If you can't answer a question or provide information that's specific and compelling, then your prospects won't feel as confident in what you're offering.

Telling someone "you'll probably improve your foul-shooting percentage a lot," inspires a lot less confidence than saying something like, "Our tests have shown the average backyard hoops player will be sinking at least 41% more free throws within the first three weeks of using this system, alone."

See how different these two statements are? See how the second one makes you feel a lot more confident, and it also gives you some sort of a personal measuring stick to get excited about?

This is the power of specificity.

Now let's talk about why this is really so powerful, even beyond this.

Being specific also gives you more credibility, but most people don't understand why.

See, amateurs think I'm referring to being specific as in saying "98.6%," instead of saying 98%... or by saying something like "Did you know most people spend 95% of their total lifetime health care costs, in the last 5 years of their life?" (Completely true, by the way.)

But I'm not talking about *that* kind of specific. I'm not talking about using decimal points to quantify everything.

I'm talking about **being specific to get your prospects emotionally involved**, by stimulating one or more of their five senses: seeing, hearing, smelling, taste, or feeling.

See, when you can be specific and stimulate your prospects' five senses, that's when you make the emotional connection in your sale, *and* in your relationship. And *this* is what triggers a sale.

For instance, here's something I wrote from a piece I did recently that out-pulled the existing control by over 50% (that's not bad, is it?):

*"Not to mention, the crushing impact things like divorce... disability... job loss... or legal problems, has on your personal finances! How can you **ever** be expected to get ahead when it's so **crazy** out there?"*

In this particular case, I'm hitting the prospect (who is in trouble financially) over the head with one specific crushing blow after another. Can you see how this gets them involved on an emotional "gut" level?

Especially when they're having financial problems?

This taps right into the heart of what they're going through at this very moment.

Not only that, but you're pushing on several emotional buy-buttons here. You're pushing on empathy, vanity, insecurity, fear, and paranoia.

This is what I mean by using specifics. Not saying "98.6%."

Specific numbers won't close your deal. But pushing specific emotional buy-buttons will.

Use this, and you'll profit from it.

- ✓ **Tell stories.** Everyone loves a good story and when you're telling a story, you're not selling something -- you're building rapport. You need to do things that put your prospects into a position where they're naturally lowering their guard. No one's going to trust you if they feel defensive or pushed up against the wall -- in person or in print.

Most people overcomplicate sales, especially in print. Selling is a very simple formula of making sure you're speaking to a qualified prospect in the first place (meaning, a prospect who wants what you have to sell), and then softly and empathetically explaining to them how you can solve their problems.

One of the most effective ways of doing this is through story-telling. Telling your prospect a good story is the easiest way to capture some of their mental shelf-space. And it's also the easiest way to differentiate yourself from your competition, by showing your prospects you're human, just like they are.

Here, check this out and see what I mean:

When Giuseppe Mascali was 14, he started getting sick. If truth be told, he had loads of gas, and an occasional upset stomach.

His mother took him to see the doctor, and as it turns out, the problem was... he had a hard time digesting the all the tomato seeds he was eating. And since he was living in Torino, a town in Northern Italy, he was eating tomato sauce almost nightly. Something needed to be done, quickly!

To overcome this, and to make sure Giuseppe didn't get

287

stomach cramps whenever she made marinara sauce, his mother
started straining the sauce at some point in the cooking
process, to remove all the tomato seeds.

The other thing she had to do, was to boil off and remove
all the oils before serving Giuseppe his dinner. See, she
came to understand, long before all the scientists and the
bigwigs at the FDA... and everyone else who's counting
carbs and watching their weight, that trans-fatty acids,
aren't easy to digest. That they don't break down inside
of you.

How some little Italian lady who presumably wasn't a
chemist, uncovered these things... I have no idea. Perhaps
it's the same way your mother always knew when you were
lying when you were a kid. Who knows, right?

Anyway, when Giuseppe decided to come over to America and
become a chef, he brought these cooking secrets along with
him, so all his meals were not only scrumptious... but
after you finish eating, it doesn't feel like you just
swallowed a pot of lead BB's that suddenly start fusing
together now that they're inside your tummy.

How do I know all this?

The answer is simple.

Over on State Road 41, just north of the railroad tracks
in this sleepy little old citrus grove town I live in, is a
restaurant called Villaggio Ristorante Italiano.

Giuseppe's owned the joint since 1999, and when my family
ate there the other night, he was kind enough to share his
story with us.

Not only that, but before our waiter came over to take
our order, Giuseppe spent some time asking us what kind of
food we liked and he made a few suggestions about some
meals he thought we'd enjoy.

Then, during dinner, Giuseppe came over to check on us a
few times, and he grabbed our glasses and got us drink
refills.

I didn't have any wine or other alcohol to drink that night (although with 3 kids in tow, you'd have thought drinking would be automatic) but if I *was* having some wine, no doubt, Giuseppe also would've made sure to fill my glass with fresh wine, as well.

Now that was a true story I just told you. And I'm not sure if Giuseppe does any marketing for his restaurant -- the parking lot is usually full, so whatever he's doing, it's working.

But if all he did was tell his story in writing, the same simple way I just told it to you... he'd have an absolute killer sales letter!

It's true!

All he'd need to do is fill in a few more personal details, perhaps about where he grew up... what kind of food his mother liked to cook most often... maybe his favorite dish even, and some information about his "business partner," who also happens to be his wife.

This way, you'd know more about Giuseppe, than perhaps any other owner of any other restaurant you've ever eaten in. And when you know (and like, admire, or respect) someone that well, you can't help but want to do business with them.

Sound good?

Great, so... what about you? Are you telling your story in your marketing?

And if not, why not?

See, if you're not telling your story, you're missing a fantastic opportunity to establish trust and rapport with your customers, which of course, lets you sell much more effectively.

Can you now see why simple stories like this are so powerful?

Of course you can!

I'm *sure* there's "something" about you -- or something in your history or your family's history -- that offers some kind of curiosity or some unusual details that are at least as exciting as Giuseppe's story. And this is what you should be talking about with your prospects and customers.

Just figure out what that story is, and then... start telling it!

✓ **Build the relationship through what you have to give, not through what you want to take.** Or, as my good friend Christian Godefroy says, "Always think of what you want to bring into this world, not what you want to get out of it." **Remember, people don't care how much you know, until they know how much you care.**

The world is filled with people who want to sell you something, and the fastest way to separate yourself from all these folks is this: **instead of being a peddler of whatever it is you're selling, like everyone else, be a provider of solutions.**

Be a problem solver.

Figure out what's keeping your prospect up at night, what their deepest and darkest fears are, or what their biggest sources of pain are, and then be the unique provider of the solution that eliminates their pain and suffering, forever.

See, the ugly truth is that in today's crazy world, "service" in the service business is nothing more than a faded memory. Mediocrity has become the new excellent, and doing the bare bones minimum has replaced over-delivering in every business, everywhere.

If you can over-deliver you'll have people who are with you for life.

Here, let me show you a couple of e-mails I recently got copied on. A client had booked a day of consulting with me, and before he finalized his travel plans and hotel, he asked me for a few references.

Both of the references he asked, copied me on their responses to him, and I was absolutely floored at some of the comments:

Here was the question asked: *"Craig Garber gave me your name and email for a reference with regard to a day of consulting with him... Please advise..."*

And here were the responses:

```
"Craig is awesome....I did a day of consulting with him a
while back and it was worth every penny I paid him!

After spending time with Craig it was obvious that my
current business was not getting me where I wanted to
be...he really helped me reinvent a new business.
```

290

Additionally, I wanted to hire him to write copy for my old business and he told me that he wouldn't do it because he didn't see how it was going to improve my current business situation. When any other copywriter would agree, Craig said no because his reputation was on the line!

I have found Craig to be very straight-forward... he is not going to BS you or tell you what you want to hear.

When I left my day of consulting I had 14 pages of notes plus I recorded our conversation. I have referred back to my notes numerous times.

My business partner is currently running the day-to-day operations of my company and I have just finished getting my Real Estate Brokers License in NC and am working with Tiger Woods on a new development in Asheville, NC.

I would be happy to talk to you in person if you like.... my number is ▮▮▮▮▮▮▮▮▮

Sincerely, Brian Deacon (Asheville, North Carolina)

And then there was this one. These folks flew over here to Tampa from Australia, solely to see me for a day of consulting.

"He's awesome. I would thoroughly recommend Craig to anyone. This guy really is THE King of Copy.

But really - apart from copywriting - his other great strength which is just as important, lies in his ability to conceptualize, design and build an automated business system. He's putting that in place for us for our ▮▮▮▮▮▮ business.

So he's not only the best, most natural and intuitive copywriter I've ever seen, but he knows how to make a business run like an automated money-making machine (so long as the value is there in your service or product of course).

He's given us a step-by-step blueprint to build our business. It is based on two-step lead generation providing leads and taking them through an automatic process that will qualify them and even sell them. Only after they have bought will we have to have contact with these people. We're going to engage him to do all the copywriting etcetera for that. He's not cheap but we wanted the best and I don't want to go through any more years of trial and error and guessing games.

The thing I found that put my mind at rest was that he asked us to send him a heap of material so he could research our business before our one-day consult. He said he likes to mull things over a couple of weeks before the meeting. I was relieved that he is the kind of guy who genuinely cares about giving value for money.

I would have been worried if we'd got there and he had to start from scratch with us. But by the time we got there he was thoroughly versed with our business. He'd even read a book on the subject! He basically had our business machine concept laid out and ready for action.

I think what Craig does is half science and half dark art. I think it requires street smarts, empathy, a strong work ethic, an intimate understanding of human nature, and an ounce of genius.

Craig has all of the above in spades. Plus he's a very genuine, lovely guy who will have your best interests at heart.

Oh, and if I were you, I'd be doubly reassured because Craig has experience in the financial industry, which can't hurt.

Cheers, Cameron" (Cameron Outridge - Queensland, Australia)

As you can see, there is "magic" in caring about what you do, and in caring about your clients and customers. **You can't fake sincerity.** If you're prepared to give before you take, you'll be loved and you'll create a huge following of loyal fans, who are willing to support you for a long time to come.

✓ **Always make an offer. <u>Remember, nothing gets bought unless it gets sold first.</u>** This is true even when you're "giving" away free things as lead generation pieces. Even the benefits of the free stuff you're giving away, have to be "sold."

One of the main reasons why most advertising never *sells* anything, is simply because most advertising doesn't *offer* anything.

Think about it, almost every display ad you see, looks just like a big giant business card. People foolishly think that simply by putting a phone number down, it means prospects are going to call.

So you wind up seeing lots of things that look like this:

Fixed Annuities	**212-555-1212**
Divorce, fast and easy	212-555-1212
Florist, 20 years in the same location	**212-555-1212**
New York's newest Mexican food!	212-555-1212

Is there any compelling reason at all, why anyone should respond to this kind of advertising?

No way, José!

Simply put, there's nothing to respond to! When you don't offer anything, you can't expect to sell anything, either!

Let's take a look at some simple offers that could have been made with each of the above ads, instead.

Instead of...

Fixed Annuities, call 212-555-1212

You could say...

FREE 7-Step Retirement "Action Plan!"
Discover How To NEVER Outlive Your Money!

Instead of...

Divorce, fast and easy, 212-555-1212

You could say...

**No prolonged legal hassles or outrageous and long drawn-out legal fees.
Now get divorced in less than 37 days, call for your FREE Report:
"5 Proven Steps To A Painless Divorce Today!"**

Instead of...

Florist, 20 years in the same location, 212-555-1212

You could say...

**FREE ½ Dozen Lovely Mixed Fresh Tulips With
Your First Bouquet Order - Tuesday and Fridays Only
Call 212-555-1212 and ask for Jenna.**

Instead of...

New York's newest Mexican food!, 212-555-1212

You could say...

FREE Margarita And Dessert On Wednesday's From 6 to 10 pm -- come on in!

See the difference here?

Almost no one is *making* an offer. Instead they talk about what they *have* to offer, and even this is done in broad sweeping terms. This is like telling your kids about all the chores that have to get done, instead of telling them all they chores they *need* to do.

Are you with me on this?

Good. So don't forget to make compelling offers, and make them as sweet as you possibly can. Otherwise you've missed an opportunity to help someone, and to make a sale by doing so. And that... is costing you... money!

✓ **Be liberal with your guarantees.** While you can't guarantee someone else's performance, you can guarantee your own. Figure out what you can guarantee and then let your prospects know about it.

The two biggest issues I typically hear about giving money-back guarantees, go something like this:

1. **If I give a money-back guarantee, people will do business with me solely to rip me off.** And...

2. **If I give a money-back guarantee, I'll lose money because I'll get loads of returns.**

Both of these are knee-jerk reactions to the concept of offering risk-free money-back guarantees, and they are both dead wrong. The truth is, you always want to remove the risk from whatever it is you're selling, regardless of who you're selling it to. Here, let me help you overcome each of these objections.

If I give a money-back guarantee, people will do business with me solely to rip me off.

Let's face it, while most people are sincere and honest, there are a few people who are consummate rip-off artists. Unfortunately, this small population of customers tends to stick out in your mind, and the memory of the unpleasant experiences you've had with them, lingers longer than you'd like it to.

Appreciate though, people decide to rip you off long before they get involved with you. The truth is, if someone's sole intention is to rip you off, they're going to do it regardless of whether you have a guarantee or not.

For example, the person who decides he's going to go out and eat a steak dinner tonight, for free... decided to do this at home, while he was getting dressed. Long before he walked into your restaurant, *NOT* while he was already there, sitting down and eating.

(This is somewhat off topic, but this is why you shouldn't be accessible to just anyone, and why you want to pre-qualify your clients as much as possible. Remember, the reason why people steal is because they're lazy. The more effort your buyers have to make to get whatever it is you have to offer, and to get access to you, the *less* likely you're going to get people who have unethical motives.)

See, your guarantees are for the honest people who *do* want to work with you, but who *don't* know you. These folks need reassurance they're not going to get scammed or hoodwinked out of their own time and money. Which is a great segue way into the second objection, which is...

If I give a guarantee, I'll lose money because I'll get loads of returns.

Again, this is incorrect, but let's look at the math on this so you can see why

Let's say your "normal" rate of refunds is 2%. This means for every $1,000 dollars worth of goods and services you sell, you have to issue $20 worth of refunds (2% of $1,000). We can ignore net numbers here, but just in case you're really anal, here's how this looks, assuming you get a 50% markup on whatever it is you're selling.

Cost per unit	$50
Number of units sold	20
Total sales ($50 x 20 units)	**$1,000**
2% Returns (2% of $1,000)	($20)
Gross sales, after refunds	$980
Net Profit (50% of $980)	**$460**

Now let's look at a different scenario. Let's say you now offer a 6-month 100% money-back guarantee. And let's say as a result of this guarantee, your sales triple, but your refunds also triple, because "people are now going to return more of your product since you're offering such a great money-back guarantee."

Let's take a look at the numbers in *this* situation:

Cost per unit	$50
Number of units sold (3 x 20)	60
Total sales	**$3,000**
6% Returns (6% of $3,000)	($180)
Gross sales, after refunds	$2,820
Net Profit (50% of $2,820)	**$1,410**

Additional net profit from a tripling of sales, AND a tripling of your refund rate:

$1,410 - 460 = $950 (206.52% more money!)

As you can see, even if your refund rate triples, **you're still $950 net cash ahead,** because while you did, in fact, get more refunds, **you also got a significant increase in extra sales you *wouldn't* have made without your new guarantee.**

The bottom line here is that you're walking away with 206.52% more money in your pockets ($950 / $460). And that is HUGE by anyone's standards, right?

I have yet to see a client offer a better guarantee and then lose money as a result of it. In fact, I offer very liberal guarantees on all my products because I realize there is a healthy (and deserving) amount of skepticism out there, especially in the marketing and copywriting arena, and especially online. Frankly, some of the products and information being sold out there aren't worth the paper they're written on.

But since my products generally deliver *more* than they promise, I have no problem acknowledging this skepticism and removing the risk from my buyers, and placing it squarely on my shoulders by offering these guarantees.

And this has paid off in spades, because our refund rate is actually much *lower* than industry standards, simply because our products are better, and also because I attract a better than average audience.

So when it comes to offering guarantees, I suggest you do the same thing whenever you can.

Coming up with a 100% risk-free way to give your prospects the downside protection they're looking for (especially new prospects), is one of the most encouraging and accommodating things you can do, to give these new folks incentive to do business with you.

Look, you can have the best marketing in the world, and the greatest sales copy on top of it. But the bottom line is, you are a total stranger to your new prospects. So some of them are always going to feel there is some element of risk or uncertainty about working with you. At least in the beginning, anyway.

Doing as much as you can to eliminate this risk (and eliminating it to zero works best) goes a long way towards you making these extra sales and getting these brand new prospects to buy from you.

Sometimes though, it's not so cut-and-dried what you can guarantee. For example, if you're a lawyer or an accountant, or if you're in the service business, you don't sell products. So what can you guarantee?

Well, one way to figure out what you should guarantee, is to guarantee these things that disturbs the users of your product most. Here are a couple of examples that'll help you out.

If you own a restaurant:

"If you don't think this is the best savory Mexican food you've ever tasted, then your meal's 100% FREE -- no questions asked!"

If you're a lawyer... or an accountant... or a doctor or lawyer, or anyone else notorious for ignoring your clients or patients telephone calls:

"Here's my personal pledge to you: If my office doesn't return your phone call and answer your question within 48 hours from the time you call in, your next visit's on the house! That's right -- if we don't get back to you within 48 hours, your next visit is 100% FREE!

Or instead of a free visit, you can give *"1 full hour of my billing time credited towards your account!"*

Can you see how much this would mean to a new patient or client? Especially if you've been hired to get your client out of a serious business or medical problem they're having?

This builds a ton of credibility and it also lets your customers, clients and patients know how important they are to you.

See, to you this might just be a job, or another case file. But to your client, it's life or death. And until you're able to see things and treat them through their own eyes, you're always going to be struggling on this issue and they'll never be 100% committed to you over your competition.

Reality is, you can guarantee anything if you put your mind to it. I've even written several job application cover letters that gave a guarantee that said: "Hire me and "test-drive" me for two weeks straight, and don't pay me a thing. If during that time you don't feel I've done everything asked of me and more, then keep your salary, hand me my walking papers, and send me on my merry way. The last thing I want to do is take even one thin *dime* from you, I haven't earned.

I realize this is a somewhat bold and daring guarantee, but guess what? I've been working since I'm 14 years old, and I take tremendous pride in what I do and how I do it. And I wouldn't even *dream* of making a guarantee like this, if I wasn't 100% sure I was able to honor it."

One last story about guarantees and how effective you can make them.

My son Nick recently ordered a bottle of bodybuilding supplements which were marketed as a "safe and legal" alternative to steroids.

He's lost a ton of weight recently (almost 60 pounds now), and he's been working out and he's getting in really great shape.

So now, like all muscle heads, he's looking to "get big" -- faster and easier than nature's willing to let him.

I told him he was basically buying a bottle of garbage, and that he'd be better off using that $30 dollars to buy himself a couple of good books on fitness and training. But no different from most new fitness buffs, he thought this might be a short-cut.

Anyway, last night we were checking out the guarantee on the side of the bottle, and let me tell you -- **it's awesome**.

Here it is:

"If you aren't fully satisfied with the results of XXX, then we'll return 100% of your money back, guaranteed."

Notice what they're doing here: They're NOT saying "If you aren't fully satisfied with how you **LOOK** after working out and taking this goop, then we'll return 100% of your money back." They're saying if you aren't fully satisfied **with the results of the pills, themselves**.

Subtle difference, but VERY powerful.

And here's why: see, if you don't see the results of the product itself, it's obviously because **you** didn't do something right in your workouts. And if **you're** not working out hard enough, that's not *their* fault, and you can't hold *them* responsible for this, can you?

Guarantees like this, that shift the responsibility of "performance" from the product to the user, are very effective, especially in the vanity industries, like health and fitness, supplements, and sexual aids or physical enhancement tablets.

Consider these subtleties when you're crafting your own guarantees -- they'll definitely be worth your while. The truth is, it's usually the subtleties of any art, that takes you from good to great, anyway.

O.K. So now that we've gone through some basic strategies of writing sales copy, let's talk about the 12 basic components of a sales letter or advertisement. (Like I said, there are really 17 different components of a sales letter or advertisement. These go way beyond the scope of this Chapter, and I typically cover them in my Ad Writing Workshops. To give you them here would be confusing. However, suffice it to say, this "dirty dozen" will put you well on your way to knowing more than *any* of your competition, for sure.)

1. Headline

Sending someone a sales letter is like crashing a party. You've only got a couple of seconds to let the host know why they should let you in the door, and that's it.

Your sales letter is in the same position as the party-crasher. You have to make a very compelling argument why your prospect should continue reading, or else the sale is lost.

And your headline is what you tell them in those few seconds.

If they like what you have to say, you're in. If not, it's out the door and "next." So spend a lot of time on your headlines. Make them bold and make them count.

Remember, never think to yourself, "I'm writing a sales letter." Instead, think to yourself, "I'm creating a relationship." This completely changes the dynamics of what you're doing and where you're going with all this.

Selling is difficult, but mostly because people are so focused on the selling. If you look throughout time, at the best salespeople, they are very at ease with conversation and establishing rapport. They're calm about what they're saying, and they're extremely methodical and disciplined in their habits, especially their selling habits. **And they are also 100% focused on their customers, not on themselves.** They want to offer sheer customer Nirvana, and they're clued in to what this means, so they can provide it.

'Nuff said, now let's dig in to these headlines.

You want your headline to solve a problem, preferably fast. And preferably, fast and easy.

That doesn't mean to use the words "fast and easy" in every headline you write (although if you look around, apparently many people mistakenly think it does mean that). What it means is that your prospect needs to know you're offering a viable solution to their problem, that can be accomplished sooner than later, and easier than harder.

Make sense?

Also, you want to add curiosity and self-interest into every headline as well. If you can make someone curious about what you have to say, then they're going to want to hear more.

And that, in a nutshell, is the real purpose of your headline: to get your prospects to read the next line, and so on.

Also, if you can somehow inject some sort of a potential for loss in there, if the prospect *doesn't* listen to what you have to say, this is also another winning strategy. Not fear of loss, in general, but a specific consequence of loss.

Here are some headline template examples so you can see what I mean:

(#) Ways, Steps To ___

7 Steps To Becoming A More Loving Husband

5 Ways To Grow Bananas In Your Florida Garden, Without Breaking A Sweat!

How To ___

How To Turn That Dull Old Antique Into Cold Hard Cash, In 30 Days Or Less!

How To Find The Woman Of Your Dreams And
Have Her Fall In Love With You In 45 Days Or Less!

How To Run A 5K Race In Less Than 30 Minutes, Even If You Just *Started* Running!

Problem: Which one of them do you want to overcome?

3 Biggest Mistakes Parents Make Raising Teenagers:
Which one of them do you want to overcome?

5 Costliest Mistakes Real Estate Investors Make:
Which one of them are you making right now?

And here are a few headline strategies that are very effective:

Specifically quantify your claims.

Now Catch 5-Pound Bass All Day Long!

How To Smoke $10 Dollar Cigars For Less Than $4!

How To Make $2,500 Or More As A Publisher... In 30 Days, Guaranteed!

Demonstrate your claims.

At Last! Beefsteak Tomatoes So Big You'll Need Two Hands To Slice Them!

Skin So Soft Your Husband Won't Recognize You.

This Laptop Is So Light You'll Think You Left It Home!

Associate your claim with authority.

What This Medical Doctor Knows About Losing Weight...
Would Shock The Establishment!

Where Do Celebrities Go When They Want Their Teeth Whitened, Here In Tampa?

Want To Know What The Last 5 Mr. Olympia Winners
Ate For Breakfast Every Morning Before Training?

Remember that for all of these examples, you can cut and combine, or add and subtract wherever it makes sense. The most important thing is to provoke curiosity and offer self-interest. If a qualified prospect sees this, they'll be interested.

Curiosity + Self-Interest =

Attention-Getting benefit-oriented headline that puts money in the bank!

2. Opening

If your headline gets you through the front door and *into* the party you just crashed, your opening line determines whether or not you're going to be allowed to stay there.

Your opening line is critical. You want to give someone a very powerful reason why they should consider making this journey that is your sales letter.

It's kind of like your body language. When you meet someone, you typically shake their hand, right? Well, what happens next is... that person is going to consider the kind of image you have and how much energy you're projecting, as their basis for determining how receptive they'll be, to moving forward with you.

Your headline is your handshake, and the opening line of your sales letter is the look you give someone as you're finishing up that handshake. It really is "make or break" time.

You've crashed the party and they've let you through the doors. Now, will they let you stay, or... will they throw you out?

There are loads of different ways to open a sales letter, but let's go over a few of them here:

Tell a story. We talked earlier about how stories are so easily remembered. And most stories are so compelling, it's hard to walk away from them. Here's an example of how you can use a story as an opener:

"6 months ago, I found myself flat on my back, laying out in the middle of the parking lot, with the rain pouring down on me. I had no idea how I got there, but even worse... I had no idea where my wallet and car keys were, either."

Few people will leave a good story right in the middle, so a shocking opening like this is very effective. Notice all the details that bring this story to life and make it real -- they're important.

Engage your prospect's imagination. The more you challenge your prospect in such a way that they get involved with your message, the more vested they become in what it is you have to say, and in who you are.

Here are a couple of ways of engaging your prospect's imagination, right from the get-go:

"Picture this. It's 4 am and you're fast asleep. Suddenly you awake, terrified and in a cold sweat. Your heart is pumping so hard and so loudly, you can't even understand how you're still alive.

Turns out, you weren't."

That's pretty engaging, isn't it?

Or something like this would also work well:

"Remember the first time you licked a frozen chocolate ice cream cone?"

Another good way to get someone's attention is to be dramatic. Here's what I mean:

"When the doctor told me I had cancer, I knew at once, my life had changed."

Or this...

"Five years ago, I was drowning in debt and six months behind on my mortgage. Last month, I paid cash for a new BMW, and by the end of this year, the mortgage on my $500,000 home will be fully paid off. Here's what happened:"

Again, the simplest way to know if your opening line makes sense is to **read it out loud**. When you do this, ask yourself, "Does this make sense?"

Also ask yourself, "If I heard someone say this, would I want to hear more?"

And if it sounds like an engaging way to start a conversation with someone you just met when you're reading it out loud, then stick with it.

If it doesn't sound good, then re-work it until it does. You can also see many different examples of great opening lines by reading almost any of my daily e-mails (if you haven't already subscribed to them, you can do so at kingofcopy.com). Or, you can check out how I start off each one of my own product or service sales letters at kingofcopy.com/products.

3. <u>**Discussion/Transition/Empathy**</u>

In this section, you're going to begin shifting from your introduction, and from your "this is why you need to listen to me" opening, to the heart of what's really going on here.

Your transition should be tied directly to your opening, and it should be a logical and conversational progression of what a well-adjusted, normally socialized person would do or say next.

Now appreciate that I highlighted that last statement in bold because many people are

304

simply very uncomfortable selling, and some people are just plain shy, socially.

If this is you, then don't freak out. Just be smart enough to know what you don't know and find out how other people in this situation act.

Read books like Dale Carnegie's *How To Win Friends And Influence People*, or anything you can get your hands on by Elmer Wheeler, John Caples and Claude C. Hopkins.

Watch videos about selling, and about how to meet new friends, and learn as much as you can about relationship dynamics. Understand the difference between what is and what isn't acceptable social conversation and behavior.

Now if you're like me, and you can pretty much can say almost anything at any time and get away with it, appreciate that this is fine in social settings. But when it comes to money, **people are dead serious about spending it!** What someone would laugh at in a bar after meeting you for five minutes, is *NOT* the best thing to say to them in a sales letter.

Because in a sales letter you're what...?

You're trying to create a relationship, that's right. I'm just trying to see if you're still paying attention here. Now let's get back to business.

You'll notice I call this section discussion/transition/empathy.

That's because you can lead with either of these depending on your story, what you're trying to do with it, or where you're trying to go, in general.

Regardless of what you're doing, though, **you must start building empathy** right here.

Empathy is the conduit into your prospect's heart and soul, that takes you directly into that little credit card that's tucked snugly away inside their wallet.

If they don't think you're empathetic and understanding about who they are and what's bothering them, then you're done, period.

There is NO exception to this rule.

Again, think back to someone you've met in person. If you felt threatened or bullied by them, or if you felt they had some sort of an agenda that has more to do with what they can get out of you than anything else... you're automatically on high alert, right?

Your prospects are no different, and if they're on high alert and defensive, they're not open to *any* suggestions you're going to make. In all likelihood, they won't even finish reading your sales letter and they won't want to continue listening to you.

Don't lose sight of this important step. Creating empathy is the most important emotional hook you can set in a prospect.

4. Credibility

This is where you want to start establishing who you are. You want to let your prospect know why they should be listening to you in the first place.

But let me clarify what I mean here. You want them to understand why they should be listening to you about **this particular topic**, not "in general" why they should listen to you because you're such a great person.

So if you were a champion swimmer in high school, and you're selling home water filtration systems, don't spend a whole hell of a lot of time talking about how grueling your swimming practices were. No one cares how you really needed to be disciplined to get up at 4:30 am every morning when you were 16 years old, while all your friends were still sleeping.

That isn't relevant to your story, so don't waste their time.

Talk about what gives you credibility to be discussing water filtration systems. Is it the fact that you're a local homeowner who was simply sick and tired of drinking water that tasted like it just came from the muck underneath someone's shoes? Did your kids get sick and no one was able to figure out why until you changed your filtration system?

What is the reason?

Hint: It can't be "Because I sell this stuff and I want to make money selling one to you."

In other words, make your story relevant to what you're offering, and relevant to the credibility you're seeking to establish and to the benefits you're offering your prospects.

See, this is often why you aren't the best person to even be writing your sales letter.

Many times, for this particular reason alone -- credibility -- the letter should be written in someone else's voice other than yours.

Often, a third party voice is the best voice to use in a sales letter. Maybe the letter can be from someone who uses your products or maybe it can be from your wife, or your business partner, or a doctor or a customer... whoever.

The point is, you need to think good and hard about credibility when it comes to who's talking, and how your sales pitch is actually going to be made. If you're not credible, then you're not going to inspire confidence. And as I said earlier, if you can't inspire confidence, then you can't inspire trust, and no one's going to buy.

Which is precisely why, today... you simply can not rest your credibility on the fact that you've been doing "whatever," for "X" number of years.

The cold hard truth is that by this point in time in our lives, we've all been exposed to so many idiots that have been doing whatever it is they do, for so long, in *spite* of their sheer incompetency, that length of service is today, irrelevant. Far too many people don't have 15 or 20 years of experience -- they simply have one year of experience, fifteen or twenty times.

Plus, there are just so many charlatans out there ready to make any kind of claim they need, just to make a fast buck, you really need to be credible for a specific reason other than "length of service."

QUALITY of your service is paramount, and this is what you want to articulate.

5. Introduction to your product or service

In this section, you start to segue way into whatever it is you're offering.

The typical way of doing this is that you've got a solution to all the problems and mishaps you've just been discussing and being empathetic about.

I like putting things into packages or making up proprietary names or systems for what I'm selling, to bullet-proof or insulate myself from the competition.

I did this with the Loan Officers in the ARMs Marketing System (you can see this at loturnaround.com/arms) and frankly, I try and do this with nearly everything I market. I've given you several examples of this, throughout this manual.

I use these proprietary names or systems as a way to be different, so this way, price has absolutely nothing to do with what I'm selling, because now I'm the only one offering this kind of a process. When you're unique, you can pretty much set your own price.

This is why good proprietary processes are like little winning lottery tickets that pay off forever.

Another problem I typically see in sales letters, is that people go on too long before introducing whatever solution to whatever problems they've been talking about. Or, alternatively, they start selling too early, before any kind of empathy and rapport has been established.

It's important to strike a reasonable balance between selling and establishing rapport, which is why you want to follow my formula and do these things systematically.

6. Bullets / Benefits

In this next section of your sales letter, you list as many benefits of the goods or services you're selling, as bullets.

There are three typical questions I get about this topic, so let's go over them. One, **"How many bullets should I include?"**

And the answer is, "As many as you possibly can, as long as each one of them is compelling." See, the thing with bullets is that you never know which particular one is going to be the trigger that causes someone to buy.

The other two issues that are problems, besides not including enough bullets, are **not creating enough curiosity in your bullets**, and **making them too short**.

So for example, to create curiosity, you want to keep your bullets what's called "blind." Meaning, you don't describe what you're selling outright. Instead, you provoke an intense amount of curiosity about what you're selling by describing features and specific benefits without revealing their exact meaning.

Let me give you a couple of examples of what I mean, from my sales letter on Lead Generation Explosion. Which I'm going to change the name of. It's far too sensationalized and doesn't really describe the product. In reality, something like "The ABC's Of Two-Step Lead Generation" would be far more accurate.

In any case, you can see the entire letter and all these bullets at kingofcopy.com/leads. Here are those bullets:

- **How to make commonplace products, very UN-common!** This makes you stand out amongst your competition and de-commoditizes your products, which is essential if you ever want to get away from the "whose product is cheapest" issue!

- **An incredibly simple technique that rapidly escalates your sales cycle!** But you've got to have an iron stomach and the ability to say "No" if you want to make this one happen.

See how the overriding emotion here, especially in the first sentence of each bullet, is curiosity? How *do* you make commonplace products, uncommon? Everyone wants to know that one, right?

And how on earth can you rapidly speed up your sales cycle?

See what I mean?

What you want to do is use a one-two punch in your bullets. The first sentence delivers a curiosity provoking benefit, and the following sentence reinforces this by delivering an even stronger and more specific benefit.

Make sense?

Good. So let me just show you a couple more examples of the final issue people typically have, which is... making the bullets too short. Here are some bullets I wrote in a sales letter that did very well in the men's dating marketplace:

- **The ONE picture you MUST MAKE SURE you include on your profile!** This one's so simple to do, and yet almost NO one does it!

- **How to describe yourself if you have a crappy job, without looking like a dolt, and without turning a woman off!** *And...* how to be 100% honest about this, even if you're embarrassed about what you do for a living!

Again, these are long bullets. But do you see how the second part of each bullet sort of "amplifies" the initial curiosity created in the first sentence? This "one-two punch" makes these bullets much more affective than just using either of these two sentences alone.

These combinations make your prospects even more curious, and the second sentence also serves to validate your initial statement. It's very important you use these two steps, even though it makes a little more work for you.

The good news is, like most things, you really do get out of this, what you put into it.

You don't need to do this on every bullet, but if I look through any given sales letter I've ever written, I can probably count on one hand, the number of bullets that aren't curiosity based, and that don't have the "one-two" combo punch packed into them.

7. <u>Guarantees</u>

We've already spent loads of time on guarantees earlier in this Chapter (pages 294 - 299), so you're well-prepared to handle this one.

8. <u>Who it's for / Who it's NOT for</u>

Why is this section important?

There are three reasons. **One, you don't want to sell the wrong things to the wrong people.** This becomes even more important if you're selling something that has the potential of having a high refund rate, like a business opportunity product, a stock-trading system, or some other kind of a money-making venture. (Not that a high refund rate alone is bad, sometimes your numbers work well even with high refund rates.)

Two, often you want to let your buyer re-validate their decision to buy. And asking them a series of questions, or offering a series of qualifying "Who this is for / who this isn't for" statements, accomplishes this. This re-affirmation also serves as a stick strategy for those folks who are uncertain about their decision, or who are on the edge of the fence about buying (as does your guarantee).

And three, you may want to take this opportunity **to further position yourself as an authority figure and remind your buyer how lucky they are to be dealing with you**, and how lucky they are you're willing to take their money.

Funny story here. When I ran our training seminar for the LOTurnaround.com ARMs System Buyers, one of the attendees made a comment to us that "I couldn't believe you guys had the balls to make me apply to give you money. I figured if you could be this good with me, you just had to be able to teach me something about how to do this with my prospects."

Positioning like this often comes from your "who it's for/not for" section of your sales letter.

And just so you know, this usually isn't a very big section of your sales letter or ad. It's almost more like a pre-close you use, to transition between the rest of the letter and the actual close.

You usually want to put these qualifying questions either in the form of bullets... actual questions or a quiz... or brief statements. And you want to be dogmatic-like in your qualifiers, not wishy-washy. Otherwise they're not qualifiers, they're "maybes."

Another sneaky thing I've done, just to really make sure the person ordering is a qualified buyer, is to list these qualifications or requirements again, somewhere on the order form -- usually on the back or near the guarantee. I'll typically do this when I have the qualifications in the form of a quiz or a Q & A, but there's no hard and fast rules about this.

At the same time, depending on what you're selling, you may not even necessarily need this section. So for example, I'm a lot more inclined to use this section when I'm selling a service or when I'm selling something high-priced or something that's at a Stage 4 Psychology of the Marketplace (from Eugene Schwartz' *Breakthrough Advertising*).

Meaning, the marketplace has seen many similar messages like this, so I'll use this section to further qualify and differentiate this particular product or service from the rest of the marketplace.

9. What it is / What it's NOT

Very similar to the last section, sometimes I'll use this instead, when I want to focus on the uniqueness of the goods and services being sold, and not on the buyer.

There are rare occasions when I might actually use both of these sections, but you run the risk of being too verbose, and setting up too many parameters for buyers to fit into, too many perceived hoops for them to jump through to give you money.

This is a judgment call you need to make, based on experience and based on how your sales copy ultimately reads. You always want to be as congruent with what you're trying to accomplish, as possible.

10. Eliminate competition (maybe)

You'll notice it says "maybe" after this sub-headline. That's because if your marketing is good, you rarely have to disqualify or even *mention* your competition.

I once asked Gary Halbert how to handle competition in your copy. His response, which I've lived by and profited from, ever since, was "If your copy is good enough, then competition really isn't an issue."

As I've mentioned several times now, I've taken this one step further by bullet-proofing myself and my marketing in nearly every promotion I've worked on, by creating proprietary processes that make whatever I'm selling, unique unto itself.

Let me give you an example of a very well-known proprietary process. One of the most well-known proprietary "systems" or ways of doing something, that made this particular product unique, was Charles Atlas' "Dynamic Tension" method.

Because this is trademarked, no one else can use this method and no one else can therefore profit from it. (In my Seductive Selling System, I actually go over one of these old Charles Atlas ads on one of the DVDs inside the system.)

And in fact, did you know that before "Dynamic Tension" existed, Atlas' business was going bust?

It's true!

Then, he met up and partnered with New York City copywriter Charles P. Roman, and boy-oh-boy did things change. Once Roman changed the name of the course to "Dynamic Tension," their business went through the roof!

If your copy is solid... and your offer is solid... and you've created a relationship with your prospect... then there *is* no competition, any more than there's no "competition" for another spouse in a good marital relationship, even though there are obviously other eligible candidates out there.

Make sense?

Much of what I've learned about creating proprietary marketing systems, comes from Eugene Schwartz's incredible book called *Breakthrough Advertising*. Specifically, you want to investigate Chapter 3, The Sophistication Of Your Market.

This is *not* an easy book to read, and should not be read by newbies or people who haven't written much in the way of sales copy, as it will confuse you. But for those of you who've been around the block, so to speak, you'll get more out of this one book, than perhaps any other marketing book you'll ever read. It's certainly one of my "Desert Island" books, for sure.

11. Closing

For many people, the hardest part of a sales letter to write, is your close. This is where all your efforts culminate and you either get the money, or you don't.

The problem for most people is how to actually ask for the money. Keep in mind though, if you've followed my formula, the transition to closing is as natural as letting the door shut behind you, after you've opened it and walked into a room.

Maybe this will help you. Most people find closing difficult, perhaps because instead of thinking about all the added value you're giving your buyers, you're instead feeling "awkward" about getting money from them. Maybe even in some extreme cases, you feel "undeserving" about it.

You're wrong for feeling this way.

Appreciate that when someone comes to you, ultimately... they're looking for help! They want *something*, otherwise they wouldn't have come around in the first place, right?

And they typically want something that eases their pain or makes their life better, right now -- otherwise they certainly wouldn't have read through your sales letter, either.

Right?

So when you're closing, just like when you're making your offer, focus on what you're giving your prospects, instead of what you're taking from them, and I bet the closing process will be easier for you.

Here are a few more things to consider:

1. **If you're still having trouble closing** because you're uncomfortable asking for money, or because you feel undeserving, or perhaps you don't want to feel like you're "taking" something from someone else... there are a few harsh realities you're going to have to face, like it or not.

First, if you don't fix this problem, you're going to be miserable and continue struggling all your life. I know this may be hard to swallow, but it's a fact. The more you close, the more money you're going to make and the more opportunities you and your buyer are going to have, to live a more vibrant and fulfilling life.

The more choices you'll have and the more control you'll have over your destiny.

Close your eyes, and picture for just a moment, how much more rewarding your life would be, if you were closing more deals, signing up more customers, and getting more business.

Pretty good, I bet!

The truth is, life has a lot less headaches, anxiety and pressure, when you're waking around with a pocket full of cash. The only people who say "Money doesn't solve any problems," are broke.

They're dead wrong. Money solves LOTS of problems.

So the first thing you're going to have to do to fix this situation, is to believe you deserve, and want, with a burning desire... the end result.

And by the way, your performance and your ability to serve your clients increases dramatically once you're making more money. Because when you're not always strapped for cash, you can focus on what you're putting out, instead of what you so desperately need.

2. Second, maybe part of the problem is you're not getting the right people in front of you in the first place.

Having an eager and pre-qualified prospect who *wants* your service, as opposed to having a prospect you "convinced" *needs* your service, makes closing a lot easier, and takes loads of pressure off you, right from the beginning.

When prospects come to you, as opposed to you chasing them down, it makes "closing" at lot less stressful, because now you're helping your prospect get what *they* want, not what you want them to want.

**I prefer being a hard opener and a soft closer,
much better than the other way around.**

When you make your prospects jump through a few hoops to get to you, or you make them qualify themselves somehow, up front, they are much more enthusiastic about working with you. You simply don't need a "hard close" in this situation.

3. Lastly, the other thing you can do, and this is HUGE when it comes to selling, is to start "positioning" yourself at the top of the mountain, instead of being the "open door" for everyone.

Only the Statue Of Liberty wants "your tired, your hungry and your poor."

You, on the other hand, should want, "the wealthy, the well-fed, and the energetic" -- at least as customers and clients, anyway.

Your job, as an entrepreneur, is to provide goods and services for a fee. You are not a 501(c)3 not-for-profit agency. The goal of any business is to make as *much* money as possible for the owners of the business, by delivering quality services to your customers and clients. Not to help every poor S.O.B who wants your help.

We talked about positioning before, conceptually. And from an implementation standpoint, the easiest way of positioning yourself is to use a two-step lead generation system.

When you position yourself so your customers have to jump through a few hoops, or in some way have to "qualify" to work with you by going through your lead-generation process, guess what happens?

You suddenly become the hot item everybody wants. **Human psychology simply dictates that what isn't easily obtainable, is always worth more.**

Got it?

In any case, please don't underestimate the value and importance of being able to close and to position yourself correctly. It is absolutely critical to your success.

12. P.S.

Your P.S. is your "goodbye handshake." It's your last chance to grab the reader by the lapels and get them to take action.

And for many of your prospects, who are not detailed readers but who instead just skim through your material, your P.S. is that much more important, because it is one of the few things these folks are almost guaranteed to read.

First, some rules about the P.S. There is really no limit to how many P.S.'s you can have, but once you get past more than two or three, your letter starts becoming overly salesy. Imagine, you're ready to walk out of a store, or ready to make your "final consideration" about whether or not you're going to buy. Your sales person shakes your hand and leaves you with one final benefit or buying consideration to think about.

That's not a problem, and if your salesperson is sharp, it's actually something you'll welcome, right?

But imagine, instead of this, your sales person keeps coming out after you, with one sales pitch after another. In this case, each individual zinger he leaves you with, actually has less and less value, because his total presentation has now been watered down and diluted.

Not to mention, if you took the time and effort to position yourself strongly, and you then use umpteen P.S.'s, you wind up destroying that positioning, by "chasing" your prospect down. You wind up looking needy and desperate, which is obviously not good.

Now in certain situations when you already have a rapport with your customers or with your list, you may be able to get away with more P.S.'s in your sales letter, but I'd still advise against it.

If you do use multiple P.S.'s, label them as follows: P.S., P.P.S., P.P.P.S. Since, P.S. actually stands for "post script," you can see why I use this labeling. And you can also see why, after a while, this gets kind of silly looking.

(If you have to make numerous P.S.'s, try combining them, so maybe one of your P.S.'s is longer or more wordy than the others.)

I also always put my P.S. in a different font than the body of my main letter, and I also put at least the first sentence of my P.S. in bold, to draw attention to it.

And what kind of things should you put in your P.S.?

Well, you have a wide variety of choices, and I'm going to show you a few of them by showing you a nice selection of P.S.'s I've written over the years. Here goes:

"P.S. Several mothers have called in asking if they could bring their children with them, and the answer is "Yes!" ▆ has hired a team of licensed and bonded babysitters to look after your children on site, while parents attend this revealing workshop."

Adding an extra benefit as your P.S. is very effective. Let me show you another example of this:

P.S. Don't forget, your investment in MCR is 100% tax-deductible, which gives you a savings of at <u>least</u> $69 dollars, if not more.

Here too, you can see the mention of another added benefit. This benefit may or may not have been mentioned before. Reinforcing something you already said is fine, as long as it's an important benefit or buying consideration (like a guarantee perhaps).

The following three P.S.'s come from a marketing system that Chet Rowland sells to Pest Control Operators. To make this easy, I'll break each one down immediately after it's stated.

P.S. Picture this: In just a few short months, I'm GUARANTEEING you'll have fresh new customers and referrals coming to you "automatically!" What will you do with all this new money you suddenly come into? How will your life CHANGE with all this newfound extra cash?

On the other hand, if you choose not to order... and ultimately, not to better *your* life, and the lives of your family -- you will simply be another statistic. You will end up looking back on this very moment, a few years down the line, as simply another "woulda... coulda... shoulda" decision you messed up.

Which position are you going to be in? The choice is yours.

As you can see, there is a lot going on here. I'm re-stating one of the many guarantees this system offers... I'm future-pacing two of the financial benefits derived from this system (having more money and living a better lifestyle). And I'm leaving the reader with a pound of regret to chew on, if they decide not to order.

P.P.S. One more thing, and it's important: Please understand, this is a private and very personal invitation. If you don't take advantage of this opportunity, you may never hear from me again -- period. So listen, and listen good:

Think long and hard about what you'll be missing out on, and what you and your family will be losing, and what you WON'T be having (that you deserve), if you pass this opportunity up!

The world is a very complicated place nowadays, but one thing's for sure:

Whether you order or not, The PCO Millionaire's Club will continue to grow and prosper. And its members, some of whom are definitely your fiercest and closest direct competitors, right now... will also continue to grow and prosper.

But if you don't order, you will never know *any* of these things, or hear about *any* of these people. That is... until they slowly start picking each-and-every-one of your accounts, clean off your books. **And by then, it will be too late and there won't be anything I, or anybody else can do for you, outside of buying whatever few accounts you may have left, for a few pennies on the dollar.**

And If You Think This Won't Happen, You Are Very... Sorely... Mistaken!

Please appreciate this is *not* hype! It is just the cold harsh reality of the consequences of you not taking action... NOW!

Here I'm using scarcity (you may never hear from me again), the responsibility to take care of your family (regret), and positioning. Also, by saying, effectively, "I'll continue making money with you or without you," I'm automatically telling them "You need me a lot more than I need you!"

Lastly, I'm future-pacing them on what's going to happen if their fiercest competitor orders, instead of them. And since this was a territorial exclusive package, this is actually a real fear, not an imagined one!

 P.P.P.S. If you think this is some kind of a gimmick, or you have any questions, then CALL ME ON MY CELL PHONE right now, and I'll give you all the reassurances you need: ■-■-■.

I know this is unheard of, and that no one ever makes such bold and daring **GUARANTEES**, and then has the "guts" to speak to you in person, but then again... I have nothing to hide! Especially since **this is the most important business-building experience you will ever encounter!**

I don't think I'd ever offer someone the opportunity to call me on my cell phone, but my client was hungry to ramp up his project and he wanted to make this offer to see how people were reacting to everything.

The problem with doing this is most of the people calling you don't believe what you're offering in the first place, and they're calling you so you can "convince" them to buy. (This is exactly what happened, by the way.)

And as you know, the "convincing business" sucks, and it's not a very profitable business, either. But this was a new venture and since hearing from customers directly gives you loads of data to work with, some folks will consider doing things like this.

Here are some more P.S.'s I wrote for a full-page dating ad placed in a local newspaper:

P.S. If you're leery about responding to a personal ad, I can't blame you -- after all, there are a lot of nuts out there. But rest assured, if I was one of them, I wouldn't be drawing attention to myself by running this huge ad in my local newspaper.

P.P.S. Maybe we'll hit it off, and maybe we won't -- no one knows for sure.

But one thing I do know for sure, is this: if you've got what it takes to shoot for the moon every once in a while, then responding to this ad may just be the most thrilling ride... of your entire life!

Thank you for reading this very sincere message.

Here, the first P.S. is used to overcome objections, and the second one resolves any doubt about having an optimistic future. This gives the prospective date additional permission to respond to the ad.

Giving your buyers hope and optimism that tomorrow is going to be better because of whatever you have to offer, is incredibly important, regardless of what you're selling.

In a harbinger of things to come, I wrote this a little over two years before the real estate bubble did in fact, come crashing and burning down, bringing the entire rest of the economy down with it. This P.S. uses fear to get people to take action. More specifically, fear of loss, tapping away at what every real estate investor fears most.

P.S. Remember, the Real Estate bubble we've been experiencing over the last few years, is definitely NOT going to last forever.

And reality is, just as sure as the sun rises in the east and sets in the west, this market WILL come crashing down on you one day.

And then what?

Because once it's over, you're going to need every single nickel you can get your hands on, just to survive. And not losing whatever extra money you have, to the tax man... may be the ONLY thing that winds up saving you!

This next one is a soft sell P.S. that makes the person real -- something every retailer in America ought to do more often. We live in a nameless faceless world, and this is nowhere more apparent than when someone tries selling you something. Being a real person is sometimes all you need to do, to connect.

P.S. When you come in, please stop by and say hello. I'm the handsome looking devil up front in the ███ ██ short-sleeved shirt. I'll look forward to meeting you!

Here, I overcame objections about being insured and licensed, since so few tree-trimmers out there actually have these qualifications. And I also used this as an opportunity to showcase his "better than risk-free" guarantee, dramatically setting him apart from his competitors.

P.S. ██████, who is fully licensed and insured, also offers the STRONGEST GUARANTEE in the tree-trimming industry: "If you're not happy -- you don't pay. In fact, if you're not happy, he'll actually pay you $50 dollars, just for trying him out."

In this P.S., I offer social proof in the form of an actual check:

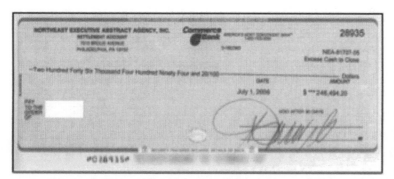

P.S. This year alone, using the techniques I've learned from ███, I produced over $737,241 dollars worth of real estate income. This check, for $246,494.20, is only ONE example of what I'm talking about. This is NOT magic. I am NOT pulling rabbits out of hats here, and there is certainly nothing illegal, unethical, or unique, about what I do. In fact, what I do is quite ordinary, and here's why: You see, successful people know the fastest way to "get the money," *isn't* by coming up with some kind of new whiz-bang way of doing things.

The FASTEST (and smartest) way to get the money, is to find a formula that works, and then use it over-and-over again. That's it.

I'm simply taking ██████'s formulas, and using them. And as you can see, this "find a formula that works and use it" idea, is quite effective, isn't it?

This is from an ad for a local dock builder. We used the P.S. two-fold. One, as a takeaway, implying scarcity. And two, to get people to pick up the phone immediately, so Kevin could determine whether or not this was a job large enough to warrant his time, or whether it was just someone shopping around or someone who was looking to do some minor repairs, which he wasn't interested in doing.

P.S. Oh, one more thing, and this is important. Because Kevin is *extremely* busy, especially this time of the year, he simply does NOT have the time to work with everyone. But don't worry, Kevin respects your time, so to make this process faster, he will ask you a few simple questions on the phone when you call, just to see if you qualify. And then... he'll let you know right there and then whether or not you're "in." **So call ██-██-██, right now!**

The next P.S. served two purposes. First, to restate the common enemy (banks and uncaring nameless faceless "suits and ties") and dredge up some more emotional venom against them. And second, to restate the uniqueness of the proprietary system I created for this project, which is only available through this offer.

P.S. Listen, please don't think of this as simply "a way out." Because frankly, it is your ONLY way out -- at least, it's your only way out if you want to control your outcome, and not leave it up to a bunch of suits sitting around a table who could care less about you and your family.

Make no mistake, the bank's *only* concerns are lining their pockets with your hard-earned cash... your home... your sweat and blood, whatever. Frankly, as long as it has a value they can measure on their balance sheet, it's *all* fair game.

Getting a FREE *(proprietary trade name consultation)* is the fastest gateway to a fresh start -- to whatever lifestyle you'd like to start living once this is over.

What I'll reveal in your *(proprietary trade name consultation)* isn't being discussed anywhere, by anyone, simply because the establishment and the big corporate fat-cats have done a darn good job of making sure these secrets *aren't* very accessible.

And lastly, here's one final set:

This first P.S. re-validates the overwhelming evidence why they need to be moving forward with this offer. And the second P.S. restates the guarantee and the no-risk proposition being put forth.

P.S. Remember, George Daniels invested 5 minutes of his time and he wound up saving $44,460 dollars. If you do the math on this, that comes out to... $533,520 dollars an hour!

That may be more money than anyone else will ever give you the opportunity to make. Plus, how much extra money are you flushing down the toilet if you don't take 5 minutes and fill in your Personal Price Quote Comparison Form? Without this, you are probably throwing away several thousand dollars a year, right now as we're speaking -- for nothing!

PPS. And with your $100 "Ben Franklin" GUARANTEE... what is there to lose?

As you can see, you can use a P.S. for any number of reasons, but don't waste this space. It's almost guaranteed to be looked at by everyone who receives your material (who's a qualified buyer).

The most effective P.S.'s are the ones that leave your prospects with an emotional dilemma or some sort of emotional discomfort they have to deal with, if they don't take action.

In my daily e-mails, however, I use the P.S. as the place to make my offers. Here's why: I always believe in giving before taking. The reason people tolerate hearing from me daily, is that I **constantly** give away good information first, *before* asking my prospects to buy something from me.

O.K., so there you have it -- my mini-lesson on writing long-form sales copy. Copywriting isn't something you're going to master overnight. It's like mastering foul shots in basketball. You can read as much as you want on the topic, but there's only one single way to become a better free-throw shooter, and there's only one way to become a better copywriter.

You do this the same way you get to Carnegie Hall (where I actually played, back in 1976): you practice, practice, practice.

Money-Making Action Steps Checklist

☐ **This Chapter's a whole book in and of itself.** Your action steps here are to study this material, over and over again, and put ALL of it to good use. Maybe not all at the same time, but implement bits and pieces as you see fit, and measure your results. This stuff isn't easy, but there again, making almost $600,000 with less than 5,000 names, isn't supposed to be, now is it?

Chapter References

- For more information about how to write compelling headlines, along with hundreds of fill-in-the-blank templates, formulas and "live" examples, check out *The Official Headlines Manual* at kingofcopy.com/headlines.

- If you want to know more detailed and specific information about how to write long-form sales letters or "Free Reports" as they are called in a two-step lead generation system, I have two detailed coaching calls on this specific subject available.

  They are included inside my Lead Generation Explosion system at kingofcopy.com/leads, and they break this process down into very detailed steps, to the point where I'm even explaining how I lay things out on the floor of my office, to organize them into the various components of your sales letter.

- To learn much more about how to be empathetic with your buyers and how to push your prospect's emotional buy-buttons, check out my Seductive Selling System at kingofcopy.com/seductive. This is the only program that covers emotional buying - which is the most important aspect of selling -- from soup to nuts.

- I have an entire program available about how to write attention-getting opening lines that suck you in, at kingofcopy.com/seductivecalls - it is the November 2006 call, and may or may not still be available at this point.

- For information about consulting, including audio and video testimonials on what you can expect, simply go to kingofcopy.com/consulting and kingofcopy.com/consultingday.

- If you want to learn about the earliest instances of how a proprietary system launched a product, get *Scientific Advertising* by Claude C. Hopkins. I've re-published this book and in this version, I've included a famous ad Hopkins wrote, and I show you exactly how to create these proprietary processes -- even if you're not necessarily doing *anything* at all that's unique! Check it out at kingofcopy.com/hopkins.

- I am constantly discussing proprietary marketing systems, and showing you how to create and apply this principle to your business and to your marketing in my Seductive Selling Newsletter. So if you're not already a member, I encourage you to take the free 30-day test-drive of the newsletter and Audio Success CD, right now. You get 18 free gifts (REAL usable gifts -- just watch the video on the web page) just for taking this test-drive, so check it out now at kingofcopy.com/ssnl.

- One of the best ways of getting feedback on your sales copy or marketing pieces is to take advantage of the many FREE critiques I offer with nearly all of my products. I encourage you to submit these and benefit from them. From time to time I will also re-write a piece sent in, and use it as an example in my Seductive Selling Newsletter.

Bonus Strategy # 24

How To Get Other People To Bring You Business

Listen, this is the first and only piece of advice I'm giving you, I didn't use myself. I didn't practice what I'm preaching on this one, but if I'm honest, I should have. And I am actively working on implementing this strategy, right now.

In fact, had I spent time doing this, I'd have made MUCH more money, much quicker.

Here's the deal, and a frank admission of a glaring weakness of mine. I happen to be one stubborn son-of-a-gun. I'm also a "bootstrapper."

Meaning, I'm the kind of guy who's always picked himself up by his boot straps, and gone out and done mostly everything by myself.

This is a blessing. But... it's also a curse. The blessing is that you're independent, but the curse is, because you're so self-reliant and (at least in my case) intuitively unwilling to accept help, you're limited in how much money you're going to be able to make. See, there are loads of people all over the world who have mailing lists of customers and prospects -- both online and offline -- that are looking for good quality products to promote.

Smart people (who aren't so thick-headed and stubborn, like me) will approach these people and look to form joint venture relationships to see if it makes sense to promote one another's products.

I've been reluctant to do this for a few reasons. Candidly, a few people approached me to form joint venture relationships and to promote their products, early on. However, most of them seemed more interested in doing a hit and run on me and my customers, than in delivering a quality service or product to my customers and clients.

I guess what I'm saying is that there was no concern over what was *being* sold, just that it *got* sold. Since you now know me a little bit, you can see how that's 180 degrees opposite to how I think and what I do.

I'm very selective about who's stuff I promote because if I'm promoting it, it needs to be a *quality product*. But that doesn't mean there aren't loads of good people out there to do joint venture promotions with.

I'm currently in the process of setting up a systematic way of finding and qualifying quality joint venture partners to work with, who are willing to promote my products. And if it makes sense, I'll promote their products as well.

In fact, if you are interested in promoting this book, or any of my products to your list, I now have an affiliate program in place, as well as a step-by-step way of contacting my office so you can do this.

All you need to do is go to kingofcopy.com/affiliate and follow the directions there. Once we receive your information, my assistant will contact you with further information about how to proceed.

My point here is that no man is an island, no matter how strong or talented he or she may be. Everyone needs help and support, and not only is there nothing wrong with getting it, it's actually silly not to seek out joint venture partners to work with.

This grows your list (and your bank account) even faster.

Why Men Crack

I mentioned this earlier, but it's worth mentioning again. After years of toiling away and going nowhere, in early 2000, at the very beginning of my direct-marketing journey, I was listening to a cassette tape of a recorded coaching call of a program I was participating in at the time. On the call, the speaker said, "Once you learn how to be a clever marketer, you really can have too much business."

This was my goal -- to have "too much" business. At the time, I also knew this was very far away from becoming a reality. However, today, this is a 100% true statement. I have way too many opportunities to look at and projects to work on, and I'd like to enthusiastically encourage you to follow the strategies inside this manual. Because if you do, you'll get to experience the same things in your life.

To become successful and make this goal your reality, however, you must focus on marketing your business effectively. You must be willing to implement new strategies and you must constantly be getting exposed to new ideas. And you also must be willing to make mistakes along the way. Remember, there's no such thing as "perfect," and most of the time you're never really "ready," anyway.

The truth is, anyone can become successful. In fact, outside of willingly accepting mediocrity, or having a poor work ethic, there really isn't a very good reason why *anyone* in today's day and age, can't move forward and become more successful than they are right now.

In a sense, it is simple -- I have given you umpteen formulas to follow in this book that all bring you much closer to where you want to go.

Simple, yes. But... not easy.

You see, success has a filter. Anyone who gives up too early, can't get through the filter... anyone who's unwilling to work hard and give 110%, also can't get through the filter. And anyone who refuses to be consistent in their application of the techniques I've given you in this book... *also* won't get through the filter.

Success filters out the weak and timid, and most of the charlatans and thieves, simply because the rewards are so great. Frankly, not everyone deserves them or can handle them, and few are willing to pay the price.

If you doubt me, then do some research of your own. After all, there are hundreds of success stories all around you, besides mine. All you need to do is go to the library or go on amazon.com and you will find no shortage of stories about successful people who have risen up from the most horrible and unfortunate backgrounds, to become who they are today.

It does take some risk, but remember what I said earlier: You've got to have some skin in the game if you want to make it.

Recently, I was going through the Forbes 400 list of the wealthiest people here in America, and the lion's share of them are all first-generation billionaires. The stories of how these folks got started, and the mistakes they made and the chances they took, are all fascinating.

Be curious about stories like this, and about everything around you, because in this curiosity lies answers to many of your questions.

Sadly though, the biggest problem for most people, and the number one reason why people fail, is because they never really give themselves a chance. They lack the same belief in themselves we talked about earlier, when we were discussing why our prospects don't buy.

Most entrepreneurs and sales people fail because they just don't believe they deserve to be successful, or they give up too early. They can't take the pressure so they filter themselves out.

In fact, many times they give up when they're on the 10 yard line -- so close, and yet so far. But see, just like in a football game, those last 10 yards are the hardest ones to get. In reality, however, that's when you really need to dig in and be the *most* resilient and the *most* persistent.

I read a book a few years ago by Steven Pressfield, called *The War Of Art*, which gives the most accurate description I've ever seen, of what's going on in your mind whenever you're getting close to a big breakthrough or a major accomplishment. (I recommend every business-owner and sales person read this book. I met Steven, and he's also a genuine guy with a great success story of his own.)

Pressfield reckons the reason you resist jumping over hurdles, especially big ones, is because of resistance. And resistance, he says, is just fear. Here, he says it best on page 55 of his clever book:

"Resistance is fear. But resistance is too cunning to show itself naked in this form. Why? Because if Resistance lets us see clearly that our own fear is preventing us from doing our work, we may feel shame at this. And shame may drive us to act in the face of fear.

Resistance doesn't want us to do this. So it brings in Rationalization. Rationalization is Resistance's spin doctor. It's Resistance's way of hiding the Big Stick behind its back. Instead of showing us our fear (which might shame us and impel us to do our work), Resistance presents us with a series of plausible, rational justifications for why we shouldn't do our work.

What's particularly insidious about the rationalizations that Resistance presents to us is that a lot of them are true. They're legitimate. Our wife may really be in her eighth month of pregnancy; she may in truth need us at home. Our department may really be instituting a changeover that will eat up hours of our time. Indeed it may make sense to put off finishing our dissertation, at least till after the baby's born.

What Resistance leaves out, of course, is that all this means diddly. Tolstoy had thirteen kids and wrote War and Peace. Lance Armstrong had cancer and won the Tour de France three years and counting." (This was written before Lance won subsequent races.)

Resistance is the she-devil of progress!

And mind you, I'm not immune to Resistance, either. I've simply trained myself to know that when she rears her ugly head, it usually means there's a big opportunity just around the corner waiting for me, and now's the time to really dig in, because the fight's about to get dirty.

In fact, Resistance reared her ugly head the closer and closer I got towards the end of this book. It seemed the more I wrote, the longer it took to write and the more I doubted what I was writing. The more arguments I had with my wife, and the less time I was spending in the gym.

There was no way I wasn't going to finish this up, though. No way in hell. I was at the 10-yard line, baby, and I was coming across that end zone come hell or high water.

But you do start questioning things, and if you question too much, or for too long, you slow down and lose your momentum, without even realizing it.

And this... is what Resistance does. Have I written too much? Too little? Will people like it? Did I write too sheepishly in the beginning? Was I too offensive and opinionated? What if no one buys the book? What if no one likes the book after they do buy it?

What if it's a flop?

In the words of Charlie Brown, "Aargh!"

Again though, because I've experienced this so many times, having been involved in so many different kinds of projects over the years -- with most of them stretching my previous comfort zone -- I know these thoughts and feelings are totally normal.

I also start three to six new projects a year, and I average one new business a year as well, and I've gone through these same scenarios with many of these projects.

But Resistance hit me maybe even more so when I was writing this book, because of the incredible amount of time involved, and because of the way I in particular, write.

See, most writers will write "X" number of pages a day, or for "X" number of hours, once or twice a day. I write (or edit) for one or two days straight until I can't keep my eyes opened.

I go until there's no gas left in the tank. And as a result, at times I'm just running on fumes, and so things are much more difficult to handle when you're in that state of mind.

Plus, the stress was magnified because I was running multiple businesses the entire time I was writing this, and had commitments to satisfy there. As well as client consulting commitments. Oh yeah, not to forget being a husband and a father of three kids... a real estate investor... yadda, yadda, yadda... you know the drill.

So the pressure does get to you. But again, since experience has already taught me all this is normal, I was in familiar territory. I will tell you, once this book was finished, I sat down outside on my dock with my wife, overlooking the beautiful lake behind our home, and I smoked a gorgeous cigar and enjoyed a Johnny Walker Blue, and it was one of the most relaxed moments I had in a while.

Anyway, my point is, if you are willing to look Resistance squarely in the eye and ignore her vicious attempts at stopping or delaying your progress, you *will* make it over the goal line. Sometimes you'll lose a few yards and get knocked around a bit along the way... but you've **got** to get back up on your feet and you've **got** to keep moving forward, no matter what.

If, however, you believe all the excuses Resistance tells you, all you get to do then, is sit on the sidelines and watch the rest of us moving ahead of you. And in this case, you get to experience the absolute worst feeling in the world -- regret.

It's up to you to decide whether you want to be a participant or a spectator. As I said earlier, one of the things that's actually helped me is that I loathe regrets. Or, put it this way -- I'd rather regret the mistakes I made than the mistakes I didn't make. For me, the pain of not doing something and regretting it, is far greater than the pain of doing something that doesn't work.

I've lived by this mantra my whole life. To be honest, it's what motivated me to fight for custody of my two sons when I first split up with my ex-wife -- I wanted sleep insurance. Back in the early 1990's, the courts were still overtly pro-mother, and I knew we didn't have much of a chance of winning. But I also knew losing would torment me far less over my lifetime, than never having tried to do the best I could for my boys.

As I told you earlier, we did lose the battle, but in the end, we won the war.

Another reason some people don't succeed is that we are all products of our environment. Many people (like myself) didn't have a particularly rosy environment to grow up in, especially as it relates to your ability to feel deserving of success.

I never heard positive messages related to success when I was younger and most susceptible to "programming." Instead, success had a negative connotation. ("Rich people stink..." "They're all crooked." And, so on....) And like a broken cassette tape that plays over and over again, when you can least afford to hear it, these negative messages always seem to play when you can least afford to hear them.

If you're in this group, then I encourage you to re-program yourself to associate success with healthy images. Like I said, the people who told me things like "Money doesn't make you happy" and "Rich people stink," were *always* broke.

You'll never hear a successful person tell you "Money doesn't make you happy." That's because money *does* make you happy because it gives you freedom and choices. It allows you to experience life on a different level - one YOU choose, instead of one you're forced to accept and adapt to.

Think about it, who doesn't enjoy being able to eat the food they want at the restaurants they want? Travel to places they want to see, and stay in nice accommodations? Who doesn't enjoy not having to worry about how they're going to pay their mortgage this month? Who doesn't take comfort knowing that if there's a family health issue, you have the money to fix it?

I've been on both sides, and I will tell you unequivocally, that having a few dollars has made me much happier, and has allowed me to give my family experiences we'd never have otherwise.

And giving my family things I never had, that make our lives easier or bring us closer from the experiences we enjoy with one another, *fills* me with joy.

It takes a lot of stamina, will-power, and courage to persevere and consistently go to bat in the face of one obstacle after another. The good news is, the payoff is worth it. I don't know *any* successful person who's ever stopped and thought to themselves, "Boy, what a waste of time that was."

Becoming successful involves a series of increasingly bigger steps that push the boundaries of who you are. The good news is, in the end, you become a stronger and of course, wealthier person, both financially and in the richness and strength of your character.

I will close this Chapter with this: implementing any of the strategies in this book increases your cash-flow and your self-esteem, and makes your business life (and therefore your personal life) much more rewarding. Implementing all of them will make you a small fortune.

It really is up to you what happens next. The only limits you have are the ones you place on yourself. There's no "money God" out there who's calling the shots saying "this much for you," "this much for her," or... "No, there's too much over there, take some back."

There is no such tethering attached to your income. It isn't limited and money doesn't have a personal preference about where it goes and whose pockets it winds up in. It doesn't discriminate based on size, race, age, or intelligence.

It doesn't matter whether you're a special education teacher or a stripper, money isn't making *any* decisions on it's own.

One little "secret" you need to know about all the marketing strategies I've given you in this book, is that having the gumption to use them is half your "mastery." Woody Allen got it right when he said "80% of success is just showing up."

Guts are worth a lot, in business and in life.

I hope you've enjoyed your time with me, and your experience. I want to personally thank you for your support, and I want to invite you to join me online at my website, kingofcopy.com. Inside, there are literally over 1,000 pages of free information about copywriting, emotional direct-response marketing, selling, success, and motivation.

You'll also find hours of audio interviews, actual sales letters and display ads, and videos -- all free. You can also subscribe to my blog by e-mail or by RSS feed at http://blog.kingofcopy.com.

I hope your life is filled with nothing but good health, happiness, and lots of success, and I hope all *your* dreams come true.

After all, why shouldn't they?

Now go sell something,

Craig Garber

P.S. Please turn to the next page to discover...

How To Get Even More... Out Of Me!

**Thanks for reading my book...
We hope you enjoyed everything!**

How To Get More Out Of Craig

Ongoing Study And Education

O.K., so what's next?

If you are new to this world, or new to me in particular, you may be wondering what your next step should be. Or you may be wondering how you can get more involved with me and how I can help you create or implement some of these strategies, or help you with your marketing, moving forward.

Good question.

If you've been taking notes, or highlighting the critical points you've read throughout this book, the first thing I'd do is go back and start reviewing these notes or reviewing what you've highlighted.

Start putting a game plan together. Begin thinking about the most apparent flaws in your current business marketing based on what you've learned, and what strategies you need to use, to stop the bleeding as soon as possible.

Next, prioritize these applications. And then... take action.

And see, it's **getting yourself to take action that's sometimes hard**. In Lou Ferrigno's book, *Guide To Personal Power, Bodybuilding, And Fitness*, he said something strikingly profound. He said something like, "Working out isn't hard -- getting to the gym is hard."

I read Lou's book when it came out over a dozen years ago, and I remember that message resonating with me even back then, as clear as day.

We are all often too often caught up in the mechanics of what we're *about* to do, as opposed to just getting on with it and then figuring out what you did wrong, later. In reality, since you can't "know" how to do something better before you do it,

anyway -- your ability to execute the mechanics really shouldn't even be part of your equation.

Remember, knowledge -- like the knowledge you've picked up by reading this book -- gives you direction and guidance. But only experience gives you wisdom. Your job now is to go out and "get wise," as fast as you possibly can.

You may also be wondering how to continue growing and developing your marketing and selling skills, and how to stay on the cutting edge, so you're on top of the newest marketing breakthroughs.

No doubt, the best resource available to help you accomplish this is my offline Seductive Selling Newsletter and Audio Success CD monthly membership. I can look you, or anybody else, squarely in the eye and say you will not find *any* other resource out there, that consistently delivers as much insight and information, along with new ideas and strategies, you can *easily* adapt to your marketing and to your business.

And if you are all about "pushing the envelope" as much you possibly can, then I will tell you flat-out, you will *LOVE* the Seductive Selling Newsletter! It's like mandatory "CE" (Continuing Education) for any entrepreneur.

And the best thing is, now you can test-drive it free for 30-days at kingofcopy.com/ssnl, and when you do, you will also receive 18 free bonus gifts, yours to keep, just for taking this free test-drive and for giving it an honest shot.

And unlike many "free bonus" gifts, each of these gifts has real value in and of itself. That's why I walk you through them on a video on the Seductive Selling which page I just mentioned.

In fact, I'm so confident in Seductive Selling's ability to consistently make you money, you even get a risk-free guarantee, just for trying it out:

Here's Your Risk-Free Guarantee:

Subscribe to the Seductive Selling Newsletter for one full year. Take advantage of every benefit, month-in and month-out, including all the sales copy critiques... the monthly examples and sales copy re-writes... the copywriting tips and strategies... and the creative warehouse of ideas that boost your response rates... and then implement these new ideas into your current marketing. **If after 12 months, you can honestly say you haven't made at LEAST an extra $15,000 dollars you wouldn't have made without these resources, then I will refund 100% of the investment you've made in this newsletter over those last 12 months.**

Is that fair or what?

But don't take my word for it, simply look at the web page and you will see literally dozens of testimonials there from many of my very satisfied long-term members. You can even listen to them live on a recorded call, at the top of the page.

Working With Me Directly

Perhaps you want me to work directly on your business, so you can profit from my experience. Like any good consultant or strategist, I look at things with a fresh set of eyes, to identify money-making opportunities you're missing, and to give you specific solutions on how to fix those things that are broken.

There are three ways of working with me:

1. On a one-on-one consulting basis:

I am available for full-day in-person consultations here in Tampa. You can find more information about this at kingofcopy.com/consultingday, but basically here's how a consulting day works:

The first half of your consulting day is diagnostic in nature. Meaning, we'll identify what's working and why, what's not working and why, and what's missing. Kind of like when you go to the doctor's office and he takes your health history. He'll ask how you're feeling... whether you exercise... what kind of foods you eat... whether you've ever been sick before... what your family history is, and things like that. Diagnostic things.

The second half of the day is more prescriptive in nature. We'll come up with specific solutions to the problems we identified earlier in the day, along with specific action and implementation steps that need to be taken, to correct or improve your situation. Usually, these improvements are dramatic, but again, don't take my word for it, listen to what others are saying on that web page.

If you are interested in coming down for a day of consulting, contact Anne in my office by phone at 813-909-2214, or by fax at 954-337-2369.

Consulting days are usually booked up 6 to 12 weeks out.

At the present time, I am still booking hourly telephone consultations, but these are limited to one-hour of time only, and they are also usually booked up 4 weeks out. Also, in the interest of full disclosure, these hourly consulting sessions may be eliminated in the future. If they are still available, you can book one hour of time with me, or find out more information about this at kingofcopy.com/consulting.

Any investment you make in consulting with me (either hourly or full-day), is 100% guaranteed. If you don't think your time has been productive or spent wisely, let me know and I will refund 100% of your investment.

2. In a group setting <u>and</u> on a one-on-one ongoing consulting basis:

I run a Mastermind Group that meets for two intense days of brain-storming, three times a year, down here in Tampa. Members of this group also meet with me individually on the phone, once a month during the nine other months of the year... and we also have a monthly group call on those months as well.

In addition, the members of this group are the only people who can e-mail me questions and have me continually review their sales copy and marketing pieces.

A couple of years ago I had some trouble with a few of the members who thought simply being in the group would make them money. They forgot they actually needed to do something. Long story short, they were disruptive at one of the meetings and I threw all three of them out.

Yes, this represented a lot of money, but not enough to sit back and take a bunch of crap from three whining babies. After this episode, I instituted an application process and the quality of the groups I've had, has increased dramatically.

You can find out more information about my Mastermind Group, including videos from members, and an application, at **kingofcopy.com/mastermind**.

3. In a group setting:

I also run a group coaching program that meets once a month for 90-minutes on the phone. The group is called Mavericks Coaching, and you get to participate on the calls and send me in questions ahead of time, which I answer on your call.

Members also get the Audio CD recordings of the call as well as a weekly fax from me. For information about this group, go to **kingofcopy.com/mavericks**.

As of right now, the dynamics of this group is slightly different than the Mastermind Group. This isn't a hard and fast rule, but it tends to be the majority of what you'll find. Some of the people in this group are folks who are either currently working in a job and trying to either get out of it, or working in a job and looking to pick up extra income in a side or part-time business which some hope to make permanent. They have joined this group to have me help them with this "other" business, or have me launch their primary business.

There are entrepreneurs in this group, but they also tend to be people involved in a number of different businesses at once, not just the one I am helping them with.

The members of the Mastermind Group, on the other hand, are all full-time entrepreneurs and hard-core marketers working on one core primary business which we work on in the group.

Copywriting

If you want me to come up with a marketing strategy for you and write the sales copy for it, you must book a full day of consulting with me, during which time we'll go over your project and your business with a fine-tooth comb, as I just explained. You'll receive a 100% credit of the investment in your day of consulting, towards your copywriting fees.

Appreciate that I do NOT take on every copywriting project that comes across my desk, simply because not every project has enough legs to give it life. If I don't think your idea has merit, or if I don't think it is a worthwhile investment for you to make in hiring me, I will be candid and let you know this up-front, during the course of our consulting day.

Since a portion of my copywriting fees are paid as royalties from gross sales, I have a vested interest in your ongoing success, and that's why I don't waste my time working on projects that don't have long-term viability. Again, search around my website and you will see this for yourself. (Specifically, you can look at the story at kingofcopy.com/leads.)

Also in the interest of full disclosure, I am *not* "looking" for copywriting clients. Although I charge a small fortune for writing copy, I do so because it is a significant interruption to my publishing and consulting business, and the money I charge has to make up for the revenue I'm losing in those businesses, while I'm working on your project.

Writing copy isn't easy and is quite time-consuming. And the simple truth is that if I can write copy and develop effective marketing strategies for my own projects I'd rather do that.

Currently, besides my kingofcopy.com publishing and consulting business, I run two other publishing and consulting companies. One provides consulting and marketing services to retail loan officers, and the other company works in niche businesses in various hobbyist marketplaces.

So rest assured, if I'm going to interrupt all this, you'd better believe it's because I think we've got a winner on our hands.

Speaking

If you are interested in hiring me to speak to your group, please contact my office at 813-909-2214, and fax your information to 954-337-2369. Provide as many details as you possibly can in order to have your information attended and responded to, as quickly as possible.

I really enjoy speaking and teaching, and interacting with audiences. However I'm a bit of a homebody and I love being near my wife and children and our lake-house. And unlike loads of authors, I don't *need* to speak, to sell stuff, including this manual. I'm out there using these same techniques in both the online and offline world, 24/7.

So to be honest, a trip to Cape Girardeau, Missouri or Shamokin, Pennsylvania, isn't very likely to get me pumped up, if you know what I mean. (Nothing against either of those two places. One of my best friends in the world used to live in Cape Girardeau, and I actually ran an audit job in Shamokin, when I was an accountant!)

But if you have an exciting group of people for me to speak with, I'm all ears!

Affiliate Programs

If you want to market any of my products, we have a very generous affiliate program available. Depending on the size of your list, we will work directly with you to come up with the most effective strategy to market the particular products you're interested in selling, and we'll give you all the turn-key copy you need, whether we're promoting online or offline.

We also regularly conduct webinars and teleseminars and will consider doing one for your group as well!

To find out how to become an affiliate, go to kingofcopy.com/affiliate for more information.

We pay our affiliates monthly, ship products out within 2 or 3 business days at *most* (all by trackable delivery service), and we handle any refunds (which are consistently at a very low percentage) and customer service issues, right away. And, we have verifiable references for all of these claims.

Customizing Products

We will customize our products for certain niches, if it makes sense. You must be a customer of mine, and you must have actually purchased the product you are interested in having customized for your niche or particular industry. We have specific formulas for doing this in any number of niches.

If this is something you are interested in, please look at the requirements for becoming an affiliate of mine at kingofcopy.com/affiliate, and then follow the directions on that page. Let us know what your idea is, and we'll get back to you.

How To Get Craig To Train Your Group

Do you want to buy bulk copies of this book for your group, trade association or company, or do you want Craig to train your group?

If so, fax your information to Anne at 954-337-2369.   Bulk discounts *are* available.

Craig is also available to give in-person, teleseminar and webinar, or other group-training sessions, custom-tailored to your organization's specific marketing or business needs. Training may be one-shot, periodic, or ongoing based on Craig's current commitments and your group needs.

Please inquire about this as well, via fax (preferably) at 954-337-2369, or by contacting Craig's office at 813-909-2214. Simply provide all the relevant details of your engagement and business needs, and any other helpful background information.

All reasonable inquiries will receive a timely response.

Feedback And Comments

If you have any comments, testimonials, or deep thoughts about this manual you feel compelled to share with me, *or*... if you want to tell me how you learned something here you didn't know, and then you went out and applied it to your business, and you wound up making a ton of cash from these ideas...

Nothing would make me happier than hearing this!

There are three ways you can do this:

1. You can call our testimonial hotline at **800-459-0663, ext. 9000**, anytime 24 hours a day, 7 days a week. Simply listen to the recorded message and then leave your comments.

2. You can fax them to us at 954-337-2369.

3. Or, you can e-mail them to us at friend@kingofcopy.com. If you are e-mailing your comments, please put "book feedback" in your subject line, so we can give your e-mail prompt attention.

Please include your name and your location (city and state, or city and country if you are outside of America), as well as contact information, in case we need to get back with you.

Note that leaving your comments via any media grants us permission to use them in our marketing material as testimonials! If, for whatever reason, you do not want us to use these comments, please let us know. Your wishes will certainly be respected.

And lastly, if you use social media like facebook or twitter or digg or any other platform, let your network know how much you liked this book, and encourage them to get a copy for themselves!

Craig Garber & kingofcopy.com® Resources

As of the date of this writing, here are all of the "How To" products I've developed and published. More information is available online, at each individual page indicated, or you can always check my online product catalog at **kingofcopy.com/products**.

Holy Cow -- it's the BIG MOMMA Of All Offers! Get your hands on absolutely every single product I've developed and save over $2,000 dollars, PLUS get a FREE hour of one-on-one consulting from me, so you can figure out how to implement all this stuff, and what your next step should be. All yours with the "Mother Of All Offers!" **kingofcopy.com/mother**

Marketing Strategies, Selling Psychology
Emotional Direct-Response Copywriting & Success

Seductive Selling® Offline Newsletter -- FREE 30-day Test-Drive Along With 18 FREE Bonus Gifts Worth Over $3,632 Dollars, including... Audio CD Interviews... Back-Issues... Live Marketing Examples... DVD Sales Copy Critique... ~~One~~ NOW 2 Free Marketing Critiques... and much much more! **kingofcopy.com/ssnl**

How To Make Maximum Money With Minimum Customers: 21 Proven Direct-Marketing Strategies Anyone Can Use! Discover all the little-known secrets and strategies I used to make a hair north of $578,000, with a small list of less than 5,000 names, in only 12 months. **kingofcopy.com/max**

Marketing Strategies, Selling Psychology
Emotional Direct-Response Copywriting

Seductive Headlines That Sell Uncover the secret to capturing your prospects attention immediately, and get the most comprehensive turn-key system available, that lets you easily create any headline for anything you want to sell. **kingofcopy.com/headlines**

The Seductive Selling® System: 47 Ways To Push Your Prospect's Emotional Buy-Buttons

343

And Get Rich Along The Way! Make 'em say "Yes!" How to choose... and use... the right emotions in your marketing and your sales copy, to get your prospects to buy what you want them to buy, when you want them to buy... over and over again! **kingofcopy.com/seductive**

Seductive Selling Monthly Coaching Program This is a structured coaching program with a different direct-marketing topic covered each month, along with a Q & A session. **kingofcopy.com/seductivecalls (Note: this program has ended... there is limited availability of existing calls, check the .pdf form at website listed.)**

Completely Uncensored Magic Marketing Research And Resource Guide Like the "Consumer Reports" of direct-marketing **kingofcopy.com/magicmarketing**

22 Ways To Completely Eliminate ALL Your Marketing Headaches... Right NOW! Rare live teleseminar with over 2 hours of rapid-fire marketing strategy. **kingofcopy.com/22ways**

Scientific Advertising PLUS... 2 NEW Bonuses, Including A Detailed Analysis Of Claude C. Hopkins' Most Famous Ad, AND... **"How To Use A Simple Sales Letter To Get ANYTHING You Want!"** kingofcopy.com/hopkins

Offline Newsletter Profits: How To Write Your Way To A Small Fortune Using An Offline Newsletter! Discover the step-by-step process of putting together an offline newsletter, either for profit, or as a free lead generating tool, and how to use it to make a small fortune! **kingofcopy.com/newsletter**

Lead Generation Programs

Lead Generation Explosion! Get the EXACT direct-mail copy I used, along with a boilerplate template mailer, and all the follow-up formulas I used (both online and offline), to generate a 42.7% response, and a 218-to-1 return on a FIRST mailing to a cold list! **kingofcopy.com/leads**

Lead Generation Explosion for Accountants! Discover how to grow your practice and expand your ability to attract success, AND how to generate more leads than you know what to do with! **kingofcopy.com/accountant**

Real Estate Marketing

The ABC's of Real Estate Investor Marketing! How to turn your part-time real estate investing business... into a full-time career! Discover the ONE reason why almost no one in real estate ever really makes the kind of money they deserve. **kingofcopy.com/abcre**

Success And Avoiding Self-Sabotage

How To Make Your Dreams Come True! Inspirational story of how I wound up working with the late Gary Halbert and how I got into marketing and writing sales copy. Includes a critique of the most valuable sales letter I ever wrote, along with the actual 40-page letter itself, plus another separate Audio CD called "Excuse Busters." **kingofcopy.com/dreamscometrue**

The NEW Science Of Getting Rich! Plus, a revealing look at some of my own struggles with success. Inside this amazing little book, you'll uncover: why you must accumulate wealth!... Exactly how to go about doing this (and yes, there are very specific rules you must follow)... How you're actually making the world a much better place, when you become wealthy, and lastly... most important, you'll discover how to become incredibly rich, without ever feeling... guilty about it! **kingofcopy.com/science**

Detailed 7-Step Sales Copy Review

7-Step Sales Copy Review And Overhaul A candid (and sometimes eye-opening) review of your sales copy, designed to transform even a mediocre ad into an eye-opening winner that consistently pulls in a boatload of cash. **kingofcopy.com/salescopyreview**

Consulting

Full Day Of One On One In-Person Consulting With Craig kingofcopy.com/consultingday

Marketing Strategy: One Hour (Only) Of Telephone Consulting kingofcopy.com/consulting

Mastermind and Coaching Programs

Craig's Mastermind Group If you are looking to take a short-cut to the top, this is the fastest way possible. You must apply for and qualify to get admission into this group. It is the ONLY way to get ongoing direct and e-mail access to me. Application and information at **kingofcopy.com/mastermind**

Mavericks Coaching Program Monthly group telephone coaching program, where I work

345

directly on your business and you also get new ideas from the other group members.
kingofcopy.com/mavericks

Copywriting Services and Public Speaking   **kingofcopy.com/workingtogether**

Index